WITHDRAWN

NORRIS DAM

COULTER SHOALS DAM (PROPOSED)

GREAT SMOKY MOUNTAINS NATIONAL PARK

WATTS BAR DAM (PROPOSED)

FONTANA DAM (PROPOSED)

HIWASSEE DAM

Norris

Knoxville

Asheville

POWELL RIVER

CLINCH RIVER

HOLSTON RIVER

FRENCH BROAD R.

TENNESSEE

HIWASSEE RIVER

K Y.

V A.

N. C.

S. C.

G A.

Atlanta

ooga

N
W   E
S

0   10   20   30
Scale of Miles

THE TENNESSEE VALLEY

D1208623

GOD'S VALLEY

ALSO BY WILLSON WHITMAN

BREAD AND CIRCUSES

GOD'S VALLEY

PEOPLE AND POWER
ALONG THE
TENNESSEE RIVER

BY WILLSON WHITMAN

1939
NEW YORK
THE VIKING PRESS

F
443
T3
W5

EARLHAM COLLEGE
JAN 16 1973
LILLY LIBRARY

COPYRIGHT 1939 BY WILLSON WHITMAN
PRINTED IN THE UNITED STATES OF AMERICA
DISTRIBUTED IN CANADA BY THE MACMILLAN COMPANY
OF CANADA, LTD.
FIRST PUBLISHED IN MARCH 1939

CONTENTS

ILLUSTRATIONS

(*The photographs in this book are reproduced with the permission of
the Tennessee Valley Authority, and are all by Charles Edward Krutch,
with the exception of the upper photograph facing page 88, which is by
Lewis Hine.*)

GOD'S VALLEY

Said the preacher at Jordan's Bend:

In the first place God made the earth, including the Tennessee Valley, and man upon it. Then He sat back to see what would happen next.

One day He saw a man digging at the ground with a stick to make the corn grow better. "Now, that fellow's got sense," said the Lord. "I'll give him a little help."

So God told the man to try digging with a sharp rock. Next thing God knew, the man began to put an edge on all the flints he could find and do all kinds of work with them. He even started a church where they said God was a rock. God didn't care much for that but He let it pass.

Then one man with a sharp rock hit another man over the ear and killed him. God didn't like that a bit. He let the river rise and drown all those men in a flood, and He started again.

This time the men went to farming along their river, and God told them how to dig ditches to water their crops. But it wasn't long before they started to worship the river, and before they were making slaves out of other men to do the digging. Some of these slaves were the people God liked best, so He let the river rise again.

The next time God wasn't having any foolishness about slavery, so He showed the men how to harness a mule and make a wagon wheel. Pretty soon the mules and the oxen were doing all the hard work. But then the men began to make chariots for war, and to

3

harness horses and even circus elephants for fighting. One of their poets said that men had two legs but horses had four legs, so they should bow down to the man on horseback and let him ride rough-shod over the other men.

It kept on that way for a long time, with God giving folks the power to do things, and them worshiping the power, whether it was rocks or rivers or horsepower or what, and then using it to hurt the neighbors. God tried them with all kinds of things from gold and silver to reading and writing, and the result was the same.

Finally—and this is coming right down to your grandpa's time—God tried them with the lightning. Some folks say He just let it slip accidentally. But anyhow they got hold of it, and, as usual, they started in first of all to say that it was God. Then they laid plans for using it to make slaves out of other people, or maybe to kill them.

This got to happening everywhere and God got worried because He thought He might have to give up. But He studied awhile and He said to Himself that somewhere in the world there must be a place where folks hadn't forgotten all the things that had happened before.

It would have to be a place, He knew, where there were flint rocks, and mules and oxen, and a river that could rise up and flood the bottom lands, and where, maybe, there had been slaves. A place where, by now, they knew about lightning but hadn't started saying it was God.

He studied and He looked over the whole earth. And then His eye lit on the Tennessee Valley.

I. MIST

The Land Lies South

In his hand are the deep places of the earth: the strength of the hills is his also.

But there went up a mist from the earth.

The valley of the Tennessee river extends, east to west, over a hundred counties in seven states lying below Mason and Dixon's line. It is not a political division but a natural one, a region marked by a water level—an intaglio island with the river's watershed for its coast. It is almost as large as England.

The course of the river, generally westward, curves down into Alabama before it flows north to join the Ohio in Kentucky; and you cross it twice as you cross the state of Tennessee. The Valley watershed is best described as shaped like a butterfly with its waist at Chattanooga. The wings of this creature, veined with big and little rivers and stretching from Virginia to Kentucky, are curiously marked and variegated. The hill folks of the eastern wing tip, who haven't changed their manner of speaking since they left England three hundred years ago, would call them pied.

There are the spots that nobody misses, the tourist centers like Asheville and Lookout Mountain and the national parks in the east wing, where Yankees drive to gawp at the natives and make jokes about moonshine stills, and to buy hooked rugs made by the mountain women and fox pelts ordered by their menfolk from Montgomery Ward. There are the sore spots, Scottsboro and Decatur and a dozen textile or mining towns well known to the League for Industrial Democracy, the Civil Liberties Union, and the Interna-

tional Labor Defense. And there are the strange iridescent spots—
Hancock county in Tennessee, where a people called Melungeons
claim to be of Moorish descent; and Madison county, Alabama,
which almost seceded from secession when they raised the rebel
yell at Montgomery, and which votes Democratic but prays Republican to this day.

The east wing of the butterfly tilts up sixty-six hundred feet to
the highest peak east of the Rocky mountains. The west wing is
lower, but not flat, and Lookout Mountain at Chattanooga will give
you a view of seven states. Substitute Mississippi for South Carolina
and they are the states of the Valley—North Carolina, Tennessee,
Georgia, Alabama, Kentucky, and Virginia.

You can be a Southerner in good standing and not know all this
country. If you come from up North, your big mistake would be to
believe that the Tennessee Valley is a part of the Solid South. You
might assume that Uncle Sam, as Tennessee's partner, has the ap-
plause of the entire section for his Tennessee Valley Authority—the
first move for real reconstruction ever made.

Some might say you needn't try to reconstruct the Tennessee Valley as a belated gesture of reparation, because of the very spottedness
of the butterfly wings. Western North Carolina and Eastern Tennessee fought for the Union, and the hills were full of horse thieves who
stole impartially from both sides. This part of the watershed is still
riddled with Republicans who resent the whole program of the
Authority. As rugged individualists they resent any authority, and
as royalists from away back they resent the Democrats. A Republican congressman goes to Washington from the town that is TVA
headquarters, Knoxville, Tennessee; a Republican morning paper
takes daily pot-shots at the leading local industry.

Farther south there are no Republicans, but a slew of Southerners
living within shooting distance of Shiloh battleground know that no
good ever came of Yankee invasion. Some old-timers in the Muscle
Shoals district, which has opened up and spread itself hopefully for
one boom after another these hundred years, feel that Uncle Sam is
no more to be trusted than Henry Ford.

There are all sorts of people in the Valley and a big lot of them, for one reason or another, don't give a hang for New Deal improvements. But now, for the first time in seven decades, there are a lot of folks up North who are turning their eyes south to see what's happening there, and maybe to meddle in Southern affairs under that curious Yankee delusion that this is a country one and indivisible. Not long ago they actually sent down a whole class of children from a New York school to see the South, especially the Tennessee Valley, for themselves, and to hear and touch and smell it. They had a nice trip, and maybe traveling over the country helped them to realize that the Valley stretches from the Smoky mountains down into the Alabama cotton country, instead of being just a little part of Tennessee. But you can't expect to understand any part of the South just by looking at it as it is today. You have to go back through the mist of history, as Southerners do. In particular, you have to look at the past if you hope to understand the people.

There was famine in Ireland, and so the Irish came to America, where the potatoes grew and England had no excise. The Scotch who had settled Ireland in Cromwell's time, never too well rooted, were among the first to sail to Philadelphia and to move south from there in search of new plantations. A third of all the Scotch-Irish in Ireland, they say, came over. There were some real Highlanders too, who had made the mistake of loyalty to the Pretender.

It's been noticed that American colonists were apt to pick on country like that they had lived in before. So it happened that the Dutch settled on the Jersey bogs; the Spaniards explored the deserts of the Southwest; the Scotch-Irish streamed down into the lower Appalachian mountains, a country of crags and mists, where, to this day, purple thistles grow along the roadside and homegrown wool is woven into clan plaids.

Families that you could call clans still occupy that part of North Carolina and East Tennessee drained by the little rivers of the Tennessee system. On the headstones in the Presbyterian cemeteries are rows of Macs, and even an occasional Dhu. The typical wayside stand isn't Tony's, but Mac's Place. And when the Campbells came to the Cumberlands, and the Boyles to the Blue Ridge, they did more than choose a congenial country; they brought with them a moral climate that was to make an Irish problem for America.

Emigrating, they no doubt considered that they had left behind forever the trade restraints of the British government, the taxes on wool and flax and hides that kept loyal Ulster, no less than the rest of Ireland, poor. As they streamed down the old Wilderness Road, they could rejoice in a rich new country. There was meat for the shooting and salt licks to season it. There was tall timber for the cutting, or you could burn it off if you were clearing land. Farther on, over the blue hills through the Cumberland Gap, there might be any-thing—maybe a passage to India by way of what Captain John Smith called "the backe sea." For the Indians said there were big waters farther west, and the little rivers all ran that way.

The Indians said too that there was gold and silver for the finding. There would be no more poverty, surely, for every man could take enough for his need. And there would be no more taxes. It was their settlements, at Watauga in 1772, and at Abingdon, Virginia, in 1775, that were first to declare against British rule in America. When they said rule, they meant taxes.

Of course, as to the question of who owned the country, the In-dians were there, but they didn't understand the ownership of prop-erty. The whole Tennessee Valley was their common game preserve, and when they let the white man in, they thought he just wanted to camp and hunt and fish, the way they did, without claiming the land at all. It seems the most civilized of the red men managed everything they had in common; they all chipped in and helped each other plant crops or build houses, and they had a common gran-ary. Then there was a special provision for widows with no men to work for them—a sort of social security, you'd call it, so nobody would go hungry as long as the nation had anything.

They traded some, getting copper from the Indians that lived up on Lake Superior. But they never thought of anything really com-plicated, like a freight differential. And with gold right there in the hills, they used shells for money, giving them a value based on the work it took to make a common shell into wampum.

But the white settlers wanted to own all the land. General Winfield Scott drove the Cherokees out of North Carolina, except a few that hid out in the woods; and Georgia got mad at the United States government because it was too lenient with the Indians they were hurrying out of there. After they found the gold in Northern Georgia, it wasn't safe even for a missionary to say a good word for the Indian claims.

Down the little rivers, the Hiwassee and the Holston and the rest, they drove them by fight or by treaty until the Eastern Band of the Cherokees was broken up. The Chickamaugas hid out for a while in the caves under Lookout Mountain, and John Ross held on at Ross's Landing, which is now Chattanooga; but they weren't satisfied with pushing the red men clear to the Shoals. That was their last stand; the Colberts in the Shoals country—they were Chickasaws with a mixture of Scotch, like Ross—held on longest. They ran the ferries on the Natchez Trace and kept on good terms with the prominent white people, but finally they had to give up all lands east of the Mississippi.

The last council of the Cherokee nation was held at Rattlesnake Springs in Bradley county, Tennessee, a hundred years ago. After that they had to move west—some down the river, some dressed in their best and riding on their horses and ponies. Those that were used to living in the hills didn't like the flat western country they had to go to, but one out of every three, they say, died on the trip.

Anyhow the Indians are all gone now, except a few of the Eastern Cherokees who hid out in the hills and were let live in the Qualla reservation over by the national park. Some say they are sort of shiftless, like the sharecroppers and mill people, though others say they were good farmers until the sawmills came. But they don't give any trouble. They still do a little farming, and lately some of them have been learning to build outhouses for the WPA. People that live in the hills around the Hiwassee dam say that you can now and then see a few of them crossing over Snowbird mountain, and that they walk single file, just as they used to, following the ghost of an old trail that a white man would never see.

The story is, too, that it's the blood of dead Indians that makes the ground so red, and they say you can still see their signal fires on top of the Smokies at sunup and sundown. But most folks know it's just the iron in the soil and the mist on the mountains.

Maybe you could argue that some sort of curse or trouble for taking the Indian lands did hang over the settlers, or you could say that it was the very things the Irish and Scotch had moved away from that haunted them. For in a little more than a hundred years this new land was to be poverty-stricken and desolate, a land of hard times and hunger, of civil strife, of absentee ownership, and above all of the tariffs that ruin trade and make for lawlessness. You can say that, today, the South is the Ireland of America—land of mammy songs as sad as "Mother Machree," of illiteracy and illegal whisky, of eternal disagreement between rebels and loyalists. The latter, numbering religious conservatives as well as political Ulstermen determined to hold to the Union at any cost, have been challenged by a literary Sinn Fein with *I'll Take My Stand* as its manifesto.

It is true that almost as many Germans as Scotch-Irish came down in the alluvial drift from Pennsylvania. Many were Lutherans from the Palatinate, but some, the founders of Winston-Salem in North Carolina, were Moravians, cousins of those who founded Bethlehem in the Lehigh valley. These Germans were stout folk, and so were a few French Huguenots who found their way down the mountains, and the little group of Swiss who settled in Grundy county, Tennessee. But somehow the Scotch-Irish, with a small but persuasive influx of English from Virginia, managed to prevail. Today philologists find in the mountains the last living traces of Elizabethan speech, and anybody can see that the hill people have Early English faces; but actually the mixture of Celt and Teuton that produced the English nation was repeated afresh on American soil, with enough Virginians to show what was right.

Experts will tell you that "hit" for it, and "et" for ate, and other peculiarities of mountain dialect which the schoolteachers try to do away with, are as respectable in their way as the homemade furniture that rich people come into the mountains to buy. For some years the hills have been overrun with foreigners hiding behind the trees in the hope of hearing a mountaineer sing the "Barbara Allen" ballad, accompanying himself on a homemade dulcimer. These survivals are going fast, now that good roads, Fords, and Coca-Cola have come to Tear-Breeches Ridge, Long Hungry, and Hell-for-Certain Creek.

It may be longer before the hill-bred faces soften. Now the young women with their firm chins and cheekbones and their bobbed hair look like page boys out of medieval chapbooks, and young men truckin' through the Big Apple at a hill dance might as well be wearing kilts and carrying targets. Old people, their mouths folded in over toothless gums, have the nutcracker face of Punch; that may be because, not long ago, there were still twenty-one mountain counties without a dentist. Their "Aryanism" is beyond question; they are skilled in yarbs and simples but they do not know the use of garlic.

Hill ways may go as the galax leaves and winter fern are going, so that every year the pickers who sell them North to the florists must go "galacking" farther into the mountains. But the hill folks themselves are in no danger of disappearing; while the hills remain sparsely settled it is only because the young folks leave home.

They have always left home. What orators called the westward march of empire, and what was actually the slow creak of ox wagons, carried this mountain breed across the other Southern states before the Civil War. Daniel Boone was born near Reading, Pennsylvania, but his folks moved to North Carolina, and the leaning beech tree marked:

D Boon Cilled a BaR On Tree
in ThE yEAR 1760

grew on a branch of the Watauga in Tennessee. Davy Crockett and Sam Houston made their marks in Texas, but they began in Tennessee when it was Washington county. All across the South from east to west went the migration, carrying ways of talking and living and thinking from the mountains and from the British Isles in the seventeenth century. The hill folks, then, are important to the Valley as a whole; the hills are geographically a small part of this area, but they were home, a century or so ago, for folks who now live as far down as the Shoals. That part of the watershed formed by the Blue Ridge holds the past of the Valley, from the Revolution to the Civil War.

And maybe it holds the future of the country. Up North the birth rate is falling because the city folks have funny customs and contraptions to defeat the plain word of God to women. Down South ten or a dozen children are still the natural result of wedlock, and so it has been calculated that in a few more years the biggest part of the population of America is going to come from below Mason and Dixon's line. That less than one percent of this population is foreign-born is of importance even to Americans free of any delusion of Nordic superiority, yet interested in maintaining certain proportions in the melting-pot formula. For, outside the South, native white American stock is losing ground, and no one has been able to invent a quota system to govern the birth rate. It is a commonplace that this country resembles the British Empire if colonies and mother country were run together, with no tight little isle to hold its own. And yet, in the Tennessee Valley, in an area roughly comparable to that of England, with a population almost equal to that of the borough of Brooklyn, we have hidden away a people more than ninety-nine percent pure even as the Daughters of the American Revolution count purity, and only too anxious to remain so. Many of these people are starving, and one authority has estimated that from half to nine-tenths of the tow-headed children aren't rightly fed. So some of their parents begin to exhibit the characteristics of oppressed people everywhere; but if their troubles are those common to the world, their virtues are unique, and early American.

There are things worth saving down there. There are tall trees left, and a few clear-running springs, and some wild birds that nobody has been able to kill off. There are hills full of rock, and bracing

smells of pine and iron in the air. There are people who still read
Scripture, and wear homespun cloth, and warm themselves by open
fires, and catch fish out of rivers, and sit and think. It is not so long
ago, as time passes in the South, since Woodrow Wilson put his hand
on a map, one finger touching the east wing of the Tennessee Valley, where the hill folks live, and said he thought the Lord must be
saving up these people against a time of special need.

Without knowing it, Wilson's administration had already made
the first move that was to bring Yankee money and Yankees themselves down into this country, and tie into one region the land from
the hills to Alabama. It was in Wilson's administration that the
government took over Muscle Shoals.

It was too bad that the South, especially the Valley, had already
had an unfortunate experience with the government of the United
States.

War without an End

*But go ye now unto my place which was in Shiloh, where I set my name at
the first, and see what I did to it for the wickedness of my people Israel.*

Shall iron break the northern iron and the steel?

In 1863 there took place in the United States a large-scale confiscation of private property by the federal government: President Lincoln
signed the Emancipation Proclamation.

In 1933 a step towards restitution was made. President Roosevelt
signed the act creating the Tennessee Valley Authority, which was
eventually to provide the South with more electric servants than there
had been slaves.

But nothing is that simple. In 1863 an army of damyankees had
invaded Southern soil and was fighting along the Tennessee river
from Chickamauga to Missionary Ridge and Lookout Mountain at
Chattanooga. When they won, defeat hammered a loose-jointed confederation of sovereign states into the Solid South.

In 1933 a handful of dam-builders moved down to save the Southern soil from floods and erosion. They have not finished fighting, but their invasion has split the Solid South into a mess of protesting politicians, "alien agitators," cantankerous small capitalists, and bewildered beneficiaries of the national bounty. Today there is about as much solidarity along the Tennessee as along the Hudson, which separates Union Square from Jersey City. But this is not the fault of the present invasion. The causes go back, as the causes of most Southern states of mind do go back, some seventy years.

A part of the Valley split off from the rest of the South at the time of the Civil War, when North Carolina and Tennessee were full of union sympathizers whose loyalty to established government was temperamental, as well as economically sound. The mountain people had no slaves; Negroes are scarce in the hills today, and with Union sympathizers as far south as Northern Alabama, the Tennessee river was a better boundary for slavery sentiment than Mason and Dixon's line.

Exaggerating some, a Yankee sympathizer wrote a pamphlet, back in 1862, to prove that the Valley would be Union if it had a chance. "Let the flag of the Republic wave victoriously at Knoxville in East Tennessee, and a Counter-Revolution will follow, restoring the Union and Constitution in the Alleghany Districts of North Carolina, South Carolina, Georgia, and Alabama." [1] The writer went on to name about half the counties in the Valley as ready to fight for the Union.

Besides having no Negroes, the mountain people generally were without excitement over the other economic quarrel, the protective tariff. Free trade wasn't important to folks who made their own furniture and pottery and dressed in homespun. Since what trading they did was back and forth over the state lines, what they did object to was a frontier dividing the states.

So the hillmen who liked fighting for the fun of it were likely as not to join the Yankees, or to form independent robber bands harrying both sides. The country was like the roof of that mountain church in the Blue Ridge, where, if a drop of rain hits the ridgepole, half of it flows into the Santee river and so to the Atlantic, and the other half

[1] James W. Taylor, *Alleghania*.

goes to the Tennessee and so to the Gulf. Some of the mountain feuds started that way, and what came to be considered mountain lawlessness. Summer tourists in the Carolina mountains always ask about moonshine stills, but not so many know that Banner Elk was a station on the Underground Railway.

This border division meant that the Valley was fought over even more than other parts of the South. They held the veterans' reunion at Chickamauga on the Tennessee river because you couldn't find a place that held more memories. And now, of course, it's the South that remembers.

Northern visitors notice that when they speak of the war, meaning the World War, the Southern listener thinks of the War between the States. Yankees could so far forget as to find in *Gone with the Wind* a story of events hardly known to this generation. But Southern children, as late as 1910, were hearing stories of coffee made from cracked corn during the war years, and of dresses made from the muslin torn from the walls; stories of burned houses, stolen silver, and wantonly wrecked pianos in the wake of the invasion; of the "uppity" Negroes of carpetbagger rule. You see, it was just as if Belgium and Northern France, where they fought in 1914–18, had lost the war and had to support an army of occupation.

The South was the battleground and the South was the loser. More, the South was subject to reprisals which have never ended. To this day it is experiencing the economic penalties of defeat, paying for a poverty that goes back to the sixties. Southerners see it as a result of the war that Yankees own most of the railroads and the industries of the country, that the financial center is in the Northeast, and that Northern capital continues to punish the South by tariffs and freight differentials. Of the two hundred great corporations that own a quarter of the country's wealth and tend to control all the country's business, all but twenty are owned in the Northeast. Ninety-five percent of the life insurance of the whole country is in the hands of Northern companies, and around eighty percent of the nation's bank deposits are in the North. Observers say that from eighty to ninety percent of the nation's wealth is owned in the North, and that this disparity between the North and the South is increasing.

The tariff to protect American industry actually protects Yankee industry. It has been calculated that, in the seven fat years before the depression, the tariff took fourteen billion dollars of purchasing power into the Northeastern states.

Southern people pay more for shoes and clothes and manufactured goods, not only because of the tariff, but because to the cost of manufacture must be added the cost of shipment South. Reverse that shipment, send Southern goods North, and the shipper meets an ingenious interstate tariff known as the freight differential. To ship a hundred pounds of freight, first class, the 645 miles from Birmingham, Alabama, to Chicago, Illinois, costs $1.78. To ship the same weight one mile more—the 646 miles from Elmira, New York, to Chicago—will cost you only $1.25. The 53 cents' difference is the freight differential, the premium awarded to the Northern shipper for being a Northern shipper.

Further to discourage Southern manufacture there was until lately the "Pittsburgh plus" price on steel. Steel is made in the South, but the steel companies are owned in the North, and the price of steel for the whole country was, until recently, figured as if it all came from Pittsburgh. A Southern firm could get its materials from Birmingham, but it paid the Pittsburgh price plus the cost of shipment from Pittsburgh.

Nor is it mere inertia that keeps the South from having more industries of its own. Destruction of capital, that horrid fear of propertied people today, occurred in this country on a tremendous scale by the passage of the thirteenth amendment. The defeated Southerner returned home to find his salable property gone; he must, from now on, pay for labor, and he had no money for payment. How could he build mills when he couldn't even afford to farm?

So came the credit system, clamping down on Southern agriculture. Crop liens and chattel mortgages are part of the farmer's experience today because they have been ever since Appomattox, when an ex-Confederate able to work could maybe get credit for his good intentions, and sign a note for the family spoons if the family was lucky enough to have any left. The printing of lien and mortgage forms makes work for every small Southern print shop, and their signing keeps notaries busy, and the resulting litigation helps the small-town lawyer and makes eventual gain for the small-town store-keeper or banker. It also keeps the farmer growing corn or cotton, because these are the cash crops.

Everybody knows what happened to Confederate bonds and currency. But farm products were down, too, with nobody to make the crops; and the Confederate officer who paid sixty percent on the money he borrowed to start farming again was charged high interest even for a cropper.

Before the war the South had more railroad mileage than the North, and it is said that the Southern roads were more solidly financed. After the war they were streaks of rust, the rolling stock gone, bridges wrecked, workshops burned—even the ties had been rooted up and piled for bonfires, and the rails twisted so they couldn't be used again. Both sides did it, but both sides did it in the South.

In the ten years from 1860 to 1870, the assessed property of the Southern states decreased in value more than two billions, or a third of the whole. Property losses by states were estimated at over $450,-000,000 for Virginia; over $150,000,000 for North Carolina, where there wasn't much fighting; over $600,000,000 for Alabama; and over $320,000,000 for Mississippi. General Sherman accounted for $100,-000,000 of the loss in Georgia; he said that $20,000,000 worth of property could be used by the Yankees but $80,000,000 was "simply waste and destruction."

And meanwhile the wealth of the Northern states had doubled.

From this a Yankee might think that the Valley, which was disputed territory at the start of the war, would have cast in its lot with the North. But you're forgetting the prejudices on both sides. When they had done the bitterest fighting of the war along the Tennessee river, and when they had tried reconstructing the Valley states, there was no longer any question; the Valley was part of the South. Today even Kentucky and Tennessee, for the most part, claim to be Southern states.

The Young Men Died

For thus saith the Lord God; Behold, I will bring . . . a king of kings, from the north, with horses, and with chariots, and with horsemen, and companies, and much people. . . .

He shall slay thy people by the sword, and thy strong garrisons shall go down to the ground.

And they shall make a spoil of thy riches, and make a prey of thy merchandise: and they shall break down thy walls, and destroy thy pleasant houses: and they shall lay thy stones and thy timber and thy dust in the midst of the water.

And this whole land shall be a desolation, and an astonishment; and these nations shall serve the king of Babylon seventy years.

Down South you naturally assume that everybody's grandfather was in the war. Up North they made it a class war by letting the well-to-do hire substitutes, so it's not so hard to find Yankees whose people went on buying and selling and sailing ships and publishing papers while the fighting was hottest. Like all the other costs, the human cost of the war was greater in the South, which was "bled white," as England was in the World War, while the North was suffering, in comparison, no more than the United States in 1917–18.

And now we know what that means politically. Wipe out a generation and you scare a country into going backwards; you can see the same thing in Europe today. So, in the South, there was the mental backsliding that always comes when there is no money for books, and all the young folks are dead.

When you have been licked, you look backward to the good old days before it happened, and you dwell on them instead of thinking of the future. Travelers smile at those Confederate monuments in the courthouse squares, the stiff cement soldier on his pedestal valiantly grasping his cement gun, with only the names in the panel below to distinguish him from his brother in the next county. Artistically these memorials are whatever you want to call them, but don't imagine they represent the taste of people who had built houses with tall fluted columns and wrought-iron railings, and otherwise qualified for the aristocracy of wealth that prides itself on loving

nice things. The concrete soldier is there because he was cheap. And
the tragic thing is that he may have been put there as late as 1910.
It took the Daughters of the Confederacy that long to save the nickels.

Of course no money should have been squandered that way, but
foolishness, like wealth, is cumulative. A government report has
lately observed that the South spends as much or more on education,
in proportion to its wealth, as the rest of the country. It has less education only because it has less to spend. You can say that Dayton,
Tennessee, showed more practical faith in evolution than Dayton,
Ohio; anyhow it didn't close its schools because it was afraid to "en-
cumber the future." Southerners who worried over debt wouldn't be
able to live at all. But foolish and ignorant prejudices remain, and it
all goes back to the fact that for seventy years the South has been sore,
with a soreness that may be recognized in European countries where
a war did relatively less damage. This soreness cankers into an in-
feriority complex, with its self-justification, anti-social behavior, and
retreat from reality.

Naturally there were other and better reactions. Energetic Southerners could and did call for a rebuilding in spite of handicaps. But
usually the best that could be imagined by the vanquished was successful competition with the victor in his own field, that is, industrialization. Let the South show what could be done with iron
and steel, with textile mills, with railroads. Perhaps Yankee money
could be coaxed to come down, perhaps the national pork barrel
would yield something for river navigation or a new post office—thus
Southern dreams around the turn of the century. These dreams were
apt to be expressed in fiery oratory, because promotion, persuasion,
salesmanship, talk, is the only action possible to the man with natural
resources but no capital. Henry W. Grady's "New South" speech
was made in 1886, but its resounding periods were being echoed by
high-school orators or stolen by congressional campaigners as late
as 1916.

That the South should accept second place with a humble conviction of war guilt was too much to expect of human nature. Yankees
might feel that they had fought to free the slaves, but in the South

the issue of the war was considered to be, not slavery, but states' rights, or the self-determination of a smaller nation. No one of any real intelligence defended slavery, just as no one today defends lynching or child labor; the question was how the evil was to be abolished without infringing on sovereign rights.

For the Southern child growing up five or fifty years after, the question was not the freedom of the Negroes but the freedom of the South, understood to be lost because the North had wanted to be boss. The Yankee orators didn't say as much about freeing the slaves as they did about preserving the Union. This was as if your mother had wanted to get a divorce while your father had objected. Talking nobly of the sanctity of marriage, father had hit mother over the head, beaten her, starved her, burned her clothes, and so forced her to submit to his decision. The original family disagreement didn't matter; it had been something about the servants, father preferring white ones to black ones. Of course, after he had beaten mother publicly, her authority in the household was so undermined that she could manage at all only because of her natural dignity.

In current relations, father was notoriously grasping and stingy. Every time mother saved any butter and egg money he took it to spend on himself. He did nothing for the children, but, adding insult to injury, reproached mother for poor management if they went ragged and hungry or missed school.

The difficulty was that Southern justifications, besides neglecting the ethical question of slavery, tended to fog the economic issue. It was an economic misfortune that the South saw the struggle in emotional terms, and it was a political misfortune that every little boy and every little girl born alive in Dixie grew up a conservative, looking backward to the good old days instead of looking ahead.

For the country as a whole, it was and is unfortunate that the standard of values in the new South was taken from the conquerors. While it was evident to surviving Southerners that their personal salvation depended on proving themselves better industrial hustlers than the Yankees, a nation-wide competition in industrial hustling was no help to civilization in the United States.

For when the South followed, it followed tardily. It is only when Northerners learn what every Southerner is born knowing, that the South never recovered from its blow, that they can understand this delay. The "Lost Cause" was well named by Southern sentimentalists, for the conditions caused by loss persist. And though the South may pay the freight, the whole country pays for the time lag in the Southern mind.

Stripped of his shirt, the defeated Southerner first of all fell back on justification in the spirit. Religious bias in the South, considered obvious today, is actually a post-Civil War phenomenon. Thomas Jefferson once made a list of qualities distinguishing the Northern from the Southern character: in the North men were sober, laborious, interested (in the sense of calculating), while in the South they were pleasure-loving, indolent but generous, and so on. Today the comparison is probably as accurate as it ever was, with one exception. In the North, said Jefferson, men were "superstitious and hypocritical in their religion" while in the South they were "without attachment or pretensions to any religion but that of the heart."

With religion largely a dead issue in the North, the South is now a land of shouting preachers, yearly revivals, denominational schools. A peddler rides in the bus out of Florence, Alabama; he carries a bushel basket full of Bibles. A fat fourteen-year-old boy looks at them with interest; he is reading a scriptural commentary. Young men on their way to school in the mountains talk, not of football, but of their "association work" during the summer; and there is rivalry amounting to coolness between the Baptists and the Presbyterians. Young people wander singing through the streets of Knoxville on a warm moonlight night; their song is "Washed in the Blood of the Lamb," and they knock on doors to ask contributions to the missionary fund. On the bulletin board in a TVA construction camp is the notice of a revival meeting in the nearest town, to be conducted by a student evangelist from God's Bible School, Cincinnati, Ohio. There is promise of old-fashioned preaching, with "Loud Speakers" in bigger type; the place is the "Big Tabernacle—Next to TVA Offices."

This is a change from the easy ante-bellum attitude described by
Jefferson, and the reason is obvious: defeat always brings a turning
to the sort of religion that offers emotional escape. The religion of
the South today is the result of a general feeling, in the last century,
that there was nothing left but God. In the same period the Yankees,
prospering, became convinced that they could do very well without
divine aid.

But besides his soul, the defeated Southerner still possessed a body,
and when he realized this he began to exhibit another symptom of
defeat as we now recognize it—a pride in the color of eyes and skin
and hair. Before the war his economic system took it for granted
that a white skin was better than a black skin. Afterwards this difference became even more important, became a hysterical insistence
on racial purity, so that the Klan in its white sheets may be considered
a forerunner of the colored shirts of modern Europe.

But it must not be forgotten that the South had a reason for racial
consciousness, in the want of tact, to put it mildly, of the Yankee
conquerors. What happened after the war was not merely confiscation
of property by freeing the slaves, but a deliberate reversal of conditions to make the freed men into voters and lawmakers without the
formality of teaching them to read. Had the Yankees instituted a
policy of emergency education such as the Russian Revolution de-
vised for the muzhik, results might have been different; but they
had to wait for the WPA to cope with illiteracy in Alabama.

Other instances of that biological pride which we now recognize
as the last resort of the defeated are also to be found in Dixie. The
tradition of chivalry was, as every Southern woman knows, preserved past its prime to assuage the hurt vanity of the male. Chivalry
never did much for women; the gentleman who sweeps off his hat
is likely to be careless where he spits tobacco. But in the ante-bellum
South ladies were no worse off than ladies anywhere. It was after the
war that a South determined to preserve old institutions shut its eyes
to women at work in fields and factories, and insisted that ladies
belonged at home.

Southern pride tends to maintain the existence of classes, for when there is not enough money to go around, it is desirable that at least a few "representative citizens" should be able to compete with the Yankees. This attitude is apparent whenever embarrassing questions are asked concerning the starving mountain folks or the mill workers across the tracks. Don't, says the "representative" Southerner, take those people so hard; don't go away and write about them as if they were typical. Maybe half the people in the county are on relief; maybe most of the people in town do work in the mill, and use bad grammar and not enough soap. But all our people aren't like that. Say, thirty-five percent of them are sort of between, and the top fifteen percent are just like educated people *anywhere*.

This pathetic emphasis on the top, the small percentage that is like, or as good as, and able to compete with, people *anywhere* is in one sense a confession and in one sense a boast of survival against tremendous odds. The trouble is not merely that the "representative" Southerner goes out to face the world like the representative of any poor family, wearing articles of apparel borrowed from his relatives. It is that, having borrowed, he feels compelled to bolster his confidence by insisting that the things are his by natural right, and by denying that the folks at home feel cold. Here the Yankee industrial philosophy, which says that if people choose to do without, it's their own fault, wins over the "representative" Southerner.

Hard Times Settled Down

And I brought you into a plentiful country, to eat the fruit thereof and the goodness thereof; but when ye entered, ye defiled my land, and made mine heritage an abomination.

But this is a people robbed and spoiled; they are all of them snared in holes, and they are hid in prison houses: they are for a prey, and none delivereth; and for a spoil, and none saith, Restore.

The main point to keep in mind is that the South, and even one section of it, the Tennessee Valley, is too big for generalizations. But it is safe to say that the South as a whole is poor.

As you go down the map, shake roofs, shaky bridges, and snake fences are the visible signs of poverty. There may be brand-new highways stretching white across the hills, and marked, as in the North, by neon lights, gasoline pumps, and hot-dog stands. There is sure to be a motion-picture theater in every town, and competing beauty shoppes get the girls ready for Hollywood. There is a "Times Square Grill" four thousand feet up and forty miles from a railroad in the Blue Ridge. But in spite of these evidences of enterprise, the old landmarks remain: the weathered Negro cabins under the chinaberry trees, with the crazy clay chimneys, the unglazed windows, and the white folks' washing on the fence; the boxlike shacks of the po' white trash, built hopefully facing the railroad tracks, with children and zinnias and primitive sanitary arrangements in the yards; the occasional big house that always needs a coat of paint. These things are unchanged from year to year because it costs money to change them.

The South does not measure its hard times by a seven-year boom-panic cycle; all its years are lean and you can't, Southerners say, feel a depression much if your natural state is lower than a fishworm's.

Nation-wide efforts to get over a depression have actually improved the ordinary standard of living in some sections of the South. Thus, in some of the mountain counties in the Tennessee Valley, three-quarters of the people were eligible for relief—always had been—and those who got it were better off than they had been before. For half the population to be on relief is common, and to the civilized eye necessary; in one mountain county the average cash income of a farm family was $45, not per month but for the year 1933; and of this amount $10 came from relief.

When you say that farm families in the Valley commonly have cash incomes of $100 a year or less it means that in one mountain county half the farm people didn't have a work animal—no mule, no ox—and that two out of five families had no cow or pig. Such people are called shiftless, but you must consider what they have to do with. A man looks easy-going if he keeps all his money in a tobacco sack, but maybe that's good enough for what money he's

WHEN CORN IS SCARCE, YOU HAVE TO MUZZLE THE MULE

WITH NO ELECTRIC PUMP, YOU DRAW WATER THIS WAY

got. And he can't mend the fence or the broken doorstep without nails, just as his wife can't mend the children's torn dresses without thread. Suppose the nickel you would have to pay for the nails or the thread meant the difference between a pound of streaked meat at fifteen cents and a pound of fatback at a dime. Or that it meant an extra half-pound of fatback, and you were sort of tired of eating cornbread and flour gravy. In fact you're sort of tired, so you don't feel much like fixing a fence today. There isn't anybody going to break through and steal anything, anyhow; there isn't anything to steal.

If you want bigger figures, the National Industrial Conference Board worked it out that the per capita wealth of the Valley is only half that of the country as a whole. Farming counties in the South can go deeper and deeper into debt every year just by getting less for what they grow than they must pay for what they use. The classic example is Grainger county, Tennessee, where somebody took the trouble to add up the profit and loss just as if the county were a private business. In 1932, before the era of "wild spending," state and federal agencies spent on Grainger county $91,000 in excess of revenues collected there. In the same year buildings in the county were considered to depreciate by $60,000, and soil and forests by $55,000, which made the total loss for the year $206,000.

When he vetoed the Norris bill of 1931, President Hoover felt sure that "the real development of the resources and the industries of the Tennessee Valley can only be accomplished by the people of the Valley themselves." This was flattering to Southern pride, but there is a Southern saying that you can't do nothin' when you ain't got nothin' to do nothin' with.

Southern poverty would be less shameful if it were unavoidable, but it is among the more ridiculous examples of mismanagement to be found in a world of bad housekeeping. In everything but money the South is big-rich. It is bad enough for a third of the nation to be ill-clothed, ill-housed, ill-fed, on a continent that is oversupplied with materials for meeting these needs and with the skill and labor for using them, even when the essentials and the needy may be long distances apart. But the bare and starving South is both the store-room and the servants' quarters of this national crazy house.

Nobody brought up within earshot of Southern oratory would willingly listen again to an enumeration of natural resources, but repetition has not altered the fact that forty essential minerals are found in the Southern mountains; that coal and iron for making steel are side by side; that ores of modern importance—zinc, chromium, nickel, and bauxite—are plentiful. Georgia marbles, to say nothing of those on the bottom of Norris lake in Tennessee, are famous and so accessible that two small towns have marble sidewalks and curbs, and one has a marble jail. Sandstones, limestones, and other building materials, brick and terra cotta clays, and clay deposits suitable for porcelain are all available in the Valley states. Southern streams, including the tributaries of the Tennessee, contain chemicals of value in the manufacture of rayon.

Southern forests were among the most valuable in America, and the uncut timber still includes oak, maple, poplar, hemlock, and balsam. Climate and rainfall are favorable to all forms of temperate-zone and even to some tropical vegetation and animal life. And so on and so on, for endless rolling periods, to prove that the Southland is the fairest flower in God's garden spot, a flashing pearl in the diadem of a peerless continent, and the only logical place for next year's convention or a runaway knitting mill.

Unfortunately Southerners do not eat flowers or pearls or iron ore, although some of the Alabama Negroes are said to be reduced to eating clay. And along with the best climate, soils, forests, minerals, rivers and harbors, and water power, the most abundant wild life and the most willing workers on the continent, the South also has the lowest per capita income, fewest mechanical farm aids, lowest production of dairy products, lowest ratio of pure-bred livestock, and lowest records for education and health.

In short the South has had to do without money, and in the effort has wrecked itself and held back the progress of the whole country. The really profitable industries—motor vehicles, meat packing, oil refining, printing and publishing, steel works, foundry and machine

shops, electrical machinery, women's clothing—carry on outside the
South. The South makes no radios, refrigerators, fountain pens, type-
writers, roller skates, sewing machines, shoes, or linoleum. Instead,
in little towns of the Southern frontier, you can still find the signs of
those who deal in raw hides, furs, roots and herbs, as they dealt a
hundred years ago.

In the South most people still try to make some sort of living
right out of the earth, by scratching the soil with hoes, bending
their backs over it, and grubbing on their knees. Only a quarter of
the people in the South live in cities, and they aren't big cities. In the
Tennessee Valley there are only two, Knoxville and Chattanooga,
with more than 100,000 people.

Plans, Booms, and the Nation

*Now the city was large and great: but the people were few therein, and
the houses were not builded.*

*For promotion cometh neither from the east, nor from the west, nor from the
south.*

Political and social changes that followed the Civil War were not
calculated to give Southerners a favorable view of federal reforms.
The carpetbaggers and scalawags were great people for irresponsible
spending, worthless money, packed courts, and high taxes. In their
day the Southern states learned to resent all federal interference in
their economy.

A burnt child dreads a Christmas candle, and there is more cynicism
in a cornfield of the rural South than can be packed into the Yankee
Stadium. Uncle Sam can come down, now, to play Providence; Mr.
Harry Hopkins can make promises in Memphis, and the TVA divide
the Tennessee river as by a miracle—but the South will wait to see
whose are the Egyptian chariots to be overwhelmed, and whether
the wrong people have been chosen to go over dry-shod.

Some progressive-minded people are able to take comfort from
the fact that, long before the days of the Tennessee Valley Authority

and indeed before the formation of the American government, there was in the Tennessee Valley an association for mutual benefit which was called a pioneer social experiment. It began when settlers from North Carolina began to fill up the country to the west. The state laid claim to all lands lying "west of the mountains and extending to the Mississippi"; the same territory was claimed, in 1772, by George III. Settlers along the Holston river, cutting free from all allegiances, formed their own Watauga Association—the first American community to declare, in formal articles, its independence of British rule.

Later, when the Revolution had begun, Watauga returned to North Carolina as Washington county; and the state ceded the territory to the infant Confederation in the hope that sister states would help safeguard a buffer against the Indians. But the realists in the Holston river region were doubtful of federal protection, and in 1784 they made another stab at self-government by forming the independent state of Franklin and electing their own governor.

By this time the days of the Long Hunters and the Avengers of Blood were passing; the Big Bend country had been settled, and the Donelson family, with a daughter destined to become Mrs. Andrew Jackson, had gone through the Shoals on their boat *Adventure*. But settlers in the watershed professed a fear that a state of anarchy would result if they had no protection other than that of the United States. They called a convention and resolved: "If we should be so happy as to have a separate government, vast numbers from different quarters, with a little encouragement from the public, would fill up our frontier, which would strengthen us, improve agriculture, perfect manufactures, encourage literature and everything truly laudable." You can call this independence if you like, but it looks a good deal like the boom spirit, and seems to provide support for the modern historian who argues that the Free State of Franklin grew out of plans for land speculation.

One proposed constitution required that office-holders believe in the Bible, heaven, hell, and the Trinity; but this radical document was rejected in favor of the North Carolina constitution, with a bill of rights declaring that no freeman was to be deprived of life, liberty, or property "but by the laws of the land." The laws were to "encourage virtue and suppress vice and immorality," and it was also provided that "a frequent recurrence to fundamental principles is absolutely necessary to preserve the blessings of liberty." These matters settled, citizens of the free state proceeded happily to clear the land by burning trees. They built iron bloomeries and forges and water mills, while those more enterprising formed a company to buy Cherokee lands and commenced a flirtation with the Spanish.

Nevertheless, it wasn't long before the Free State of Franklin dissolved in a contest of rival parties, with courts set up by both sides. When agreement became impossible, they finally decided to become a part of the state of Tennessee. So ended an effort which Theodore Roosevelt so optimistically commended in his *Winning of the West:* "It is this fact of the early independence and self-government of the settlers along the headwaters of the Tennessee that gives to their history its peculiar importance. They were the first men of American birth to establish a free and independent community on the continent." The rugged individuals of the region knew how to trust in God and keep their powder dry, but they had not learned to co-operate with each other to form a government.

There were other attempts at co-operation but they came from the outside. In the eighties, Thomas Hughes of Rugby sent over a party of five well-educated young Englishmen to start what he referred to as an "experiment" in Tennessee. Hughes spoke of "the power of association to lift the masses of the people in every country to a fuller and higher citizenship," in short to a more abundant life. His colony was to practice diversified farming but have a common herd, and it did get as far as establishing a free public library and the Arnold School for Boys, before the Britons gave up. It might have gone further and lasted longer if, the critical natives whispered, the English public schools had taught young men how to start sheep farms without sheep and co-operative canneries with nothing to can.

In the nineties, the Ruskin Co-operative Association worked hard to establish itself on Yellow creek in Middle Tennessee, its inspiration coming from the writings of Edward Bellamy. The Ruskin colony ran a farm and a store, and used a currency based on work-hours just as the Indians had. They also printed a newspaper, *The Coming Nation,* since they saw in the teachings of Bellamy, Ruskin, and Marx the only hope for civilization. But Bellamy himself predicted the colony's failure because society could never "be redeemed by a few people shutting themselves away from it on the principle of hermits in caves." They did fail, through internal dissension; they had a strike on the paper, and some of the colonists said that the charter they had to work under was too capitalistic. In the end a Nashville capitalist bought the farm. So ended two reform movements hopefully planted in Tennessee by foreign theorists.

But you have to believe in something; while distrusting the federal government the South developed a desperate hope in salvation by private enterprise. Down South all the "representative" people have what might be called the white-collar mind, worried over money, determined to keep up appearances, distrustful of social change, and easily won by flattery. It is the mind that makes booms and crashes, and independent of nation-wide depressions, certain parts of the South stage their own little booms and slumps. Muscle Shoals on the Tennessee river is one of these hopeful areas; there the "Tri-Cities" of Florence, Sheffield, and Tuscumbia are little towns tired out by one boom after another, going back to when Madison was President.

They were booming Shoals real estate then; General Jackson, who had crossed the river there on his way to New Orleans, owned some of the property and gave it as his opinion that it was an ideal spot for the national capital. Town lots in the woods started at three hundred dollars, and soon went as high as two thousand because it was plain to see there would have to be a big city built. By 1828 they had a railroad, Tuscumbia got its first thousand population, and civilization was established, with flour selling for eight dollars a barrel and whisky for fifty cents a gallon.

But nothing much happened for a while, and during the war the Shoals saw their share of trouble. First one side, then the other, took the county; the Yankees burned the railroad and what factories there were, also a college they were mighty proud of, and a library, and the courthouse, and some other houses at Florence.

After the war, another railroad was promised and Sheffield boomed over that; a capitalist from Atlanta paid nearly eight thousand dollars, that time, for one city lot. The bankers who were financing the railroad went broke, but there was talk of iron furnaces. Birmingham got the iron, but around 1902 they had a boomlet in which they began to talk of doing something with water power.

Then, of course, there was the World War boom, when they built Wilson dam and planned to take nitrates right out of the air. Later still there was the Ford boom at Florence, which everybody remembers—that's when they built all the city curbs you'll find out there in the bushes, making it hard to plow. Henry Ford said: "The destiny of the American people, industrially, for centuries to come, lies there on the Tennessee river at Muscle Shoals."

They hoped most of all from Mr. Ford, down in Alabama, and they say he might have got the Shoals if only he hadn't talked too much. He said he was going to sell cheap aluminum, and that stepped on Andy Mellon's toes. Mr. Ford was going to build a railroad right down from Detroit, and to hell with the freight differential; and the railroad people naturally didn't care for that. In Alabama they don't think you have much chance of succeeding at anything if you talk against all the big moneyed people that run the country.

So they weren't any too eager for the government to step in, down at the Shoals, and the city of Florence wasn't in any great hurry to take TVA power. They signed up finally, but they held out for a special rate; they hadn't forgotten that Thomas Edison had said: "The completed Muscle Shoals will be worth more than all the gold and currency in the world. Its possibilities are so great I cannot tell them."

The industrial history of Muscle Shoals summarizes that of the South. You could say it was extra unlucky, or if you believe that stars fell on Alabama, and know for a fact that one old-timer living in the Shoals district has the gift of second sight, you may prefer to think that the Shoals country is haunted. One of the first things the white

settlers did there was to massacre an Indian village. Then two men,
fighting a duel, shot and killed each other. And one more thing
happened after that; they sold out the Nation.

The Nation? It was a stretch of land near Florence, called that
because the Indians, driven westward, made a last plea for a place
where they could come back to the Shoals just to hunt and fish. Of
course they never did come back, although to humor them and get
rid of them the white men promised. The country was good fat farm
land, settled like any other and sold over and over during the booms,
but for a long time folks spoke of it as the Nation.

And you could say that the spirits of the Indians who saw no sense
to private ownership did come back to claim the place, to haunt and
hold it for public hunting and fishing.

2. WATER

The Floods Came

The floods have lifted up, O Lord, the floods have lifted up their voice. . . .

The waters stood above the mountains.
At thy rebuke they fled; at the voice of thy thunder they hasted away.
They go up by the mountains; they go down by the valleys unto the place which thou hast founded for them.
Thou hast set a bound that they may not pass over; that they turn not again to cover the earth.

Maybe you never saw a rabbit sitting in a tree. Maybe you never went to work in a rowboat, and found you had to tie it at the second-floor window of the office building. Maybe you never went home to cope with the problem of digging mud out of the inside of a piano.

Some parts of this country have dust storms instead of floods, but you can't say that rampaging rivers are confined to any one section. Back in Hoover's day, when the Mississippi set out to show what it could do to the levees, there was some talk as if flood losses were, like hookworm, a Southern complaint. But later on, the rivers up around Hartford, Connecticut, and Pittsburgh, Pennsylvania, took their turn.

Down South some think the trouble with the Tennessee is that it's a Yankee river. That seems a mean thing to say, but there are arguments that go to prove it. Just look at the way the river comes along and takes the good rich topsoil off the land. Isn't that exactly like a big company from up North coming in, to cut the trees and mine the coal out, and leave nothing but stumps and holes in the ground? Then look at the way the floods are always bringing down the tall

33

trees and the good soil from up on the hills, and putting everything on the bottom—turning things upside down, like the Yankee with his ideas of social equality. The river hasn't got any respect for people's ways of living either. It just makes a big bend towards the South to fool you, but in the end it flows North.

It gave itself away way back when it took sides during the war, right there at the bend at Chattanooga, when they fought the battle above the clouds at Lookout Mountain.

You recall that they'd already fought at Chickamauga; General Rosecrans had played a low underhanded Yankee trick of coming in from the Southwest when everybody looked for him from the North, where Yankees ought to come from. But General Bragg outsmarted him and pushed him into Chattanooga, and then moved up on the mountain himself. It looked as if Bragg was bound to win then, because while the Yankees had the town, he had both the better position and the railroad. His men were right where they could roll rocks down on the heads of any Yankees so foolish as to come up the mountain, and while maybe that wouldn't hurt a Yankee, they did stand a good chance to starve without the railroad to bring in supplies.

But there was the river, making its bend. And you know what they did? They built a boat up at Bridgeport and brought it down to Kelly's Ferry with truck to eat. They called it the *Chattanooga,* and people living along the river called it the *Chicken Thief.* But that boat saved the Yankees and gave them strength to climb the mountain, and it proved the river was on their side. Because it carried their boat right on, when all it had to do was go down for dry weather as it so often does and they couldn't have navigated. You can say the Yankees were smart as hell to build a boat, but it took hell and high water too for them to do the job.

The thing is to find some way to make the water work for you instead of against you. Dr. Harcourt Morgan, chairman of the Tennessee Valley Authority, came down from Canada half a century ago and picked Tennessee as a good place to live because he liked the big rainfall. But he says that big rainfall is either the Valley's biggest blessing or its biggest curse, according to how you manage it.

Members of Congress have been known to doubt the wisdom of interference with nature, and one Ohio town subject to floods just gave up and moved. But the act creating the Tennessee Valley Authority says it is "to control the destruction of flood waters in the Tennessee river and Mississippi river basins." A Yankee wondered in print why such an enterprise should have been undertaken in a region relatively free from floods. Tell that in Chattanooga, where they've seen steamboats in the streets and where TVA men, charting the course of the flood of '67, planted their tripods in front of the Hotel Patten in the heart of town.

It was good news to the whole Valley that in the floods of 1936 and 1937, TVA engineers cut from three to five feet off the crests at Chattanooga. This meant a foot off at Paducah and six inches off as far down as Cairo, at a time when they had sandbags and mud boxes on top of the levees there. You have to remember that an inch on the crest of a flood may be as important as an inch on the end of a man's nose.

In 1937 only one dam above Chattanooga was working. Hiwassee dam will take another two feet off the crest, and with the whole series they expect to cut it down twenty feet. Differences in the Ohio and the Mississippi should be proportionate, according to the estimate made in 1927, when they said that from fourteen to twenty percent of the big river's surplus came from Tennessee.

Opinions differ about the best means of flood control; people have suggested digging holes through to China to drain off the water. Some engineers are faithful to the levee idea even after what they saw along the Mississippi. But the army engineers officially abandoned the levee plan in 1927, and Dr. Arthur Morgan had made up his mind when he worked out the Miami river project in Ohio. Building dirt walls and messing with sandbags is clumsy and primitive, like trench warfare. In fact it was warfare of the worst kind when Mississippi valley farmers crossed the river to cut the levees so other folks' fields instead of theirs would be flooded.

But if you want flood control by dams you must build them in the upper reaches of the river; this means that dams on the Tennessee will help in Ohio and Mississippi floods just as a dam on the Hiwassee affects the Tennessee. One engineer, not working for TVA, considered that the effect of the whole TVA system on the lower Mississippi should be comparable to that of the Bonnet Carré spillway at New Orleans. Engineers for the Authority say it should take two feet, at least, off the big river below Cairo.

By its dams the Tennessee will, in the words of one of the TVA engineers, "flow down a giant stairway from one end of the Valley to the other." It will be gauged and guided; even with work in progress in 1936, they managed the floodgates at Norris and Wheeler to prevent flooding the coffer dams at Pickwick Landing. They don't depend on finding catfish up the branches or seeing boll weevils dig in; they post daily schedules in the TVA offices, and even the schoolchildren at Norris study river-gauging.

Considering all this, it is surprising that TVA is inclined to discount the importance of dams in its water-control program. The dams are necessary, they say. But to do the thing right you must catch the water where it falls.

The Earth Melted

Wherefore gloriest thou in the valleys, thy flowing valley, O backsliding daughter?

There shall be an handful of corn in the earth upon the top of the mountains.

For the waters of Nimrim shall be desolate: for the hay is withered away, the grass faileth, there is no green thing.

Therefore the abundance they have gotten, and that which they have laid up, shall they carry away to the brook of the willows.

Sightseers at the dams, going as close as they are allowed to the big steel shafts and feeling the pulse of the power, think that the power starts with this machinery. Actually the machinery just harnesses the power of water so it can be used to drive more machinery, or wash the clothes, or cook the waffles. The power was there all the time, and for years it's been pushing down on the topsoil of the Valley—a light soil, tilted every whichway so that the water can carry it right off.

Stories of the North Carolina farmer who fell out of a field and broke his neck, and of his cousin in Tennessee who always tied his mule to a tree before he began to plow, don't seem far-fetched when you look at the country. If you insist on farming those hills you have to plow slopes that look dangerous to man and beast, and are dangerous to the land. Over in North Carolina they tell how it took generations to teach corn to climb the mountains, and that should have taught them corn was never meant to grow up there. Water runs off corn land several times as fast as it runs off grass or woodland, and instead of traveling alone it elopes with the topsoil.

In the old days they knew so little about erosion that they plowed straight up the hill and let the water race down in ditches between the rows. After a while it seeped into their minds that it would be better to plow round and round the hill. But a lot of Southern farmers got to where they couldn't grow enough corncobs to stopper the jugs before they decided it would be better not to plow at all.

Bottom lands, of course, grew fatter as the topsoil from above came down. But on the rich bottom farms the corn is drowned when the water runs wild, and the floods these days are fiercer and more frequent.

Now, why is that? The average rainfall is just what it was, and they say 50 inches is just about ideal for vegetation. It's what they have at the source of the Blue Nile in the mountains of Africa. But the Tennessee Valley's maximum variation, 40 to 80 inches, isn't enough to account for the extra damage done when the creeks and rivers start cutting new ways through bare land. Old folks in the Valley all know the land washes worse than it used to, and the floods are worse, too. Most of the creeks and branches are so muddy, even in ordinary weather, that you can't see anything of a swimming turtle except his head. In flood times, you expect them to run like mean-dispositioned claybank horses, with sticks and cornstalks and even tree trunks tangled in their manes.

To find clear water and the sandy bottoms they used to have in Dixie, you've got to go way up in the hills and woods, where leaves and moss and roots still act as a filter. Any railroad cut or roadside shows you what happens when they go; you'll see roots holding the soil at the top, and hanging in the air where it has washed below. But if there are no roots to take hold, the ground washes into gullies, and that shows you how it is that the plowed land bleeds to death. There are places now where you can hardly tell what color the top-soil was; what you see is the red clay underneath, the color of raw beefsteak, with shattered bones of limestone sticking through.

People notice erosion more than they used to, and it's got around that the Mississippi takes an acre a minute into the Gulf, so that travelers who exclaim over the changing color of the water at New Orleans are seeing the United States in solution. Milk bottles in TVA's hydraulics laboratory show what the various branches of the Tennessee contribute to this burden, and all the people who be-lieve in fighting to defend American soil should look hard at those bottles of silt.

The Tennessee Valley Authority is interested in erosion because it silts up reservoirs and buries dams. They say Deep river, in North Carolina, silted up eleven out of fifteen private power reservoirs built there in less than fifty years, and a private power dam on the Ocoee is filling up now. Dr. Arthur Morgan feels that the danger has been exaggerated in the case of the TVA dams, and they say that Norris lake is good for at least seven hundred years. Neverthe-less, they aren't taking any chances.

Leaping into the breach, in its first year the Authority put CCC boys to work building 59,000 little "gully dams" on dry land. In bad cases the boys put down wired mats of brush to hold the ground, and some farmers ready to move off decided to stay awhile, in case the scheme should work.

Tractor-drawn terracing machines were brought in, too, and they got the cost of terracing down as low as $1.75 an acre. Some of the steeper slopes can't be helped that way, but it works down in the rolling cotton country where they have sheet erosion.

Of course you've still got people who can't be worried about it or who consider the land will last their time. But even the bottom lands suffer in time, as the washing goes on in the hills. Under the top-soil lies clay, and it washes too. Some of this clay can be used for making fine porcelain, but none of it is suitable for agriculture; and when the kaolin coats the bottoms they will have to mine for good soil down there.

People who think that the job of the Tennessee Valley Authority is building dams and nothing else are inclined to minimize the importance of the fight against erosion, but the TVA staff, from the chairman down, emphasizes that part of the job. They are struggling to pry loose the grip of a giant whose gnarled red hands, gouging deeper, are tearing the Southern hills apart and crumbling them into the river.

You can figure it out in acre-feet or tons of pressure and find they're right when they say that the underground reservoir, meaning the ground drainage, is the biggest one in the Valley—bigger even than Norris lake, which could cover the state of Pennsylvania with a foot of water.

Steamboat round the Bend

He gathereth the waters of the sea together as an heap; he layeth up the depth in storehouses.

And there shall be upon every high mountain, and upon every high hill, rivers and streams of waters.

An orator at Knoxville objected to the arrival of the steamboat *Atlas,* on March 3, 1828, because it would bring outsiders into Tennessee. He wasn't alone in his hostility; the state had to have a law against throwing rocks at steamboats.

But most Southern politicians like the idea of river navigation,

and steamboats in the golden era on the Mississippi were the fore-
runners of dream boats on every creek and branch and bayou from
Florida to Texas. The Tennessee, coming after the Mississippi, the
Ohio, and the Missouri as the country's fourth navigable river, was
an obvious subject for hope.

Flatboats, in the early days, went down by way of the Ohio to
New Orleans; they didn't try to make the return trip, but were
broken up to make the wooden sidewalks the Creoles called *ban-
quettes*. Some called the flatboats "arks." Keelboats, which were nar-
rower, could come back upstream by bushwhacking, which means
grabbing at the branches overhead and pulling along that way. But
of course there was always trouble at the Shoals.

So it was seven years after the first steamboat got to Florence, in
1821, before one got up as far as Knoxville. They made all sorts of
plans for getting over or around the Shoals; one man took out a
patent for putting steamboats on rollers, and they dug or started
more than one canal; the last one was begun by a young engineer
named Goethals, who afterwards did a good big job of canal-digging.
But the Shoals jinx defeated him, and they ran out of funds, as usual.

Their best plan was to run one boat line up to the Shoals and another above, and that was the way they managed around the time of
the Civil War. They had enough boats then to make what they could
call an armada for General Grant, when he managed to get the river
on his side. After the war, in the eighties, they never did much with
passenger boats, but the freight traffic was considerable, and some
people think it might have kept up if the railroads hadn't got control of the boat lines.

Anyhow the army engineers who studied navigation on the Tennessee before the days of TVA estimated that, with proper development of the channel, the river traffic in 1950 could amount to 17,-
800,000 tons, with an annual saving of $22,800,000 in transportation
costs. Everybody now agrees that this was too optimistic, but it
sounded well to Southern congressmen.

So "to improve navigation in the Tennessee river" is one of the
legally constituted objectives of TVA, although it was cannily ob-

WATER DAMAGE: WHEN THE FLOODS CAME TO PADUCAH

FIRE DAMAGE: SOMETIMES THEY BURN OFF THE TREES

EVERYTHING IS SHIPSHAPE DOWN AT WHEELER DAM

served by the first chairman of the Authority that "TVA did not
originate the policy of making the Tennessee river navigable. That
policy was established by the national government through congressional action under a Republican administration before the TVA
was born."

Dutifully carrying out its mandate to do what Congress authorized in 1930, the Authority is making a nine-foot channel from
Paducah to Knoxville; and now the little river excursion steamer,
the *Golden Eagle,* can get past the Shoals.

Republicans and sinners who like to talk about the unnavigable
Tennessee can take even less comfort from the freight traffic, which
passed the 2,000,000-ton mark in 1936 and is rising right along. Last
April the Gulf Refining company started sending tow-loads of gasoline and oil from St. Louis down the river to Perryville, Sheffield, Decatur, and Guntersville, because they found they could do it for about
half the railroad rate; there were rumors that the Standard Oil people were planning to send barges up from Baton Rouge.

So when the Southern railroads petitioned the Interstate Commerce Commission to abolish the freight differential, they cited the
Gulf Refining company's shipments as competition to be met, although Perryville, Tennessee, isn't even on a railroad.

Conservative Southerners who don't think so much of government
interference admit that if TVA gets rid of the freight differential, it
will be paying its way. And while Southern politicians will vie with
each other to claim credit for that achievement, it seems clear that the
Authority has done more than any other agency to bring it about.
Southerners had been working on the problem a long time, but TVA
built the dams that provided the competition to turn the trick.

Besides that, the Authority has been a convincing witness in the
controversy. In a survey issued in 1937, it pointed out that it costs 39
cents *more* to ship a hundred pounds of freight from Atlanta to
Chicago, 731 miles, than it does to ship the same amount 890 miles
to Chicago from New York; that you must pay 41 cents more to send
the same package from Atlanta to New York than to ship it the
greater distance from Chicago to New York; and that it costs two

cents more to send it from Atlanta to Louisville, than it does to send
it 403 miles farther, from New York to Louisville. These things are
no news to you if you grew up in the South, but it seems you have
to put them down in black and white before the Yankees will believe it.

The TVA book tells you also that the freight rate per hundred
pounds is a dime more if you ship to Nashville from Smithville,
Georgia, than if you shipped from Chicago, although the distance is
exactly the same. Stoves made in Sheffield, Alabama, cost 10 cents
more a hundred pounds to send to Chicago than stoves made in Detroit cost to send to Reading, Pennsylvania, six miles farther. You
must pay 7 cents more to send a hundred pounds of Tennessee
marble from Knoxville to Newburgh, New York, than you would
pay to send the same weight of Indiana limestone seven miles farther,
from Indianapolis to New York. You pay these differences for no
explicable reason except that the Yankees charge what the traffic can
be made to bear. Certainly they have no relation to the cost of freight
transportation, because it is also shown that costs are lower down
South.

Of course the South moves less freight, but if they want to charge
more because they ship less, they also ship less because they charge
more. Moans and groans never did any good, but now big corporations have started buying river terminals, and they say that Atlanta,
built on its railroad traffic, got excited enough to ask about water-
front connections at Chattanooga.

Another study made by TVA shows that the prosperous parts of
the country are those with access to deep water, along the coasts or
the Great Lakes and the Mississippi. So far there's nothing nautical
about Tennessee, but the dams do remind you of big ships in port.
Maybe it's the cleanness, and the paint, and the railings with life pre-
servers.

And of course the working of a power dam is easier to understand
if you see it as a steamship in reverse. A ship's engines work to turn
the screw, which turns the propeller, which moves the ship through
the water. A dam stands still and lets the water run through it. But

the rush of the water moves the turbines, and the power goes out to
work engines on the land.

On the Just and the Unjust

Hast thou perceived the breadth of the earth? . . .
Who hath divided a watercourse for the overflowing of waters, or a way
for the lightning of thunder?

He putteth forth his hand upon the rock; he overturneth the mountains by
the roots.
He cutteth out rivers among the rocks. . . .
He bindeth the floods from overflowing. . . .

He hath compassed the waters with bounds, until the day and night come to
an end. . . .
But the thunder of his power who can understand?

Water, falling from heaven on man-made boundaries, washes them
out. A good many people have been struck by the thought that the
Valley watershed violates the constitution in the matter of states'
rights. Little drops of water from the Powell, the Clinch, the Holston, or the French Broad may pour, in flood times, into cellars in
Paducah or nibble at foundations in New Orleans. Little grains of
sand from a cottonfield in Alabama can travel by water until deposited on the floor of a hotel in Cairo, Illinois. Norris dam, if it were
silted up, would be filled with soil from North Carolina and Virginia
as well as from Tennessee.

So flood control of the Tennessee river system is, in the words of a
TVA engineer, "engineering on a scale hitherto unattempted in
America."

The nearest thing was the Panama canal, but except for the malaria
problem the jobs are very unlike. In the Canal Zone lines can be
drawn firmly and Uncle Sam has the say-so, beyond question, on
his side of the line. In the Valley the state and city and county authorities are there to have their say, in the American or anyhow the
Southern language, and no dividing line keeps the rest of the country out.

Instead they are making an effort, for the first time in the history
of the country, to go beyond what you might call a job of plumbing
repair to study its relationship to the whole house. Up to now we've
been considering every job separately, with some queer results. Dr.
Arthur Morgan told about a dam on the French Broad river authorized by the government in 1929. A year or two later other federal officials, at the request of local and state officials, approved a million-
dollar bridge just above the dam site. The bridge and three million
dollars' worth of highway would be drowned out by the dam.

This is the sort of thing that planning on the TVA scale is meant
to avoid. So far, going slowly and studying the records of previous
floods not only in the streets of Chattanooga, but on the Danube and
in the Nile valley, the Authority has managed to hold to a general
program; and it has yet to make an error as costly as that of the private company which found a better site for a dam after it had spent
six millions in one false start.

Anybody can see the sense in planning for water control over a
wide area; you don't stop a flood at the river mouth or erosion in
the bottom lands. But another kind of breadth to the TVA program
is harder for folks to understand. That is the spread into the economic field that takes in power production along with flood control
and navigation; they call them "multi-purpose" dams.

Any dams are expensive, and Yankee taxpayers, who are putting
up most of the money for TVA, stand their only chance to get their
money back through the sale of power. But some people, seeing that
the allocation figures finally charged a little over half the costs to
power development, wonder if it wouldn't have been cheaper to
leave the power out. The answer is that to build dams for flood control alone may be reasonable, but once you include navigation, it
would be plain foolish not to include power.

Either high dams or low dams will keep back floods, but to make
a deep channel for navigation high dams are better, because you don't
need so many. The army engineers made two plans for the Valley,
one for thirty-two low dams, the other for seven or more high dams.

The low dams would have lengthened the navigation time from the river mouth to Knoxville by eleven and a half hours.

Deciding to build high dams, TVA provided for flood control, shortened navigation time, and got power as a by-product or any-how as an unavoidable consequence. Back in 1903, when he vetoed a bill for a private power franchise at the Shoals, President Theodore Roosevelt said: "Justice to the taxpayers of the country demands that when the government is or may be called upon to improve the stream, the improvement should be made to pay for itself, so far as practicable." Thirty years later Dr. Arthur Morgan observed that, if dams to make a navigable channel could also develop two or three million kilowatts of energy, "how stupid it would be to throw it away."

You do have to stretch your mind to think of several things at once, and people who can't do that always assume that over-all planners are bound to fail. Even Dr. Arthur Morgan, so confident of possibilities that he wanted TVA to find a way to save the power companies from loss, began to be nervous about using dams for both flood control and power as soon as he had to turn the management over to other people. But he thought they were all right as long as he had control.

While you use the same dam for holding back flood waters, and for storing water for navigation and power production, of course you can't use the same reservoir space. So you must provide extra storage capacity for your multi-purpose dams. This has been done by TVA; it was not done in the Ohio district where Dr. Arthur Morgan built a dam marked with a much-quoted warning:

THE DAMS
OF THE MIAMI CONSERVANCY DISTRICT ARE FOR
FLOOD PREVENTION PURPOSES.
THEIR USE FOR POWER DEVELOPMENT OR FOR STORAGE
WOULD BE A MENACE TO THE CITIES BELOW.

To insure complete flood protection under the TVA system, you need only make sure that the dams are not worked too hard; that is, that the reservoirs are not kept too full. This works out automatically if the installed generating capacity of the dam is in the right proportion to the size of the reservoir, considered from the standpoint of flood expectancy. Dr. Arthur Morgan has expressed his confidence in the safety of the dams as built.

Anybody just looking at the river, particularly around the Shoals, would say it was naturally intended to provide power but not very promising for boats. The little grist mills all over the Valley—one near Norris dam is over a hundred years old—show that early settlers with common sense saw what to do with a river that drops a foot a mile from the mountains to its mouth. Water boiling over the rocks at the Shoals was working hard, only it wasn't earning much.

But of course the river had to be trained to work regularly, day in and day out, the whole year long. Sometimes, left to itself, it would get down to a trickle; then in a few weeks it might be a flood half a mile wide. At Florence they measured and found the big flow over a hundred times the lowest flow. Engineers called it a "flashy" river.

Now all that is changed; the TVA engineers figure that Wilson dam takes care of daily, Wheeler of fortnightly, and Norris of seasonal variations. So there's no reason why the river shouldn't punch the clock regularly, and in fact they're fooling it and making the same water that started work at Norris keep working all the way down. Maybe you could have let it go its own sweet way and still cut flood losses by building low dams, growing crops on the bottoms except in flood season. But that would have introduced another hazard; you'd have had to get the farmers out in time. It's easier to regiment the river.

And once you start managing the water, there seems no end to what you can do with it. Look at one little item they seldom mention: malaria control. Southerners living in the river bottoms had been slapping mosquitoes for years and thinking nothing of it; of course the children generally had chills and fever, off and on, but what could you do about it? The Yankees, though, are fussy about little things and can't seem to stand trouble; as soon as they came down, they established a special TVA division to deal with malaria. They sent up airplanes to dust Paris green over the swamps, and they ran around in motor boats putting oil on stagnant water. They drained some of the marshes and limestone sinkholes where the water stood. But after they got the dams built they found the most effective way was to raise and lower the water level in the reservoirs about a foot, during the breeding season. That put out the sensitive young mosquitoes so that eventually, they hope, the druggists won't be able to sell so much of that patent remedy called "666" that you see advertized on all the fences. Down in Alabama some people were afraid the mosquito campaign would hurt the fishing, but they said not. And in their Yankee way, they actually figured out that farmers might lose from $12 to $40 on one spell of fever, counting lost time and medicines.

But how would you figure what proportion of the cost of TVA dams should be charged up to killing mosquitoes?

Just as it's hard to separate the parts of an organic whole, which the project seems to be, it's hard to say that one part is more important than another. Some people, either for or against, see the power program as the big thing. Others say that phosphates will be more essential than power, in time. Some think that nothing is as important as ridding the Valley of mosquitoes and the freight differential, at one fell swoop.

But all these come back, one way or another, to what the Authority calls water control. With flood damage the foolish waste that it has come to be in this country, and with erosion worse for the soil, they say, than dust storms, it's hard to think of anything they could do better than managing the river and the run-off on the land.

That is the view of visitors from a country that has long served as an example to flood and erosion fighters. In China, they say, it is too late to do what they are doing in the Valley. Knoxville has the usual number of laundries run by exiles whose presence in a far country might be traced to the fact that the rivers of China were not harnessed in time. But one of the most interested sightseers at Norris was the Honorable Fo-liang Chang, director of rural welfare in the province of Nan-chang.

And on South Gay street in Knoxville is the Norris bookshop, "the first Chinese bookstore in America." Its proprietor, a graduate of Vanderbilt university who was born in Canton, is aware of the importance of TVA but is able to understand other views. He cites a Chinese proverb to show that in his country too, some people were distrustful of outsiders.

3. ROOTS

Nature Takes Its Course

The whole land is made desolate, because no man layeth it to heart.
The spoilers are come upon all high places through the wilderness.

They shall march with an army, and come against her with axes, as hewers of wood.
They shall cut down her forest, saith the Lord, though it cannot be searched.

A man was famous according as he had lifted up axes upon the thick trees.

On a summer Sunday in the Cumberland Presbyterian church at Fayetteville, Tennessee, the young preacher mentioned God's bountiful gifts. The earth, he said, blossomed and bore fruit for us, and he was right because Fayetteville is in Middle Tennessee, in good farming country.

But it was not enough merely to accept the divine gift of a bountiful harvest. We must, said the young preacher, do something about it. He waved his hand, and it just happened that he waved towards an old red-brick house used as headquarters for the AAA and the Farm Security Administration, and for the office of the county cooperative selling TVA power.

Some people feel that doing anything about it is wrong; all these government planners are going against nature, maybe against Providence. Man was put here to till the ground where he wants to and as he wants to, without orders from Washington. Let the New Deal bureaus come and go; farming will go on as it always has.

Nature's cycle by which rain makes the plants grow, the plants feed the animals, the animals fertilize the soil and in turn feed the plants, seemed bound to last. It was broken by the animal that

49

learned to use other animals and plants and minerals in excess of his own needs. Sometimes the break is temporary, but sometimes the land itself is washed out, worked out, gone.

The abomination of desolation mentioned by the prophet is in Eastern Tennessee. They say it might have been in North Carolina, but when they were marking the boundary they ran out of whisky and had to make a trip down into Georgia after it. This accounts for the jagged corner where the three states meet, and where the copper mines are.

People who have seen Western deserts aren't so astonished by this area, in which sulphur fumes from copper smelting killed off the grass and trees and poisoned the ground, and laid a blight on the country so that for miles around Copper Hill and Ducktown no green thing can grow. But the local people, used to a decent cover over the nakedness of the earth, are shocked by the sight; and anybody should give thought to the fact that this imitation of a Western waste wasn't made by centuries of erosion, as the natural deserts were. This desert was man-made, of recent memory. They stopped the sort of mining that made it when a power company sued because its reservoirs were being filled up, and now the fumes that killed the trees are turned into acid that sells for more than the copper ore. But the desolation is left, mile after mile of it, raw red gullies as far as the eye can see. The earth still washes, exposing roots to show there once were trees, and the creeks cut deeper into canyons to be bridged by the WPA.

And within an afternoon's drive is the other extreme, the land as God made it. Climb up into the Joyce Kilmer Memorial forest, in North Carolina, and you can see nearly 3500 acres of virgin hardwood—poplars and hemlocks six or seven feet through. Nobody can slash them with a saw or poison the air they breathe; they are safe on their reservation, forever.

The odd thing is that the natural state of the Kilmer trees is due to planning, while the desolation around Ducktown is due to letting nature, human nature, take its course. Thanks to human nature the destruction throughout the Valley, as throughout the country, differs from that of Copper Hill only in degree. In time, lumbering and farming can do what mining did.

While the pioneers were eager to kill off the birds, buffaloes, and Indians, they had a lasting grudge against trees. The pioneer cabin stood in a "clearing," and indeed it was necessary to clear a cover under which wild animals or Indians might lurk, as it was to clear the fields before they could be plowed. But from this woodchopping there came a habitual attitude of enmity, so that tree-cutting, except in the case of cherry trees, was represented as a virtue in stories told the young.

This determination to get out of the woods was not peculiar to the South. In the far West, men cut down the biggest sequoia—the oldest living thing on earth—just for the fun of it; and in New England, not so long ago, mischief-makers hacked the heart out of a historic elm. A Frenchman traveling in New York in 1831 noticed "a general feeling of hatred against trees. . . . They believe that the absence of woods is the sign of civilization." This belief made Yankee cities cut the elms on Main street even before Southern towns removed them from the courthouse yard. There are little cabins sitting under the Southern sun with no more shade than they get from rows of cotton, and maybe it's that low-growing cotton no higher than a bumblebee's knees. On the other hand, it was a good old custom to leave or even to plant an avenue of trees leading up to the big house, and in some parts of the South where the Yankees burned the houses you can still see those double rows of oaks or cedars or magnolias, leading nowhere.

Of course the Lord did give the South an extra-fine stand of timber. It's been figured that in one Kentucky county the original growth would now be worth $3750 to every person living there. Farm family income thereabouts is less, today, than the interest on that capital. But there as elsewhere the lumber companies came in, paying two bits to five dollars an acre for the land, and then giving men seventy-five cents to a dollar a day to strip it off. Now the big companies are gone and the work is gone, and small farmers are cutting out dogwood to sell for twelve dollars a cord. Some people

don't like the idea of destroying dogwood, but twelve dollars is a
lot of money to a farmer, and it seems they use the wood in making
machinery for textile mills.

It is now recognized by the utilitarians that large-scale destruction
of the trees was bad business. It seems the trees served a purpose in
catching clouds, breaking winds, and holding down a fugitive soil.
So they had been a help to the farmers who were so glad to see
them go, and the soil was poorer and the floods worse after the
lumber companies cashed in on the slow growth of centuries under
their policy of "cut and get out."

Since this expert opinion is not generally held, there are parts of the
South and of the Valley where you have to persuade them to let
the little trees grow. In Western North Carolina, only last year, it
was reported that half the forest fires were deliberately set. They
have a mistaken idea that burning off the trees helps the land; or
sometimes hunters do it to scare out game. Anyhow, on one tract
that they fired, over ten thousand acres burned.

Of course the game never had a chance. Back in the days when
Andy Jackson was a young man, Reelfoot lake in Tennessee—just
over the edge of the Valley—was made by an earthquake. That lake
and the cypress swamps around it attracted all sorts of birds and for
a while there weren't enough settlers to kill them off. They made
up for it later, though. They killed the swans and shipped them in
box-car loads to Nashville and Memphis, where they sold for two
bits apiece. They killed the egrets. Now just to mention Reelfoot to
some people is enough to make them cry.

But over the eastern rim of the Valley they are bringing wild
life back to the national parks; they have deer and wild turkeys
and ravens and eagles in the Smokies now. As with the trees, it
appears to take some sort of planning to get back to a state of nature.

They say the Indians are multiplying too, but there is a good
reason for not planning to bring them back in any force. Back in
1733 the trustees of Oglethorpe's colony in Georgia made a treaty
under which they promised to make restitution for any damage
done by the settlers. If the Indians were ever to present a bill for

damage done the forests and the soil, the streams and the birds and beasts, in Georgia or any other Valley state, it would be embarrassing.

Even partial restoration is a job to keep several government agencies busy. The Tennessee Valley Authority is welcomed in reforestation circles; it grows 18,000,000 seedlings a year in its nurseries and oversees their planting by the CCC boys. Fish hatcheries established by the Authority supply the river and the reservoirs; bird sanctuaries and game reserves have been marked out along the new shorelines or on the islands. The Forest Service is doing the same thing, but it can use reinforcements.

These little trimmings just touch the real trouble, which is that of the wasted soil. You can grow trees, not a primeval forest but ordinary hardwood for commercial cutting, in two or three generations; it takes centuries to restore lost land. Up to a point you can turn wornout lands to pasture, so eventually restoring their fertility, but there comes a time when even grass refuses to grow. There are places in the Valley where no cover crop will grow without fertilizer; and so, in the new cycle being set up to take the place of a natural cycle that has been destroyed, the making of fertilizer by water power at Muscle Shoals is one stage.

You can start following a cycle anywhere and come out the same place, but there is something reassuring about beginning on the ground. TVA may be able to replace the broken natural cycle— the old simple rhythm of rain to plants, plants to animals, animals to soil—with its own new rhythm of rain to river, river to power, power to fertilizer, and fertilizer to crops. But in this new pattern you can see that the dams and the fertilizer factory together do only what a good soil would do: they hold the water, and combine it with crushed rock to make plant food.

Earth Saves Itself

The earth also is defiled under the inhabitants thereof; because they have transgressed the laws.

Ye that follow after righteousness, ye that seek the Lord: look unto the rock whence ye are hewn, and to the hole of the pit whence ye are digged. . . . For the Lord shall comfort Zion: he will comfort all her waste places.

On Dr. H. A. Morgan's desk in Knoxville, between his pipe and one of those birds the woodcarvers whittle up in the mountains, is a chunk of something that looks like hoarhound candy. Actually it is TVA's proud achievement called "metaphosphate." From the standpoint of distribution, what is important is that this product, which is nearly two-thirds plant food, is less bulky to ship than ordinary fertilizers. It is not affected by a little weather, so it can be moved like coal, in flat cars or barges. And from the standpoint of manufacture, it is important that this concentrated fertilizer can be made from low-grade phosphate rock, not hitherto considered to be of great value. Dr. H. A. Morgan feels that the TVA process, which made available for use large deposits of this low-grade ore, has contributed immeasurably to our natural resources. If you must measure, maybe it's worth more than the whole cost of the project.

As he talks, Dr. Morgan scribbles the signs for the chemical elements on a yellow pad, until even a city-raised person can understand that phosphates are no patent medicine, but something necessary to a fertile soil.

In parts of Tennessee the crops and gardens languish, and the land looks exactly as if it needed water, but the rainfall is abundant and the fact is that hunger is counterfeiting thirst. Land needs water, but it also needs nitrogen and phosphorus, as part of its regular diet; dirt farmers can say they never heard of such a thing, but the land nowadays seems to know about it, the way a modern child will ail if it doesn't get enough vitamins. It may take the diagnosis of a soil specialist to show what element is lacking, and the proportion in which it should be supplied. But you have to accept the idea that the basic soil elements are as essential as water and air and more essential than dirt as such; the new-fangled dirtless farm puts these elements into the water.

That TVA has undertaken to supply phosphates instead of nitrates, as provided in the original plan for Muscle Shoals, is explainable on several counts. By growing the right cover crop you get five pounds of nitrate for every pound of phosphate you add to the soil. So every phosphate-demonstration farm in the Valley becomes the nitrate factory Uncle Sam had intended to run at Muscle Shoals, with clover or lespedeza to do what the German manufacturing process was supposed to do—pull the nitrates right out of the air.

Furthermore, the clover or the lespedeza or whatever cover crop you plant solves another problem, that of hitching the fertilizer to the ground. Over in the Appalachian country they tell about one man who put on a lot of commercial fertilizer, and his neighbor said: "Nice cotton land you're making there." When the hill farmer disclaimed all intention of planting cotton, the neighbor explained that he didn't mean the cotton would grow until the fertilizer had washed down the river into Alabama.

But anchor the fertilizer with a cover crop, and maybe you've got it; at any rate you've helped TVA stop erosion, which is the part that fertilizer is supposed to play in the reclamation cycle.

As for what the phosphates will do on the ground, all you have to do is look at a field in any one of the demonstration farms. There are over twenty-three thousand of these farms in the Valley and in states over the country—farms where TVA phosphates are being used in accordance with conditions laid down by the Authority and agreed to by the farmer. On these farms, crop yields increase, weeds give up, and farmers note the miraculous appearance of dormant legumes. One said: "I didn't sow nothin'. Tell me, where was that clover?" In one of the mountain counties where they have copperheads, a woman farmer said that when she crossed the pasture she always walked on the part where no phosphate had been applied, because the grass was so thin there she could see the snakes. And of course the smart farm animals prefer a phosphate-flavored pasture.

But nobody claims that phosphates are a panacea. The TVA men are fond of making an example of Middle Tennessee, the part of the state known locally as the "dimple of the universe." (It was the whole state that Governor Fiddlin' Bob Taylor called the diamond breastpin on the shirtfront of the world.) Even a non-agrarian from the outside can see the difference, going over the rim of the Cumberlands and down into this section where they have fat barns, like Pennsylvania, and bluegrass, like Kentucky. Almost anything will flourish in Middle Tennessee, although there's no telling what will happen if they keep on growing corn on the slopes and hay in the bottoms.

Any Valley farmer knows that the dimple of the universe was favored by Providence with good soil, but the TVA men reveal that the secret of this soil is phosphates, put there like a present from Providence. Middle Tennessee is where TVA gets its phosphate ore. Dig out that Middle Tennessee mud, refine it at Muscle Shoals, and you can make another dimple anywhere—anyhow, you can grow bluegrass. If, that is, phosphate is the missing element. Of course it does no good to put phosphates on a farm in Middle Tennessee, where they are already.

Also the dose for soils needing phosphate will vary, and tests are required to determine the right formula. That is why TVA makes soil maps and is co-operating with the Department of Agriculture and the land-grant colleges in a soil survey of the Valley.

It is one reason why the phosphate program is not being rushed through, but the chief reason for that is that you can't get anywhere if you try to rush farmers. Especially Southern farmers.

How They Teach Evolution

If my land cry out against me, or that the furrows likewise thereof complain. . . .
Let thistles grow instead of wheat, and cockle instead of barley.

Be ye ashamed, O ye husbandmen; howl, O ye vinedressers, for the wheat and for the barley; because the harvest of the field is perished.
The vine is dried up, and the fig tree languisheth; the pomegranate tree, the palm tree also, and the apple tree, even all the trees of the field, are withered.

The CCC boys squirmed a little as the man began to talk; they liked movies better than speakers. But this man started telling about a place called the Carlsbad Caverns.

He told about a trick they have of making it dark down under the earth, darker than you ever thought it could be even before the world began, while the choir sings "Rock of Ages." That trick may seem pretty funny to sophisticated people from up North, but the tourists take it seriously and so did the CCC boys, the way it was told.

Then the speaker switched to the Grand Canyon and how it grew. All this was to explain how long it takes to make rock; it was freshman geology for the CCC. Since it was the first time most of the boys had heard anything of the kind, they listened. They listened all through the mosses as the start of vegetation, and how mosses and trees broke up the rock to make soil; how "countless generations of plants and animals have spent their life span on or in each soil, enriching it by the influence of their life, and by giving their bodies back to the soil in the end that a better plant or a finer animal might follow them in the use of the land." It was sort of a graveyard talk, but the boys liked it; when the speaker was through, they got up from their seats on the ground so reverent towards what they had hitherto regarded as plain dirt that they were a little shocked by one who said, wait a minute, he had to brush some rock of ages off his pants.

With bright-colored lantern slides and carefully picked anecdotes the TVA men make speeches through the Valley to CCC boys, to farm groups, or to business groups in farming communities, and over the radio. They are, in fact, preaching the gospel of evolution in Tennessee; there are sixty-four demonstration farms in the county where the "monkey trial" took place.

There is not much doubt that all the TVA people believe in evolution. Dr. H. A. Morgan likes to draw pictures of how everything depends on what went before; he'll make a big X on his yellow pad and show you how, through the ages, came first minerals and then vegetable and animal lives, each one standing on the others. It seems we're right at the crossroads now, with man's intelligence taking everything but not putting much back. According to the TVA chairman, what is ahead of us depends on whether we put this expensively produced intelligence to restoring some of the resources we used up getting here.

The reason Tennesseans stand for this sort of evolutionary teaching is that it sounds just like preaching, only more sensible. It warns, as religion warns: "Look out there, be careful, watch what you're doing." It urges decent treatment even of the lowly dust under your feet, which it hails as the most valuable antique in a country given to worship of the past. And it promises that if you do right there will be a reward.

Also, of course, it does have to bring to the farmer a conviction of sin. Farmers have always been preached at; farm papers did it, and the Department of Agriculture bulletins did it, and the agricultural colleges, and the county agents. Still they failed to convince farmers that growing the wrong crops in the wrong way could hurt the land past saving. Some of the preachers didn't realize this, themselves. They preached crop rotation, but sometimes as far as they got with that was to insure a few volunteer cornstalks in the cottonfield; rotation was understood to mean corn one year and cotton the next.

It's easy enough to get indignant at the way the Southern farmer treats his land. Up in Pennsylvania they say years of farming never changed the soil; they've put back what they took out. But down South they always seemed confident that they could move on, if necessary, and you've got farmers who don't so much farm the country as infest it. Where these parasites have lived for a generation or two, the landscape begins to look ragged and mangy, and first thing you know it's bald and bare, then scrofulous and peeling.

Dr. Arthur Morgan wanted to tell farmers like that to get off the earth. He said: "A man has no natural right to inherit good land and pass on a waste of gullied hillsides to those who come after him." He felt that "laws of land ownership should be changed so that men shall not be allowed to own and occupy land unless they will manage it in the interest of a permanent agriculture." He noted that "while the government is spending millions of dollars to prevent soil erosion, the small-scale mountain farmers of this region, hard-pressed for sources of livelihood, are clearing steep mountainsides for three or four corn crops before the soil is washed and the land destroyed. It is therefore a question as to whether the expensive repair work of the government is keeping pace with this destruction going on in the same region at the same time." It seemed to be with some regret that he added: "At present the TVA law does not provide a legislative basis for meeting this problem."

But the other directors weren't for such extreme measures. They figured that in most cases it was ignorance instead of cussedness. Or maybe the farmers knew well enough what should be done; they just couldn't afford to do it.

Some of them may still regard erosion as an act of God, but you don't have to tell Southern farmers that fertilizer is a good thing. The fertilizer companies have been doing that for a long time; it was back in 1905 that the Tennessee Valley Fertilizer company published at Florence, Alabama, a touching little fable called "How Henry Allen Won His Wife." Read it and you'll find that Henry won her by buying fertilizer for the Allen farm. The only trouble about buying fertilizer is that it takes money. At that, hard-up Southern farmers buy more than twice as much fertilizer as do farmers in all the rest of the country; and they pay two to three dollars an acre for it, as against an average cost of 30 cents an acre in Yankee states like Iowa, Wisconsin, Illinois. They have to use more and more of it, too—commercial fertilizer sales reached a new high only last year. It's one of the things that keeps the Southern farmer hard up.

Of course if you go back to causes, it's erosion that made fertilizer necessary in most cases, but the damage has been done, now, until on those little farms, mostly under a hundred acres and the average around seventy, less than thirty acres ought to be cultivated.

They could use more cover crops, which are feed crops; more than eight million dollars' worth of hay is brought into the Valley every year. But a feed crop isn't a cash crop and the farmer has to eat too.

"Over in Grainger county," said one of the men in TVA's agricultural division at Knoxville, "we've got a farmer who is anxious to save his land. The trouble is it's not very good land—you know Grainger county—and by rights he ought to put nearly all of it into cover crops. That will increase the value of the land eventually, but what will the family live on meanwhile? There are eleven young children, and while you save the soil you're starving them."

At present the TVA approach is most tactfully made through fertilizer, which the farmer wants and which the Authority is willing to give him—on conditions. The free distribution is necessary because the farmers can't afford to pay and also because Uncle Sam isn't going into the fertilizer business, at present. He is having enough trouble with power companies without getting the hundreds of manufacturers of commercial fertilizers on his neck. The TVA fertilizers are no longer in the experimental stage as regards manufacture, but they are, the agricultural division will tell you, still experimental as regards use by the farmer on the land.

The farmer gets the TVA phosphates free (except for carrying charges) but he must promise to use them only on cover crops; and he must make his farm a demonstration farm for the benefit of his community. Land use must be in accordance with drainage and soil surveys; this may well mean turning everything around, putting clover where the corn was or turning a cottonfield into pasture. Records must be kept—this is the hardest part for many of the farmers, and TVA has learned to call on the wives for clerical help, or maybe the children in school. And the farm is open for inspection.

So they earn their phosphates, and it is testimony to the value of the fertilizer that they are meeting the conditions. The farmer doesn't himself apply for the honor; the system is to call a community meeting at which the Authority's ideas for better land use are explained, and farmers attending select their own representatives for the demonstration. Then the candidates make plans with the help of the county agent, who must approve the application for phosphate and see that the plans are carried out. There is nothing compulsory about the program, but when the farmer stops, the phosphates stop.

In other words the phosphate is a persuader, or you might call it a downright bribe, except that it's to everybody's interest to save the land. The point that proper land use is the main thing is stressed by the Authority, and no effort is made to keep from the farmers the fact that they will have to work, and wrassle with figures, and maybe even make less if they meet the conditions.

The real difficulty, even where farmers are willing, is to equalize what must be asked of them. On one demonstration farm in Grainger county a farmer was co-operating in every way with the Authority. Big brown-paper plans drawn before and after showed how he had changed crops, moved fences, and terraced fields, operating on a shoestring to improve a place in bad condition through no fault of his, for it had been far gone before it came into his hands. The changes he made meant a real sacrifice of income in the beginning, although his books now showed a profit.

Twenty miles away a richer farmer had been doing well enough before TVA came along; his land was good and he always had practiced crop rotation. To make his farm qualify as a demonstration farm, few changes were necessary; he merely accepted and used the phosphate. To him that hath can be given with little extra effort.

But what would you do with an application from a man with six children and a thousand-dollar debt; a 75-acre farm, 51 acres in use, mostly poor soil at a slope of thirty degrees? Or with another one where the farm is 116 acres, described as four flat, 36 steep, the rest rolling; livestock, two mules; family budget for the year, $100 for food, $75 for clothes?

The applications must tell all these things; they even ask how many pigs and cows and chickens, and how many children. But they put it in a general way about the children; they ask about ages— how many "Over 12? Under 12?"

Along with the application blank must come a plan of the farm, showing land use at present; and the county agent is there to help with soil tests. In fact it must be seen that this whole arrangement leans heavily on the county agent and on the agricultural college where the applications are classified. TVA prides itself on close co-operation with these existing agencies.

To an outsider, it does occur that some of the county agents have, of recent years, been put under a pretty heavy strain. Ten years ago the average county agent in the South was a well-meaning chap who had maybe gone to agricultural college, but hadn't taken to actual farming; if he was really conscientious, he drove around the county in a rattletrap Ford and got to know the farmers, and maybe, if he was a diplomat, he could persuade one or two of them to read his printed bulletins, though it was asking a good deal to expect them to take his advice. If he was lazy, he sat in his office in the county courthouse, with the prize-winning stalk of sorghum and the red ear of corn on the wall over his desk, and let the bulletins gather dust in the corner. It didn't matter much, either way.

Then came the AAA and the Bankhead Act and other complications, and the agent got to be a man of some importance. He had to hold elections on quotas and see about a lot of things, so he was worked to death unless he got help. If they gave him assistance, he got to be a bigger shot, and anyhow the complications tended to turn his sympathies towards the bigger, better-off, more intelligent, and successful farmers in his county. The small fry always had been too dumb to learn, and now they got all balled up in the red tape and made nuisances of themselves. Of course all the agents weren't alike; some would work as patiently on the case of a one-mule farmer as if they had been consulted by the biggest cotton-grower in the county. But it was natural for a lot of agents to feel that the little man was licked before he started, and to assume that the benefits of the AAA and the farm loans were intended for the people who had proved they could farm at a profit.

You won't get TVA to make any complaints about the county agents; they have nothing but praise, in Knoxville, for what the agents do. But in order to keep from overworking the agents the Authority supplies, in those counties where co-operation justifies it, an assistant to the agent. This assistant, presumably, does most of the work in connection with the demonstration farms. He also works with the Authority in other matters, such as relocation in the reservoir areas, or the various experiments and surveys they make.

And the assistant has to pass the TVA tests for social attitude. This doesn't mean that he will have high hopes of immediate regeneration for the ornery, malarious, plug-chewing, shambling, snaggle-toothed illiterate that a Southern farmer can be at his worst. Like the county agent or the university-extension worker, the TVA man is apt to remark that farming is a complicated business requiring considerably more intelligence and training than a man would need to run a bank or a store. The difference in attitude is mainly that the TVA man feels you can't afford to let the shiftless, no-'count farmer continue in his way. You've got to do something about him, not so much on his account as for the sake of the country.

Anybody who undertakes to change the minds of farmers knows that, just as you have to contend with what they call acidity in the soil, you need an antidote for an acid condition of mind among men who have worked hard and got nothing to show for it. With the possible exception of Vermont, the Tennessee Valley leads the country in the conviction that things are terrible and nothing can be done, especially by outsiders. Having continued on his way unimpressed by county, state, and other federal educators, the Valley

farmer saw the TVA, at first, merely as a new target for cackling
rural wit. Did you hear how they had a wild-life bureau, run by
college boys from the New York night clubs?

But some of the TVA college boys had studied psychology, and
they had a patient man at the head of the Authority's agricultural
activities. Dr. Harcourt Morgan had nothing to learn about Valley
farmers; he had been dealing with them for nearly fifty years.

So in one way or another, here a little and there a little, they have
made progress. They hold meetings in counties where the only public assembly is at church; they show movies where films have never
been, and generally educate by the project method, and with gadgets, as the county agents couldn't afford to do. They arrange for
public demonstrations of terracing, and afterwards are happy to
compare a neighborhood attack on gullies to the log-raisings of
pioneer days. They beam when a farmer says a gully is "healed."
They seem to think that, as a child in a modern school is supposed
to learn without knowing he is learning, the farmer can be induced
to absorb necessary knowledge painlessly or even pleasantly. The
idea maybe isn't so much to impart knowledge as to suggest new
habits and attitudes of mind. All the record-keeping on the demonstration farms is designed, of course, to enlighten the farmer as well
as the Authority. He is supposed to learn how to take stock of his
assets and liabilities, and to regard his land as capital to be lived
on, not run through.

As evidence of success, the Authority now points with pride to a
community on Poplar creek where 132 farmers of Roane and Anderson counties, Tennessee, have organized themselves into a board
of trustees responsible for the land. The community called Wheat
has become, you might say, one big demonstration farm. Surveys
and soil analyses to determine land use have here been made by
TVA on a community scale: first an air-mapping to show the woods,
then a land-ownership map, then a cover survey for the study of
erosion in the watershed, and finally a soil survey. The farmers added
the usual case histories required on the demonstration farms, and
went into further details about the community life.

Wheat community knows, now, what its soil will do, how many trees it has, how much livestock, how much relief is paid, how much mortgage money owed, what crop-control benefits are to be had, what goes to pay the salaries of teachers and preachers, and even how many people aren't getting enough to eat. This exposure may be regarded by some folks as indecent, but the attitude of TVA —and of the 132 farmers who decided to co-operate—is that such a stock-taking is the first step in managing the business of living along Poplar creek.

In another five years, they figure they'll make another survey to mark progress. In the meantime they set themselves short-term objectives: so many acres to be limed, so many to be treated to phosphates, so many houses and mailboxes to be painted. In the check-up so far, it's noticeable that while they almost made the grade on most of these objectives, the one where they went over the top was in the application of TVA phosphates. But they had to pay the freight and put them on.

In other words, TVA came to the conclusion that farmers were like flies, to be caught with molasses instead of vinegar; for molasses, read metaphosphate. But if you can get them to talk in the agriculture division at Knoxville, they may confide to you that one thing they are trying to do is to find out if the ordinary farmer can afford to farm at all; or must farming be subsidized, like the merchant marine? If the government is to stop gambling on each crop and hire the farmers regularly to do their jobs in the best way, what should be the details of such an arrangement?

The Authority, in time, may be able to persuade the nation to the same sort of stock-taking they now have on Poplar creek, and for the first time in its history the country will be farming with its eyes open.

INTERCULTURAL EDUCATION WORKSHOP
204 EAST 18th ST., NEW YORK, N. Y.
TEL. ORCHARD 4-3199

Consider the Cow

Thus saith the Lord God to the mountains, and to the hills, to the rivers, and to the valleys, to the desolate wastes . . .

Behold, I am for you, and I will turn unto you, and ye shall be tilled and sown. . . .

And I will multiply the fruit of the tree, and the increase of the field, that ye shall receive no more reproach of famine among the heathen.

Suppose you educate your farmer so that he knows as much as a county agent, and can put a fancy name to the soil instead of just rubbing his toe in it and saying it's crawfishy. Suppose he gets to know as much as a TVA man, and is willing to put fertilizer on a pasture, and worry about whether his land is sliding out from under him. Suppose he moves as fast as the land, or even a jump ahead, and manages to hold on to it. What is he going to do to make a living?

They say that Southern farmers have stopped suing each other over boundaries because the land is too poor to support the lawyers. But when the farmer gets his land in good condition, he grows more crops. When he grows more crops, he makes less money—everybody, nowadays, has heard about that. When he gets the biggest possible return from his land, what's to keep him from starving to death?

You have no right to say you've solved the problem of land use when you've saved the land and made a survey to show what crops will grow on it. You've got to determine what crops the country can use.

Southern farmers are noted for their heedlessness regarding the market problem; it is customary to say that they go on growing cotton year in and year out, whether the world wants it or not. But the truth about the cotton business is that Southerners have long memories, and nearly all of them can recall a year when people did make money in cotton, big money. So they gamble on doing it again. Remember how before the World War there was a campaign for charitable people to "Buy a Bale," and how those that did it were rewarded with a huge profit? Remember how during the war they urged you to plant food crops, and then potatoes went for nothing while cotton continued to soar? If the sun shines and there aren't many weevils and the bale they set on the floor of the Cotton Exchange at Memphis is only the first of a bumper crop, of course you'll have a bad year. But you can always sell cotton for something, because the brokers are gamblers too and they know it will keep. There may be another war.

In the southern part of the Valley they take chances on cotton the way Yankee office workers buy sweepstake tickets, or Harlem Negroes play the numbers racket, and you've got to let them have some entertainment. They may be right, at that, in their stubborn feeling that people ought to use more cotton. It's been said that if they used the crop just to make enough sheets and pillow cases for folks who can't afford them, that would take care of it. Or you could do something to counteract the advertising for artificial silk, up North, that makes even Southern women buy dresses made of the stuff. You might even start a campaign for lisle stockings to help the Southern farmer instead of to spite the Japanese.

But with established buying habits fixed in the North the way they are, it might be smarter to find a new cotton industry. Suppose you use cotton for building materials, or paving, or paper? They can use the whole plant in some of those new processes, and when they do that, cotton can cease to be a row crop harvested by hand. It will be grown like wheat and cut the same way.

These are bigger changes than growers have seen since a Yale boy invented the cotton gin. In any case it's coming to be understood that the cotton-growing of the future will likely involve machinery, and so be done more easily on the flat fields of the Southwest. The largest cotton-growing county in Alabama is in the Valley watershed, but instead of building dams to grow more cotton, as they did on the Nile, they hope that dam-building on the Tennessee will have the opposite effect.

Corn, as a crop, hasn't got the fatal fascination of cotton and it may be easier to get rid of; of course, it's worse for hill farms than anything they could grow. But suppose you get rid of corn and cotton, what are you going to plant?

On the Holston river in East Tennessee the early settlers found a place they called Strawberry Plains, and you can still see wild strawberries growing on the lawns in Knoxville, or on the campus of the University of Tennessee. Berries and small fruits are the obvious suggestion for a country of small farms, with a long growing season, plenty of moisture, and relative proximity to city markets. Because strawberries seemed indicated by nature, because their habit of growth and the methods of mulching plants makes them a cover crop, and because electric refrigeration could prove a useful factor in marketing, TVA and the University of Tennessee have worked hard on a quick-freezing process that they hope to make a big success. They started with refrigerated trucks, then built a refrigerator barge to run on the river, and they say the process works not only for strawberries but for other fruits and vegetables.

In the hills they have runty little apples, mainly good for cider, but maybe they could grow better ones if they had the right nursery stock. Peaches have been tried without doing much in the eastern part of the Valley, but you could grow them in the southern part, and of course any kind of vegetable truck. The problem is marketing—unless your farmer is a good business man he can find these fancy crops a more dangerous gamble than cotton. In fact one farmer can't do it because the shippers won't fool with him; you've got to get a whole community to specialize in one thing.

So far, TVA has taken the obvious course of stressing fruit- and vegetable-growing for local use. Co-operative canneries and community refrigerators are a big help with the county food supply, if you can just get people to try them.

These new possibilities come with the electricity, and so do other farm improvements that the farmer is quicker to see for himself. They are finding out that you can warm seed beds, hatch baby chicks, cure tobacco, dry hay, and grind corn with electricity, and some like to put a jolt in the fence wires or rig up insect traps. Along with these changes TVA hopes to see other improvements in farm methods, and with the college experts they have worked on experiments for better sorghum, ensilage, and cottonseed processing. Also, in line with reforestation, TVA has suggested tree crops, not for sale but for feeding, and the idea of letting the small fruits and nuts fall to the ground to feed the pigs appeals to the Southern farmer's natural sense of economy in labor. Anybody knows it's a good idea to put the pigpen under an oak tree. Persimmons, Asiatic chestnuts, mulberries, and "hicans," a cross between pecans and hickory nuts, are other possibilities mentioned by the experts.

They can think of lots of refinements and make pretty plans for what Southern farmers could or should do, but when all is said and done, it seems too bad that Valley folks weren't converted to the Hindu faith. Because the Hindus worship cows, and it would have been a fine thing for the Valley folks if they had taken cows more seriously.

People who say that civilization follows a calf trail aren't so far wrong; there are figures to show that cars and telephones and radios and the other signs of rural prosperity follow the cow. In the good old days, of course, the South had plenty of cows and chickens, and it may be exaggeration to say the Yankees stole them all. After the war it was said that there was no use growing chickens for thieving Negroes and carpetbaggers, but one ex-Confederate officer managed to bring the first Jerseys to a farm in Maury county, Tennessee. In Alabama, in the nineties, they had a party for the cow Lily Flag, who had won first prize at the Chicago World's Fair; wreathed in roses, Lily Flag received the élite of Huntsville in her stable, and then the guests danced under electric lights strung for the occasion by the Alabama Power company. But maybe that was the trouble; Lily Flag was a party cow, running with the rich, and not much more important to the agricultural progress of the Valley than that early exploring trip made by the governor of Virginia and his Knights of the Golden Horseshoe was to its settlement. The élite greeted Lily Flag, but when it came to buying stock they were more interested in the new electric lights.

As late as 1895, one observer noted: "The dairy and poultry products of Georgia are worth half as much as the cotton crop. . . . The interesting part of it is that while cotton is going lower and lower, milk, butter, eggs, and chickens are firm and advancing." But they were firm and advancing because they were getting scarce.

Maybe one reason for this was that raising cows and chickens was traditionally woman's work, and women never have been able to conserve capital for next year if it means starving the children now. So when times got hard they sold the cow, and maybe they killed the last of the chickens for unexpected company, or when the preacher came for Sunday dinner. Anyhow the cows and chickens went, so that milk and eggs are no part of the Southern rural diet, and billboards along the Valley highways advertise Wisconsin butter.

Look beyond the billboards at the country, and you can't help being reminded of more prosperous regions that it seems to resemble. There are parts of the Valley that could be in the south of England— the same rolling hills and fields dappled with cloud-shadows are there, and at a distance you don't notice that the houses and fences are of wood instead of stone. At a distance you can't see, either, that the trees are mostly second-growth instead of the oaks they saved in England because, though they painted themselves like Indians and killed each other off instead of holding elections, the Druids worshiped trees.

But from a long way off you can tell there is something missing from the Southern fields, a lack that explains as well as excuses the fact that some of the fences have fallen down. There aren't enough cows.

But They Still Study War

Proclaim ye this among the Gentiles; Prepare war, wake up the mighty men,
let all the men of war draw near; let them come up:
Beat your plowshares into swords, and your pruninghooks into spears.

But in the last days it shall come to pass, that the mountain of the house of
the Lord shall be established in the top of the mountains. . . .
And he shall judge among many people, and rebuke strong nations afar off;
and they shall beat their swords into plowshares, and their spears into pruning-
hooks: nation shall not lift up a sword against nation, neither shall they learn
war any more.

And the work of righteousness shall be peace.

When the Tennessee Valley Authority had first called attention
to the state of things in the Valley, a traveler from France looked
at Tennessee and said: "All the international wars waged in Europe
since the fall of the Roman Empire did not do as much damage to
the European soil as the Americans managed to inflict in three centuries on their own earth." [1] That's harsh reproof, but the thing
you wonder about in the Valley, now, is whether efforts to restore
the soil can get anywhere before interruption by another European
war.

You can argue, of course, that without the World War there would
have been no Tennessee Valley Authority. It does seem unlikely
that Congress, back in 1917, would have authorized the spending
of $150,000,000 at Muscle Shoals just to make nitrate fertilizers. It
was because they wanted the nitrates for the war that Uncle Sam
didn't count the cost of Wilson dam and the two factories.

Of course, no nitrate fertilizers or nitrates for war use ever were
produced at Muscle Shoals. Two plants, numbered One and Two,
were built there for $68,000,000. But before anything could be done
with Plant Number One, the process it was built to follow became
obsolete. This is one story; another is that the German patent never
fully revealed the process and so failed in performance just as other

---

[1] *A Foreigner Looks at the TVA*, Odette Keun.

properties seized during the war were found to fail. At any rate, Plant Number One proved even less useful than the good ship *Vaterland,* and couldn't even be sold for scrap.

Plant Number Two, the largest cyanamide factory in the world, tested and found fully capable of producing nitrates, was left in idleness until it was taken over by TVA. It is now making phosphate fertilizer, but it must be ready for wartime use as a nitrate plant if required. It is said that the plant could, with a few weeks' warning, provide enough nitrates to meet the requirements of an army of a million and a half men.

The Shoals seem peaceful now; the buildings that were army clubs house the TVA offices and the school. But in the former nitrate plant, where the furnaces cook phosphate ore at a temperature of 2750 degrees Fahrenheit, it is easy to feel the lethal possibilities. Phosphates have their own war uses in the making of poison gas and smoke screens. The acid that runs in little rivers into a big tank gives off unpleasant fumes, and visitors are warned not to step where it's wet. Phosphates can be used to make the clover grow, but they can also be used to kill men.

Actually the Tennessee Valley Authority has taken this country's first step towards government manufacture of munitions. Shortly after the Muscle Shoals chemists announced the new metaphosphate, it was said that the army planned to make the Valley the fortified center of armament-making for the country. Already, few and scattered as industries are in the South, a surprising number of those essential to modern warfare are in or near the Valley and the army likes to play its war games there. And there are people, firmly opposed to the government planning that involves tree-planting and strawberry barges, who would welcome as proper preparedness the military administration of the Tennessee river system.

Farmers might miss the fertilizer, but war would send the price of lowland cotton kiting, and give an occupation to the tall tow-headed boys in the hills. In another way, you can say that a war is just a matter of fertilizer, for export.

They don't like to think of things like that in the Valley. "We don't want no war," they say at the crossroads or on the buses, if you mention it. Even the TVA people, better able to understand how importation into America of a German process for making rayon can affect both the Japanese silk market and the Southern cotton market, hate to consider that hungry Japanese and inventive Germans may one day threaten a peace that makes the Tennessee Valley seem another Shangri-La.

It seemed ungrateful to suggest to Dr. H. A. Morgan that his plans for making farmers phosphate-conscious would be interrupted if Muscle Shoals should be put on a war basis. And his first reaction was that of any administrator of a peacetime project—somebody else would have to bring on the war. But after a moment he reached in the drawer of his desk and pulled out a map. It was one of those flat projections of the globe, and it had been hand-colored to show the distribution of phosphate ores in both hemispheres. Dr. Morgan's forefinger moved over the blue, green, red, and violet patches.

"See—the world's important deposits of phosphates are owned by four countries. They are exported, of course, because the countries without them must import them, either for war or for peace. We export ourselves—mostly to Italy, Germany, and Japan, the countries without a natural supply.

"The natural deposits are in this country, in the British and French possessions, and in Russia. We have the most; Russia has the largest single field, near Archangel. So these four countries—the United States, Great Britain, France, and Russia—could by acting together virtually control the world supply. These four countries could declare peace."

These four countries could declare peace—the sentence was arresting, but he said it casually, for Dr. H. A. Morgan is no propagandist. He believes that the world grows slowly, by evolution. But there may be a time when, to prevent a catastrophic change, you have to speak out. The 1937 annual report of the Tennessee Valley Authority recommends mildly that "the determination of the quantity and destination of phosphate exports should therefore be a function of the Federal Government as a matter of foreign policy." But

if Dr. H. A. Morgan is right about the importance of phosphates
(there is no dispute about the distribution), then that is not enough.

It is not enough to consider thankfully that Providence gave the
phosphates to the right people. It should be shouted from the house-
tops, in this country, in England, in France, in Russia—that by acting together, merely in this one matter of the good earth God gave,
"these four countries could declare peace."

Since Dr. Morgan said that, in the summer of 1938, international
events have made it clear that England and France will not act with
Russia; but the earth God gave us remains. Now more than ever
it may be important not to sell phosphates to every comer as trust-
ingly as savages swapped pearls for calico. The yellow ore they give
us in return won't make the bluegrass grow, even if you bury it in
Kentucky.

4. ROCK

Moving the Mountains

He stood, and measured the earth: he beheld, and drove asunder the nations; and the everlasting mountains were scattered, the perpetual hills did bow.

The mountains skipped like rams, and the little hills like lambs.

To understand a dam you want to catch it young, when the steam shovels are taking bites out of the mountainside above the river, and making funny faces as they spit out mouthfuls of rock into the trucks that take it to be crushed. Most of the tourists go to Norris, but that dam is finished now, and quiet, while last summer you could see one being built by going up into the hills to Hiwassee.

The job is just what one of the TVA engineers called it, moving a mountain half a mile or so from a place where it serves no useful purpose to a place where it can do some good. These hills have been here so long it may seem a hard thing to move them; but after all they are dead rock now. The dams are new rock, growing right under your eyes.

There is a big raw gash in the side of one hill, where the dam is to sit; and along the river a piece there is another gouged-out cliff where they are quarrying the rock, with the help of a steam shovel named Bucyrus. Another kind of shovel that can work in the water is browsing on the river bottom; this semi-aquatic monster ought to be a brontosaurus. The rock is being dug out of hills and rivers by machines that remind you of the animals that were here when the rocks were laid down.

For both the high dams, Norris and Hiwassee, the rock was right handy; it looked as if Providence, knowing there would be no navigation up there, had kindly planted a mountain of dolomite to do the job at Norris, and there was a similarly useful cliff at Hiwassee. Down the river where there are no mountains you can send the rock in barges, and use floating mixers, right on the water, to make the concrete.

For the high dams they strung cables across and rigged up a new kind of concrete-carrier that holds seven cubic yards. Mrs. Roosevelt took a ride in the cable car at Norris, first thing. Now the same outfit is working at Hiwassee, but none of the congressmen who were there investigating cared to travel that way.

TVA had a little cement war when it built Norris, which it won by threatening to make its own cement down the river at Sheffield. They did get the lumber for the forms right out of the reservoir area, where it had to be cut anyhow, and they kept that up at the other dams, building out of what the land-clearance people chopped up. At Wheeler they filled the coffer dam with rock and clay from an excavation for the power house, and for a highway cut. So it got to be mainly a case of rearranging the country, just using what they had and putting it somewhere else.

After the steam shovels the thing to watch is the rock-crusher, an especially soothing sight if you are mad at anybody. At Hiwassee they spray water on the rock to keep down silica dust; then the crushed rock travels on conveyors to be graded and crushed finer, till some of it gets to be sand, and it all goes to the cement-mixer. A little toy train takes it from the cement-mixer to the cableway, and then they do their tight-rope stunt high in the air, with one cable tower moving and a man on the ground telephoning across to tell them where to land. From the height of the cables the load of wet rock looks too small to count, and you start doing arithmetic to see how many trips the carrier will have to make. But remember they dammed the Nile when a man could not carry in a day half of what the bucket carries in one trip.

After they dump the cement, it's like setting a sidewalk, just one of those jobs that attracts rubbernecks fond of watching other folks work. But the dam-builders themselves, in safety helmets and sometimes goggles, are something to see. They say it took persuasion, at Norris, to get the men to use all the safety inventions that TVA provided, but now they are easier to convince because the safety records are good. A big blackboard down by the drinking fountain lists accidents, but the totals are so much lower than usual on such jobs that they are something for ordinary builders to think about. At Hiwassee, in the summer of 1938, two men had been killed; at Chickamauga, the year before, the record was higher—they had lost six—but the dam was nearer done, and the engineer in charge was rightly proud of his safety record. The same was true of Pickwick and Wheeler and Guntersville. When Wilson dam was built in the old careless wartime days they killed 57 men there, as a memorial tablet will tell you.

Besides having all sorts of training in safety, with men rotating on safety committees so that everybody gets the idea, they take the trouble to put railings on all the steps and on the concrete forms. Also there are posters, here at the dam and in the community house and the cafeteria, telling the men not to hurry. The Southerners know about that, and the Yankees learn.

It takes some sort of skill for even the simplest jobs because the working equipment is complicated, and there are all kinds of special skills necessary. So, besides the people from the neighborhood and the engineers, they have men from all over to make a dam-construction camp a little world in itself. Perhaps their last job was in Seattle and their next will be in China, or Hawaii, or Canada. At Hiwassee, the man who set the diamonds in the drills had mined for diamonds, and for gold too, in South Africa in the days of Rhodes and Jameson and Oom Paul.

They have more natural scenery around a camp than in a city, and at the TVA dams they take care to keep it; but they have more machinery than you see in most cities, and an odd combination of all the useful ways to do things that men have discovered. Over in Lincoln county, Tennessee, a man has used TVA power to electrify a blacksmith shop. Out at Hiwassee, right across the river from the toothy grins of the steam shovels, is a smithy where Mr. David

Lilienthal hasn't yet sold any electrical equipment to replace old-fashioned red-hot coals. But the blacksmith isn't making horseshoes; he is doing the hand-forging still necessary on modern tools.

They work here at night, with lights on the towers of the cableway and up the side of the mountain. And every so often, mostly at night, you will hear the boom of the dynamite blasts. After you've stayed at the construction camp for a while, you realize that the biggest difference between it and any city you have seen, these times, is that everybody is working.

They say that TVA employs some thirty different kinds of engineers, some of them of course being concerned with the land-reclamation program, and some with power, but you can see how a lot of them are needed just for one dam. They begin with mapping, up in the air; the army engineers did a lot of that and TVA carried on to make the Valley one of the most-mapped regions of the world. Then the geologists have to dig down under the earth.

After they pick a location and design a dam to fit it, the planners make scale models and the hydraulic engineers run water through to see what it will do. They float confetti to show the course of the currents, and move carefully calculated amounts of silt; and in one case they saved themselves the trouble of dredging out an obstruction because they found that the water, in its new channel, would do the job for them.

The geologists go to work again on the river-bed, when piles driven in have changed its course so they can work on the bottom where the dam will be. They drill to test the rock and fill in flaws as you'd fill a tooth—"grouting," they call it; one of the things invented on the job at Norris was a special tool, a sort of feeler, for this purpose. They're so sure of what is under the dams that they draw pictures of it.

The new rock they are making must be tested, too; every batch of concrete they mix has to be sampled before it is poured. These dams are meant to last.

And still, when you watch them, you can't believe they can do it at all. If it's a high dam, it looks as if they never could bridge the hills with their little cables and buckets. If it's a low dam, with the big river that got there first flowing right where this construction aims to be, it seems just as unlikely. In either case, as you stand on the bank and watch the machinery slowly but surely having its way, tended only by ant-sized men, you may feel that the machinery is pretty wonderful and the men are pretty small.

If you were the engineer in charge, you might get to feel almost like God, because you are certainly making over God's landscape. Only it's you and a lot of other people. The little ants are hard at work, but maybe they could gang together and sting. There are more ants in faraway factories making the machinery they use. Then there are the men who invented the machinery, and made some of the rules and took some of the risks first; some of those are dead men, by now.

Also there are local ants who must move out when the rocks are moved, and who can give considerable trouble unless you are careful not to step on them.

Moving Quick and Dead

And it shall come to pass, that like as I have watched over them, to pluck up, and to break down, and to throw down, and to destroy, and to afflict; so will I watch over them, to build, and to plant, saith the Lord. . . .
And the whole valley of the dead bodies, and of the ashes, and all the fields . . . shall be holy unto the Lord.

Most folks don't think of building a dam in terms of moving graveyards. But before they could swing into place the million cubic yards of concrete they put in Norris dam, they had to move the gravestones and the bones from Bull Run Creek and Hogskin Creek and Caney Creek, from Sinking Springs and Dripping Springs, and from Black Fox Ford and Dead Mine Bend. Norris lake has fingers that go far up into the hills, and little coves and inlets show where there were hollows and valleys before the water came. In those places were little cemeteries that would be covered with water, or would be where nobody could get to them except in a boat.

So in Raccoon Valley and Hickory Valley and Poorland Valley, in Elbow Hollow and Kettle Hollow and Powder Mill Hollow, the TVA men surveyed and mapped, and where there were burying grounds or just family plots with two or three graves, they made notes and took pictures of the gravestones. Then they talked to the relatives to decide what was to be done. They moved more than a hundred Stooksburys and Snodderlys and around fifty Hatmakers out of the Norris churchyards without getting them mixed.

They saw the preachers too, and the preachers were a great help in explaining it to the people. The Authority offered to move the graves to any place within twenty miles, or to allow money for the families to do it. In most cases they just left it to the Authority, and TVA built up new cemeteries at New Loyston, New Baker's Forge, New Indian Creek, and Big Barren Memorial. They had all local men to do the work, and in all they moved more than five thousand graves out of the Norris area.

Then there were the dead Indians, some supposed to have been there since before Columbus came to America. Nobody had ever paid much attention to the grassed-over Indian mounds, but the Authority said it wouldn't do just to let the water cover them, because then nobody ever would know what was inside.

So they got archaeologists from the universities, and WPA workers to do the digging, and they went to work. In the Norris area, at Caryville, they found the first temple site to be discovered east of the Mississippi. They found relics too, cooking pots and counters used to play a game like checkers, and of course they found lots of skeletons. The men that built the temple, and lived in caves along the Powell river, where more bones were found, weren't Cherokee Indians; they went a lot farther back than that. So they said three civilizations would be flooded by Norris lake.

Down the river, the Pickwick dam would drown out part of Seven Mile island, the way the island of Philae was drowned when

the English dammed the Nile at Aswan. So they went to work on
the mounds there, and in the summer of 1937 what looked like a
village of Indian tepees turned out to be the tents of white diggers.
A mound was being sliced into cross-sections and plugged, at promising points, just like a watermelon. That day over-energetic WPA
shovels had dug into a skeleton, and the conscientious young man
in charge, who had started with the CCC and was anxious to make
good on his TVA job, was afraid it wasn't in the best condition. But
the men who knew could make learned guesses from its position
and the slant of stripes in the surrounding clay.

Farther along the island were shell mounds, made by Indians who
lived where the mussels were and who had accumulated the natural
containers as the modern world dumps its tin cans. On top of these
past and gone settlements came the era of the fighting Cherokees, and
mementos of them, in the form of arrowheads, an occasional ax or
spearhead, and plenty of flint chips, were to be picked or plowed up
right on the ground.

All this attention to dry bones took some time and trouble, but if
the tactful TVA men were to tell the truth, they'd say that moving
the dead is a whole lot easier than moving the living. Engineers know
how to handle clay and dust and lime rock; it's living creatures that
worry them.

Because it is careful, the Tennessee Valley Authority does its most
varied and diplomatic work in what is called relocation, meaning the
removal and resettlement of people from the reservoir areas. Uncle
Sam is doing a good deal of this sort of work right now, but in the
Valley there are special conditions.

In the first place, the Authority has a right to condemn land, and
rising water completes the argument. On the other hand, the land
required for the reservoirs is not always waste land unsuited to any
other use—in fact it's only too often the other way round. If it were
possible, certainly it would be better to take a wornout mountain farm
than to flood the bottom lands, which are the best farm lands, and
all the men on relocation work wish that water would run uphill.

In the early days at Norris, where the farming was nothing to brag

about, the main objections were from people who just didn't want to
move. Some of the hill folks did feel that they'd rather starve than
be disturbed. The story of the old lady who said she'd just sit right
there in her rocking chair until the water came up to drown her went
far and wide, losing none of its sorrow in the telling. A song printed
up North was mighty sad:

> From this Valley we soon will be leaving;
> How we will miss our old friends and our homes.
> For they say that the waters will cover
> The place where we all love to roam.
> There's the aged old father and mother
> Who have spent many years here in toil;
> They have reared up the little children
> On the products of old Clinch river soil.

But of course they weren't the first folks to have to move out for
such a reason, or the last. Now they've started flooding some Catskill
mountain villages for New York City's water supply, and some in
the Swift river valley, in Massachusetts, to get water for Boston.

In the hills it was also true that some of the young people, especially, were glad to see things change and all ready to ask for jobs on
the dam. Their side of the story had its own ballad:

> My name is William Edwards, I live down Cove Creek way.
> I'm workin' on the project they call the TVA.
> The government begun it when I was but a child,
> But now they are in earnest and Tennessee's gone wild.
> All up and down the Valley they heard the glad alarm;
> The government means business—it's workin' like a charm.
> Oh, see the boys a-comin'—their government they trust.
> Just hear their hammers singin'—they'll build that dam or bust.

As for the true rights of the case, you have to admit that nobody
has found a way to have progress and keep sentiment. If you spend
only a short time in one of the reservoir areas, you find yourself thinking it's too bad that these trees, these cardinal flowers and wild roses,
even this honeysuckle and fern and jewel weed, will soon be lake
bottom. There are lonesome chimneys left standing where the houses

have been moved away. Take a drink of clear, cold water from the spring, ticketed as "safe" by the Authority scouts; you may drink here now but not next year, for then there will be too much water.

And if it were your own spring, that you had known all your life, with the world over the hill an undiscovered and unwanted country, of course you'd hate to move. Yet there are people in such places who welcome a chance to see more folks, and cars, and hear a train whistle.

Few who came to look at Norris in the early days failed to mention the Stooksburys, who became the standard example of a sturdy mountain family uprooted from its native soil. There were pictures of one of the Stooksbury houses, and of Mrs. Jacob Stooksbury at her spinning wheel, and of other Stooksburys doing the washing in a three-legged iron pot. The Stooksburys, said the stories, had lived apart from the world since the days of Daniel Boone.

Nobody took the trouble to go a few steps off the market square in Knoxville, where two Stooksbury brothers were keeping a store. They are still there, as they were before TVA came to town, and this year, while he gave a good measure of peaches, Mr. Stooksbury said that as far as he knew most of the Stooksburys who had moved out for the lake were doing as well as or better than they had before. Most of them hadn't gone far, just into the next county. Of course he'd got out earlier himself, so it wasn't exactly true that the Stooksburys had never heard of the world outside until the dam was built. For that matter there's a Judge Stooksbury in Knoxville, too. But Mr. Stooksbury the grocer could understand how these writers tried to make things picturesque. As for TVA, it was certainly a great thing for this country.

There was an indication right on the map that the Stooksburys and the Snodderlys couldn't be quite as isolated as some people thought they were, because one of the crossroads places that was drowned out was named Shanghai. A TVA man who had given the matter some thought suggested that one of the natives of this fighting region must have gone to foreign wars and got as far as the Boxer Rebellion. Now the TVA gave them something to do at home.

Considerable effort was made to keep those who had to move from being cheated while they had in their hands the cash that Uncle Sam had paid for their farms. County agents, knowing the people, were a big help here; their advice was offered and in some cases accepted. Working with the Authority, they listed available farms in the near-by counties, and made their own appraisal figures. Farmers who had to move were driven around to look at the possibilities, and some of them were suspected of being extra hard to please just to get free rides.

The removal men did what they could to help families living below what they considered a normal subsistence standard; one reason people were on the whole so willing to move was that so many of them thought things couldn't be worse. In the more desperate cases the Authority looked around and sometimes found long-lost relatives who agreed to help, or furnished a link with the outside world.

Three years after the removal a charity worker in the area, in no way connected with TVA, gave it as his opinion that the families moved out were on the whole slightly better off than they had been before, and certainly in no worse condition. A survey showed one out of five to be dissatisfied, which is a low percentage of dissatisfaction anywhere.

You have to consider that almost any big company coming in would have taken less care about disturbing people than Uncle Sam did. At just about the same time that they were relocating people at Norris, up in New Jersey a woman said she wasn't going to allow a privately owned power company to cross her farm. And deputy sheriffs shot and killed her.

A lot of the lessons they learned at Norris could be put into practice down the river, when they moved people out of the other areas. But the down-river country was different. They were lucky, in the first place, in not having so many people to move—less than a thousand families at Wheeler, around a thousand at Guntersville, eight hundred at Chickamauga, and less than five hundred at Pickwick. The trouble was that down there they had to flood more good rich bottom land.

However, down in the cotton country most of the farmers were
either tenants or croppers, in no position to argue about what was
done. And in dealing with the owners it could be argued truthfully
that, while this was pretty good land, it was also the area of flood
damage. Relocation was assigned to see that the tenants got, if possible, a fair chance elsewhere. And they did what they could to
adjust removals to crop seasons.

Down where the river is really a river, a certain amount of river
industry had to be considered. One fisherman at Pickwick fixed
things for himself; he had lived some distance from the water because
you could never tell where it would rise to, but now, with the river
under control, the TVA engineers could tell him where it would
come. So he moved right by the water line, where setting his trot lines
—across the river for cat, up-river for buffalo—would be less trouble
than it had been before.

Objectors to the big Western dams made a lot of fuss over what
would happen to the fish; but TVA had no romantic salmon to deal
with, and the catfish of the Tennessee, slipping over the spillway at
Wheeler dam, soon recover from their surprise. The reservoir lakes
are being stocked with real fish, bass and bream and trout, so that on
the whole it is understood throughout the Valley that TVA is the
fisherman's best friend.

Northern papers did mention sadly that the mussel industry was
being ruined, but you wouldn't worry much over that if you were on
the ground. Nobody eats mussels; the Indians did, but that was before the white man turned the river into a sewer. At the Shoals,
mussels could be gathered by lowering an iron bar with short lines
and hooks attached. The mussel grabs and holds until he is hauled
up; he is thrown away to rot while his shell is sold to make pearl
buttons. A ton of shells sells for $20 to $50 when the shell boat makes
its rounds, and some farmers added to their income that way, as did
some of the fishermen on the river and the people living on Seven
Mile island. Deep water will mean no more mussels, but on the
whole the industry was not as important as some of the papers made

it sound. Most of the river people wouldn't even take the trouble to grade the shells; they left that to be done on the boat, though they might have made extra money by sorting them.

Seven Mile island is, or was, a strip of jungle in the river near Pride's Landing, accessible only after various works of man had begun to conquer the Shoals. Before the TVA men came, part of it was farmed, but tall cypress and tupelo gum trees were left standing along the shoreline, with wild grapevines looping to the tops to tie together water, earth, and sky. In the old days, with the matted grass and creepers for a screen, eyes peered suspiciously at all strangers who landed, because the real industry of Seven Mile island was bootlegging.

Relocation of the bootleggers was, by the nature of the enterprise, left to them. But the TVA launch was welcome, and an ex-bootlegger passed the time of day amiably enough as he worked at calking a boat he meant to use for legitimate business when they got navigation on the river.

In the Hiwassee area of North Carolina the relocation men found another set of problems. This country is more like the Norris country, although there is no city as near as Knoxville is to Norris. In the hills around Persimmon Creek, Hanging Dog Creek, and Bear Paw Church, you will find sledges used for transportation and see oxen plowing the fields. But some say a steer is better than a mule, because you can use the meat and tan his hide when his day is done. Maybe a farmer who lives in a log cabin and plows with a steer will dig up a thousand dollars out of an old sock when he has to move.

Then, too, this area is one where national parks and forests have already accustomed people to dealing with Uncle Sam. Over the line in Georgia some of them moved once for a park, and now they're moving again for the reservoir. But of course the state of Georgia started as a resettlement project.

On the Carolina side many of the people are of Cherokee descent, and the land titles of the Dockerys and the Stileses and other families of the area go back to Indian grants. One Indian treaty was signed at Tellico Plains between Knoxville and Hiwassee, and while it's a little late, it's interesting to know that Uncle Sam is at last paying fair prices for Cherokee lands.

Most of the work of the Authority is specialized, but a relocation man has to know a little of everything. He meets the most objections and makes the most friends. As one onlooker down in Alabama put it: "First come the engineers to survey—they go right across and pay no attention to anybody. Then the men come to value, and nobody's satisfied, because if a TVA man walks across a field, of course it doubles in price. Then come the people cutting wood. And then the relocation people have to smooth it all out."

First of all, the relocation man has to remember what TVA plans to do—how the lake will run and when the reservoir clearance will begin. Relocation men get contour lines so well fixed in their minds that they can look at wooded hills and cornfields and talk of islands and peninsulas. Then it is necessary to know enough about farming to judge the value of land. Land acquisition is a separate department of TVA, but in dealing with the people it is important to understand whether a man is moving from a good farm to a bad one, or vice versa. It also helps if you know enough about the man to know when he is lying and when he is telling the truth.

Then you must understand the customs of the people. It does no good to leave a man on a farm if you drown out the road that gives him access to markets, so local trade routes must be studied, not on maps but on the ground. The maps may show as a road a trail that you couldn't get a sledge down; the way to find out is to drive your own Ford over. And remember that the farmer may not have a Ford— he may have to walk.

When it comes to deciding removal dates, you must try to adjust to the crop year and the length of leases. In some cases, after buying the land, TVA leases it back for one last crop before the water comes. But will it be safe from flood damage while the dam is being built? You must talk to the engineer about flood stages.

With such details given attention, there always remains a general problem about transplanting farmers. They are broke already; how can they sell a mortgaged farm for enough to finance a new place? Under the present procedure, not only the county agent and the university-extension man, but a representative of the Farm Security Administration is also likely to be called in.

And will the farmers flourish under transplanting? There may be a resettlement project elsewhere in the state with plenty of room for them, but will they like it there? Will their wives like it? Most of them want to stay in or near the same county; it is the exceptional mover who thinks he'd like to seize this opportunity to take a look at Venezuela or Brazil. Yet the near-by farms may be scarce, and undesirable from the expert's point of view.

In the case of small industries, the usual practice is for the owner to move to higher ground and build himself a better shop with the proceeds of his sale. In Murphy, near Hiwassee dam, the local laundry is rehoused in style because the old frame shack it occupied will go. The man who owned a small mill moved it too, but just as he got his nice new building finished, and before it was insured, it burned to the ground. TVA fire-fighting apparatus had helped put out a fire in the talc mine near by, but they couldn't save the little mill, and the relocation men were unhappy about it.

Besides raising a lot of individual problems, large-scale planning has to consider whole communities. Most of the little towns drowned out at Norris were mountain crossroads, with a population of a hundred or so and no local industries unless you count the church. One town, Caryville, had a population of a little over a thousand but only fifty of its houses would be flooded by normal high water. The people wanted to stay, and the local industry, coal-mining, was considered good—as far as coal was concerned—for another hundred years. So TVA moved seventy-three houses, just to be on the safe side in the case of a big flood, and also moved a nine-room brick school and the Baptist church. The planners went further; working through a local committee, they gave Caryville a park and a playground and a town common it hadn't had before. Also the town found itself on the edge of a lake.

Near Hiwassee, the town of Murphy will also gain a lake, and this

NORRIS DAM HAD TO DISTURB FIRESIDES LIKE THIS

BUT IT'S EASIER FOR MA TO COOK WITH ELECTRICITY

AIR-COOLED IN SUMMER TIME; WHAT ABOUT THE WINTER?

NORRIS HOUSES FOLLOW OLD STYLES, BUT IN A NEW WAY

town expects to be benefited; as a sign puts it: "Welcome TVA—Make Our Store Your Headquarters." Nevertheless, the lake that the dam will back up to Murphy's ball park will be a lake for only part of the year. The "draw-down" for navigation and power purposes must at other times leave Murphy adjacent to mud flats, and how will Murphy like that?

Down in the Shoals district, bad luck has dogged the little towns that were smaller rivals to the not-so-large "Tri-Cities." Riverton, a product of a boom in the eighties, was too far gone to save. But Waterloo was doing a legitimate business with farmers in the flooded area before TVA arrived on the scene. The town was left above the water line but its trade was gone. Now the chief hope is that the highway to be built along the Natchez Trace—a highway that may or may not be worth two million dollars, but does share with the Chisholm Trail and El Camino Real the romance of a good road name—will come through and give Waterloo citizens a chance to sell postcards.

To be fair, to do as little damage as possible, and to do a little improving wherever possible, these are the gentle purposes of the relocation staff. To achieve these ends you must have more than good intentions; you must have knowledge and firmness and tact, and a sense of proportion.

You must also have luck, either direct from Providence or through some other agency, because big as TVA is, there are limits to what it can do. Whether the Natchez Trace highway should be built, and where and how it should be built, is the concern of other government agencies, federal and state, all mindful of other problems besides those of Waterloo.

Building on Rock

Woe unto them that join house to house, that lay field to field, till there be no place.

Except the Lord build the house, they labor in vain that build it.

But the house of the righteous shall stand.

And an highway shall be there, and a way . . . the wayfaring men, though fools, shall not err therein.

That the best-laid plans may gang agley is humbly admitted by everyone in the Authority and often illustrated by the housing at Norris, so highly praised by enthusiasts when the town was new. The houses, of course, are as good as ever. But like most government housing ventures of those early days, they cost too much.

As an experiment is expected to cost more than the standardized product, this in itself doesn't greatly matter; the Authority is using the Norris experience on all subsequent housing jobs. Also it can be said that intelligent dam-building saved, on the Norris job, more than was spent on the town. And to see why an experiment in housing and town-planning should have been undertaken at Norris, you have only to look at housing all over the South.

Before the war, the Civil War, they built good private houses, but the South never studied civic planning. There were few garden cities or even good suburban developments before 1933. Instead, the average Southern town boasted one or two good houses left over from the good old days, respected by the women's club for historic reasons, but usually in a state of disrepair. There would be crazy shacks, built anyhow, occupied by the Negroes and the poor whites. And if the blessings of industry were enjoyed, there were rows of identical company houses, with a modern brick house for the boss and some bungalows for the white-collar workers. A Southern town counts itself a real city when it gets one or two duplex houses and apartments; as for architecture, people who get their ideas from the movies see nothing much wrong with filling stations.

Railroads, worked for and welcomed, might cut right through the town, as at Knoxville, or pass so far off, as at Asheville, that the traveler goes half-way to the next stop to catch his train. Knoxville is probably one of the worst-planned, or least-planned, towns in the country. It sits on a maze of railroad viaducts, with the trains puffing soot into people's faces. Public buildings are so well hidden they have to use directing signs, and the new post office is in a neighborhood of churches. Farmers drive into a public market, but when they have backed in their loads of flowers and vegetables, there is no room for a buyer to drive through. There are houses anybody would like to live in, but from the Southern viewpoint the residence section is oddly placed, because some of the best white houses out by the university are in a hollow where shrubbery grows lush and Bob Whites call, but no breeze blows; while the colored population lives high above the business district on a tree-shaded hill.

So it wasn't unreasonable that the Authority tried to make Norris what a small town in the region should be. If the ideas were just a little highfalutin for Tennessee at the time, give the folks a few years to catch up.

Of course, looking around you in the South, you can see that the cheapest kind of house is a frame shack. Anyhow it's the cheapest if you don't mind using up timber, and hiring cheap carpenters, and either using a lot of fuel or freezing in the winter. So common people leave brick to the rich folks.

But the Authority tried brick, and stone, and a newfangled cinder-block construction, and even their plainest wooden houses had improvements that ran up the cost. They talked to women, who spoke for screened porches to work and eat on, and plenty of shelves. They talked to health authorities, who suggested cross-ventilation. And they even talked to mountain people, who said of course you ought to have a fireplace; you could set up a stove just to warm by, but you'd have no place to look, and no place to sit, and no place to spit.

They didn't listen to people who might have fancied Swiss chalets or Spanish bungalows; there isn't one in the town. Mostly they took their designs from the oldest hill cabins, and built what folks call "dog-trot" or "shotgun" houses, with a hall or "breezeway" right through and rooms on each side. They don't look like the Northern houses that people try to copy, but they are comfortable to live in.

Then they used board-and-batten construction, and some of the hand-split shingles or "shakes" that were used in the Valley in early times. Nowadays farmers are apt to leave the shakes on the outbuildings, and put a nice tin roof on the house.

But they put in insulation because they wanted to heat with electricity, and they used copper sheathing because people were having trouble with termites. This ran up the expense, especially when they tried out different heating systems to get a good one. They used copper screens too, and copper pipe. The Yankees thought copper pipe wouldn't freeze in the South, and they wouldn't listen to folks who told them any pipe would freeze in a Tennessee winter, but they found out about that the first year.

And about the most expensive thing they did was to pay carpenters and masons a union wage.

When they went to set the houses on the ground, they made no effort to line them up, but turned them according to the slope of a hill or the situation of a tree. This didn't cost any more, although, before that, it was done only with well-to-do places like those in Melrose Park in Knoxville. Then they curved the roads, and put in paths and stepping stones instead of cement sidewalks, and put garages under hillsides where they wouldn't show. The road from Knoxville, called the "freeway," was part of the planning. They said it was to be just a "wide rural road," but Uncle Sam bought enough land on each side to keep off the hot-dog stands and the Coca-Cola signs.

Around the town they left a tract of woodland, a "green belt," they called it, of community forest. There weren't any big trees left, but there were middle-sized pines and some hickories that turn yellow in the fall, and some dogwood that blooms in the spring. They offered people land for community gardens, and plants for their yards if they would put them out. The soil at Norris is worn out and it takes a lot of work and fertilizer to build it up, but a big improvement could be noticed last year.

The offices for the town management, and the school, were put right in the middle of the town. Any town could be proud of that school. The building is two stories high, but they backed it up against a hill so the children on the second floor can walk out without having to use stairs. Inside they left the plain brick walls but painted them cream-color. They put in an electric heating plant, with humidifiers for the air, so even the janitor could have a college degree and a white-collar job; and they trained a trick "electric eye" to turn on the lights in cloudy weather.

But the main thing is the way the school is run. The children have no books to carry home; instead, they do their studying in the library from a lot of different books there. Grown people in the town use the same library, as well as the school auditorium and the woodworking shop.

Instead of using report cards they decided to write letters to the parents about how the boys and girls were getting along; they put down grades only in case some child might be transferred. And instead of keeping up the attendance record, if a child comes to school with a cold they send him home with a note saying, please keep him there. It seemed unusual to most people, but the children did well with their work.

Some of this work wasn't like ordinary schooling. The science class, for example, used the weather-station readings to make forecasts about the river. Then the school went into business; they formed a company which delivered the Norris news bulletin, in return for which the town contributed a five-acre plot of ground. So they organized the Norris School Produce company to raise vegetables. When they needed capital, they raised $50 by selling five hundred ten-cent bonds, paying three percent interest. Stock in the company, though, was obtainable only by work—eight hours for one share. Company production was supervised by the science teacher, accounting by the mathematics teacher, and sales by the social-science teacher.

Other school ventures were a towel service, and a lost-and-found service for the town. The student report on these activities found them profitable as services, but not as commercial ventures—a distinction which suggests at least some study of social science. Although some of the engineers' children from other places might have seen such schools, it's been a real novelty in Tennessee.

Besides the school, the community center has its own fire department, and a post office, and a grocery store, and the prettiest drug store you ever saw, designed so it doesn't look like a drug store at all. They show moving pictures in the school auditorium, and there's a little announcement board in the drug store, but no big posters—in fact, if you don't count pictures of the TVA dams, there isn't a sign in the whole place advertising anything. It looks unnatural, that way.

Instead of building three or four churches, they decided, by a ninety-nine percent vote, to have a "Religious Fellowship" to include all denominations and meet in the school auditorium. Some people got excited about that; there was an article in the Chicago *Tribune* headed "Churchless Norris," and a Kentucky congressman opposed to TVA brought the matter up again this year. Actually, they have had services every Sunday from the very first.

Norris folks voted unanimously against selling liquor, which made them different from the rest of the state, because they not only voted dry but actually drank milk.

They did queer things in other ways. An Englishwoman came to Knoxville in 1935, to speak against Fascism. That didn't sound right to Knoxville authorities, so they didn't allow the use of a hall in town. Miss Jennie Lee, Labour member of Parliament, spoke at Norris instead; but afterwards people got more broad-minded and next time she came she spoke in Knoxville.

You have to consider Norris a sort of suburb of Knoxville now, because that's what it got to be after the dam was built and could almost run itself. People working for TVA in Knoxville like living in Norris, and as many Knoxville people as could rent houses have moved there. You can't buy a house; Uncle Sam owns the place in perpetuity. And while building houses and a good school for Knoxville people wasn't what they started out to do, it's a nice town, and they've never had a crime there, unless you agree with the Republicans who say it was a crime to build it in the first place.

Of course a lot depends on who does the building. Down at Wilson dam, started during the World War and carried on by the Republicans, they've got some good houses that were built for the army people. In fact, they had two sets of community buildings because they had army engineers and also an ordnance department, and the two didn't mix. So TVA uses for its offices one headquarters, called the million-dollar officers' club, and the other is a school. They are just one-story frame buildings built around courts, but they are the right thing for that country, and well built because nobody counted costs.

But when TVA built Wheeler dam down there, they resolved not to attempt anything fancy. They had to build in a hurry to provide employment in Alabama, and part of the job was let out to private contractors. Later they wished they had done more, because a little town called Red Bank that mushroomed up on the outskirts of Uncle Sam's property was no credit to the job. But they built some temporary housing, and some they intended to be temporary is still there because it was better than people had before.

Chickamauga dam was close enough to Chattanooga for people to live in the city. At Guntersville they ran short of houses, and people who tried to live in the near-by towns of Huntsville and New Hope found that rents and prices climbed away up; when taxpayers save on TVA housing, the dam-builders lose.

At Hiwassee and Pickwick Landing they struck a half-way policy and built houses but kept the costs down. At Hiwassee they had some that cost, complete with plumbing, less than a thousand dollars. There still weren't enough, and sometimes, as they say happened in Russia, married couples have had to separate for dormitory life; you have to put up with temporary inconvenience in a new world. But with vines and flowers, tennis courts, swings and sandpiles, and a pitch for horseshoes, Hiwassee is a pretty and a pleasant place—"a fine place," said TVA's Irish police chief, "for the children."

Pickwick, having many Negro workers, has also a Negro village, where colored carpenters did the building. They did a good job, too. Nothing was done in the way of Negro housing at Norris, which bothered radically minded observers from New York, but the fact was simply that the Authority employs colored workers in proportion to the local population, and there weren't many in the Norris neighborhood.

Another problem where you have temporary housing is what to do with it when the dams are done. At Hiwassee some of the planners are already wondering if the dormitories can't be used as a permanent camp for 4-H boys and girls, or for Scouts. However, for the people about to go to work at Gilbertsville, they are moving some houses down the river from Pickwick Landing—floating them on barges, which will be something new in navigation on the Tennessee, and quite a change since a federal invasion burned houses along the river instead of building and saving them.

If it weren't for being accused of extravagance and over-activity generally, the Authority would no doubt have done more with permanent housing at the later dams. There could have been a lot more of the simple building they are doing now, which is still superior to much of the local construction.

Of course, if you were born in the South, you find unpainted cabins picturesque. You like to look at the mud-chinked log ones, whitewashed, that they have in Virginia, and the Tennessee-to-Alabama version made with sawed boards but with a clay chimney. You notice that in the mountains, where they like to whittle wood, they don't run to other frills but are apt to put a fancy-cut railing on the gallery. They all look nice even when the steps are broken, the fences falling down, and the yards grown up in yellow lilies.

But if you've got any sense you stop to think what those places are like to live in, and for the women to work in when they aren't working in the fields. At Hiwassee they were showing off some new cottages built of a patent composition wallboard, insulated to make it comfortable, and easy to handle; they said they had just put up the walls in sheets and cut holes for windows and doors. Made that way,

there were plenty of windows in the cottages. But only a few miles
down the road there was a weathered cabin with four or five people
looking out through the door when they heard a car. That place
was no concern of TVA because it was outside the reservoir area.
But the TVA men knew the family situation anyhow, which was not
good. And they pointed out that the house had no windows at all.

5. BEASTS

Why Croppers Are Sorry

What profit hath he that worketh, in that wherein he laboreth? . . .
I said in mine heart concerning the estate of the sons of men, that God might manifest them, and that they might see that they themselves are beasts.

For what hath man of all his labour, and of the vexation of his heart, wherein he hath laboured under the sun?

For that which befalleth the sons of men befalleth beasts . . . as the one dieth, so dieth the other . . . so that a man hath no preeminence above a beast.

Up in the Carolina mountains they have a custom of muzzling the plow mules; it's a Bible-reading country, but they never seemed to reason that what was said about not muzzling the ox would also apply to a mule. And of course nobody ever thought the passage referred to the sharecropper. But there would be no need to consider that, because he can't eat what he raises anyhow, or give cotton and tobacco to his hungry children.

It would take a smart person to figure out any way to make life harder than it is for croppers. They have no choice about what they grow. They don't know what the price will be or what the grade will be; other people decide that. They don't know how much they will get of what is due them, because somebody else keeps the books. It would do them no good to be better farmers, because one of the first rules of good farming is diversification, which they wouldn't be allowed to practice. And yet you'll find people who say the trouble with croppers is that they show no initiative.

A lot has been said about the sharecropping system and you could

say a lot more without explaining just how bad it is. You have to
see it, and you have to think about it. A lot of Southerners see it
without thinking, because the people it produces are such sorry-
looking folks that it is taken for granted that such people would be
in trouble anyhow. But there are more of these people than there
used to be. Just in the last few years it's got so that more than half
the farmers work for other men, and in the cotton country sixty
out of a hundred do.

They hire out by the year, but they don't have much chance to
better themselves when they start the year in debt. One university
survey showed that forty percent of the croppers started owing
about $80; that may not seem like much money but it is if it amounts
to your yearly cash income. In Alabama, another count showed over
half the croppers starting even, and only a quarter of them ending
in debt, but not one in ten made as much as $80 a year.

When they borrow, taking the advance in goods, the store mark-up
can be as high as fifty percent. The croppers don't complain; most
of them don't keep the accounts. They wouldn't be allowed to anyhow, but most of them don't know how; they just let the commis-
sary man have his way with the doodlum book.

Cotton-planters will tell you they are shiftless people or they
wouldn't be croppers. You can't get good tenants. They've got no
ambition, no gumption, no sense of responsibility. You can't treat
them like other people. Anyhow nobody does.

But for the Yankees to sit up there and consider the landlord a
tight-fisted money-grabbing scoundrel, living in luxury off what he
makes from other people's work, is plain foolish. A book that a lot
of people read took that attitude and talked about the plantation-
owner summering at Biloxi as if Biloxi was a fashionable resort like
those the Northern capitalists go to, when everybody down South
knows it's just a little Gulf Coast town where anybody can go that
isn't working right then. It doesn't take money, or the cotton-planters
wouldn't go there, because a WPA survey showed that the average
net income of the plantation-owner was $2572 a year. Up North they
wouldn't consider that put you in the capitalist class. Moreover, a

tenth of that was in goods grown on the plantation and used at home.

The survey took in prosperous country, too, good rich Delta farms. In the Muscle Shoals district the incomes were lower, and the owner made, on an average, $1340 a year. That's better than the tenant makes, naturally—he would average something like $350 for his work at the same time. So the proportion isn't fair, but just the same it's true that the landlord isn't what you could call well off himself. In fact a Muscle Shoals cotton-planter wouldn't have to pay an income tax in New York state, even if he wasn't married, and the planter making the higher average for the whole survey area would be exempt if he had a family.

Besides realizing that nobody makes a fortune in cotton any more, people outside the South have to distinguish between renters, croppers, and wage hands. The renter can pay a cash rent or he can be a "third and fourth hand," supplying everything but the land and paying a third of the corn or a fourth of the cotton as rent. The cropper furnishes labor only, and gets half the crop. The wage hand just works by the day in hoeing or picking season, and of course he won't make over a dollar a day, so some people think it wrong for the WPA to pay $6 a week to people that should be picking cotton.

The WPA survey found that the average net income for croppers was $312 a year. For cash renters it was $354, and for wage hands $180. This wasn't cash money, of course; a third of it was in food. They found that about a quarter of the plantations ran their own commissaries, but they didn't all make their tenants buy there. The average tenant lived for two-thirds of the year on an advance of $13 a month.

Houses, naturally, weren't much. Mississippi had the fewest painted tenant houses, but tenants don't expect paint. Alabama had the most log ones. A majority of the owners had screens while a majority of the tenants didn't have them. But ninety out of a hundred places lived in by landlords and tenants alike had what the WPA surveyors called inadequate sanitation.

Tenants move, of course—white ones at an average of every four years, Negroes every six. But when they do move they seldom go outside the county.

The tobacco market is less of a gamble, and the labor is considered more skilled, although picking off worms and even picking the leaves is a mean job they like to give to children. But thirty years ago they had a sort of tobacco war, with night riders who acted like the old Klan—this was before the Klan was revived as a commercial proposition in 1916. It was before so many farmers had to take to tenantry or cropping; they were still independent producers convinced of their right to bargain. When the tobacco company fixed the price, they held on to the crops of 1906 and 1907, and the night riders burned barns where farmers refused to co-operate in this crop control. The struggle went on for some time; there were said to be ten thousand organized tobacco farmers in Kentucky, and grand juries wouldn't indict them for burning warehouses and cars of tobacco or even for stopping the fast train to Memphis. It got to the point where only two men planted tobacco in the biggest tobacco-growing county in Kentucky. So there was worry over how the liberty of the farmer was being menaced, and the governor of Kentucky finally declared martial law, exactly as in an industrial strike nowadays. The outcome was a victory for the farmers in the matter of price, and they had to give the night riders credit.

Not that anybody who does the actual work in the tobacco business makes money out of it; when the president of the Tobacco Association complained that the wage-hour law would double the wages of people who did hand-stemming, that meant they made less than two bits an hour. Tobacco company payrolls run to around one-tenth the amount of the company dividends, and farmers get less for the whole crop than the net profits of the big companies.

But tobacco, like corn, is usually just part of a Valley farmer's living. It's the cotton-grower who stakes everything on one gamble, as he has a right to do except for the risk to the tenants and croppers and wage hands who have to depend on his judgment.

Some time ago a Southern judge with sense ruled that a cropper is not a partner but a wage hand under annual contract. This was a

recognition that a cotton plantation is more like a mine or a factory
than a farm. If the federal government had understood this, it might
have managed differently with AAA, instead of fixing it so that a big
paying plantation like the Delta and Pine down in Mississippi would
get the biggest checks for crop control. Tenants and croppers began
to understand they were just wage hands when some growers forgot to divide up the AAA checks, or just applied the amount on the
annual debt. That did more than anything else to make the croppers organize.

The Southern Tenant Farmers' Union has done more already than
a lot of people realize, publishing a paper and getting help from the
WPA to cut down illiteracy, and making health surveys. Then they
got 'way ahead on studying what machinery would do; while the
National Association of Manufacturers was arguing that the tenancy
figures must be wrong—surely fifteen or maybe twenty-five percent,
not sixty-five to seventy—and while the president of the American
Cotton Association was suggesting an appropriation of $10,000,000
to check the migration of labor from the cotton belt, STFU was
reporting on the probable effects of the Rust cotton-picker.

The union also undertook to educate its members about the government, and to establish friendly working relations with government agencies. Deputy WPA Administrator Aubrey Williams,
speaking in Memphis shortly after the mayor had warned the CIO
to stay out of his city, was one of the first to wish them well.

There wasn't much use, of course, in their trying to work with
county governments; one county agent, invited to put a farm worker
on a county farm board, said, what for—you wouldn't put a chicken
on a poultry board, would you? Nor did the states do much, down
South. Back in 1936, when the papers had a lot to say about the
tenant situation, the governor of Arkansas appointed a commission
to study the problem. But the governor of Mississippi disclaimed
knowledge of any tenant difficulties in his state, and it was true that,
while the Mississippi papers had just reported the killing of two people in an eviction, it was right over the line in Tennessee. The Mississippi commissioner of agriculture said: "It might be a good idea

for the friends of the South to get together and stop all the propaganda about sharecroppers that is hurting the South." Some of the
other states were more interested in doing something, but even the
governor of Arkansas forgot to appoint any tenant farmers to his
commission.

In spite of this snub, STFU went to work anyhow and made a
long report of its own, which for clarity and common sense would
do credit to any investigators. So when the President appointed a
committee of forty to suggest a national farm tenancy plan, he put
a member of STFU on the committee. This representative made a
minority report that again presented facts of considerable importance
—the tendency of county agents to speak for landlords or business
interests, the questionable responsibility of state administrations—and
suggested that Department of Labor jurisdiction might be prefer-
able to that of the Department of Agriculture. The report asked for
tenant representation on boards, and for extension of the Wagner
Labor Act and the Social Security Act to agricultural workers. With
regard to efforts to solve the problem by resettlement in small hold-
ings, it looked at its own investigation of machine production and
observed that the small homestead is now an "economic anachro-
nism."

Later on, the union made a report to the National Emergency
Council that was connected by some people with Mr. Hopkins's
promise, at Memphis, to find part-year employment for farm workers.

Why Mill Hands Are Ornery

*Behold, we are servants this day, and for the land that thou gavest unto our
fathers to eat the fruit thereof and the good thereof, behold, we are servants
in it:*

*And it yielded much increase unto the kings whom thou hast set over us
because of our sins: also they have dominion over our bodies, and over our
cattle, at their pleasure, and we are in great distress.*

Back in 1768 the Indians reluctantly consented to the settlement
of the Tennessee Valley in what was called the treaty of Hard La-

bour creek. That has been the condition of life and people are used
to it; for years now the industrialized North has condemned Southern "laziness," while Southerners have been busy working from
sunup to sundown for wages that a Yankee would consider carfare.
The truth is that man and nature too must work longer and harder
down South. The crops and trees grow for a longer season, the rivers
keep churning over the shoals with no time out for ice, and people
get to their jobs early in the morning and quit late. It isn't that they
don't work, it's just that the crops don't sell for much and the water
power has always been wasted, and the wages are low.

Before the Civil War the New York *Herald* said that the twenty-
eight cotton mills then in Georgia employed boys and girls from
twelve to twenty years old, and paid them four to six dollars a week.
The paper added: "On an average they are better paid, and worked
easier, than is usually the case in the North."

But maybe the *Herald* was over-optimistic. Even in the fifties there
was talk of a differential; a North Carolina congressman claimed
that labor costs were a hundred percent cheaper in his state, and a
Tennessean argued that, while in Lowell, Massachusetts, they might
have to pay men 80 cents a day and women $2 a week, with board
besides, Tennessee workmen got along all right on 50 cents a day,
and women on $1.25 a week.

Also in the fifties there was fear of labor unrest, particularly on the
part of people who had observed that poor and presumably discontented people, non-slaveholders, were in a big majority. At that time
they had no real restrictions on voting, such as afterwards disqualified the hard-up white folks along with the Negroes. So a writer
in *DeBow's Review* worried some because "the progress of the
world is 'onward,' and though in some sections it is slow, still it is
'onward,' and the great mass of our poor white population begin
to understand that they have rights and that they, too, are entitled
to some of the sympathy which falls upon the suffering. . . . It is
this great upheaving of our masses that we have to fear, so far as our
institutions are concerned." But the writer had a way out. Manufactures would employ all those in want; and "the active industry of

THIS TOWN'S OUT-OF-WORK MINERS HELPED BUILD DAMS

COTTON IS ONLY PART OF THE CROP, IN THE VALLEY

WHITE WOMEN PICK THE COTTON NOW, OFTEN AS NOT

a father, the careful housewifery of the mother, and the daily cash earnings of four or five children, will very soon enable each family to own a servant, thus increasing the demand for this species of property to an immense extent." So, of course, people already blessed with slaves could sell them at a profit.

Another theory regarding Negro slavery as an accompaniment to keeping the poor whites in their place was advanced about the same time by one of the cotton-mill owners of that period, one celebrated for his enlightened management. William Gregg said hopefully: "In all other countries, and particularly manufacturing states, labor and capital are assuming an antagonistic position. Here it cannot be the case; capital will be able to control labor, even in manufacture with whites, for blacks can always be resorted to in case of need."

But the Yankees fought a war to stop that, and for a while everybody in the South was so poor there wasn't much talk about the poor whites. By the time they got to describing them again they were "The Best Cotton Mill Labor in the World, Working under the Best Conditions in the World." Under this headline the *Manufacturers' Record,* in a special edition published during the boom of the twenties, described the Southern mills as "a great missionary force," under which workers "developed mentally, physically, and spiritually."

Plenty of mills moved South then because, as before, the Yankees were first to denounce the union. Back in 1919 the University of Tennessee made a survey of wage levels, accepting $4.70 a week as a living for a man, $3.70 for a woman, $2.80 for a child eleven to fourteen, $1.90 for children under ten, or fifteen dollars for a family of five. A survey of 1415 families showed over two-thirds of the whites and over half the Negroes to be under these levels. No wonder that, in the words of Mr. Walter S. Gifford, the East and North turned their eyes to the South, and the South of the commercial clubs was seen "grooming itself to meet this outpour of money and this expression of confidence on the part of Northern business men and large corporations, and to fulfill every expectation." In the North wages were going up, but in the decade that saw the textile industry shift to a Southern center, Southern wages decreased.

Of course it was only a matter of time until the Southern workers would hear of what they were paying up North, and be discontented. Look at Happy Valley, on the edge of the bigger Valley of the Tennessee, and containing a little town called Elizabethton. Campaigning in 1928, Mr. Hoover made a speech at Elizabethton and promised great things if folks would vote Republican and go to work in the German-owned rayon mills being built there. So they did both; but inside of a year the mill people were dissatisfied with a $5-to-$12 wage scale and ungrateful enough to strike.

The governor of Tennessee broke the strike with troops commissioned as policemen, and with army equipment. Happy Valley folks had fought for the government at King's Mountain and Buena Vista and Shiloh, and in the World War, and they didn't know how to fight against it. The strikers were jailed and then blacklisted, the mill built a ball park for its loyal workers, and everything seemed to be settled. How did it happen that in another ten years the mill had a contract with TWOC, the textile workers' affiliate of CIO?

Ten years ago, down South, a union was a union, and an American Federation of Labor organizer would be kidnaped as quick as any other. Yet the snooty preference of the A. F. of L. for high-salaried workers kept them from doing much in Southern mills, and today the mill-owners know the devil is personified, walking on earth in the shape of John L. Lewis; his minions are Russian Communists invading the Southland to stir up contented working people and force them to join the CIO.

A lot of the people who worry themselves into a lather along this line never saw a CIO organizer, or wouldn't know one if they met him—or her—in the road. There's no use telling them that most of the CIO representatives are mild-mannered folks whose worst vices are drinking Coca-Colas, smoking hand-rolled cigarettes because they are the cheapest kind, and keeping scrapbooks of newspaper editorials adverse to them.

Nowadays the organizers aren't even Yankees. In times past it might have been necessary to import people to talk about the wages they paid and the hours they worked up North. Now there are plenty of Southerners who know, and organizers in the Valley are mostly born there.

Anybody who still visualizes the labor leader as a so-and-so meddling New York Jew should have heard a gentleman from Georgia imitate a speech made to a group of textile workers last year. " 'Come, choin up mit me and I see you vass treated right,' he says, and all they do is stand and laugh at him. It was pathetic," said the Georgian, managing a fair East Side accent between bites of watermelon. "He didn't get to first base." And the point to this performance is that the man from Georgia was a CIO organizer. The ineffective exhorter from New York was the factory-owner, who came down to urge his employees to join a company union.

Yes, they have company unions, now that the labor struggle in the South has come to conform to a recognizable pattern. First there was, probably, some ineffective striking years ago, as at Elizabethton. Then came hopeless endurance, until the short-lived intervention of NRA. With the right local people in charge, NRA didn't make much trouble, and sometimes, asked to choose between low wages and work, the mill workers themselves agreed to get around the codes. Or delay would help, as when Georgia cotton gins asked leave to go on paying fifteen cents an hour, knowing the ginning season would be over before Washington could refuse. When they had to observe the codes, they learned from the North to put in new machinery or the stretchout and fire folks, beginning with the Negroes.

But it did some good, and many mill workers look back to the Blue Eagle as fondly as brokers remember Hoover prosperity. Maybe they'd be ashamed to tell you what they worked for before or afterwards. "But we done right well," they'd say, "under the NRA. Twelve dollars a week!"

When NRA was invalidated, there were wildcat strikes. Ten

years ago people had just quit; now they just sat down. But Southerners are seldom hard-boiled enough to sit down effectively, so
the mills and factories just stayed closed.

As for organizers, Southern property-owners reasoned that the
thing to do with an unwelcome visitor was to take him, or her,
out of town with maybe a little rough handling and a warning not
to come back. This kidnaping trick was tried again and again;
last year, in a little one-family fief called Cleveland, Tennessee,
they went so far as to kidnap a government conciliator.

Some other towns just pretended they weren't organized. Take
Florence, Alabama, where the Chamber of Commerce handed out
a leaflet saying: "Wage rates more moderate than are in effect in
more congested areas make possible a superior standard of living
to the worker in this area." This sentence is one to mystify students
of social science or even of rhetoric, but the context makes it
clear: "The type of labor available in Florence, Lauderdale, and
adjacent counties . . . is intelligent, native born, English speaking,
willing and anxious for employment. . . . Open shop conditions
are in effect, and no recent labor strife or agitation has been ex-
perienced. State labor laws are favorable to industry."

There was no CIO office in Florence, but by going to a barber
shop and getting a haircut, and talking to the right people, and
hiring a car to drive out into the country that night, you could find
the president of the local in one of the textile mills. Sure enough,
he was intelligent, native-born, English-speaking, and able to say
with some pride that his mill was doing pretty well now. They'd
had one lock-out, and made the company stop using water from the
sewage canal in the humidifiers, which had made it unhealthy to
work in the plant. They had better wages and hours than the
other two mills in town, which had no unions. He'd like to try
organizing there but he couldn't undertake too much, because he
had to think of his own family. He figured it would take time to
convince folks.

He was right, because this year they were having more trouble
in Florence—the situation had progressed to the next phase. Under

that the mill closes down, explaining that it has no orders, or is losing money by paying the union scale. It stays closed for the four weeks it takes for unemployment benefits to come through. Then it starts up, using fewer people maybe, and arguing that now they must be hired as individuals—to organize, start over. This way of killing unions reminds you of TVA's method of killing mosquitoes by opening and shutting the dam sluices, and it was being tried all over the Valley last year.

When the national government tried to make conditions uniform by the child-labor amendment, of course the states could just vote it down. But then came the Wagner Act and the NLRB and the wage-hour law, and first thing you knew the union organizers were able to tell members about federal laws bigger than any picayune local practices. Southern business men were slow to believe that a union could have legal rights, and usually it takes at least one Labor Board hearing to convince them. So it's easy for the union to get evidence of intimidation and discrimination and such interference as the government now disapproves, although it appears to the mill- or factory-owner to be just his own way of running his business. All the organizer has to do is to persuade the workers not to strike, but to hold their heads up, take it easy, and tell their troubles to the lawyer.

So, just as there is hardly a town in the Tennessee Valley where you won't find a little cotton or hosiery mill, so there is hardly a town that hasn't had a Labor Board hearing. They've had hearings for knitting mills and lumber mills, for silk and woolen mills, furniture and garment factories, and pipe and stove foundries. Cities like Chattanooga have had twenty or thirty appeals pending at once.

And now the word is getting around that for some reason Uncle Sam believes that even a CIO organizer should be let live. There are Southern towns where the TWOC headquarters actually hangs out a shingle. In fact, it's almost as safe, now, to have to do with a union in the South as in the North. Last fall, when a sheriff shot into a picket line and killed a hosiery-mill worker, it was up in

Pennsylvania; the pickets were protesting removal of the mill to Virginia.

Yes, things are changing. Down South in the old days they used to make biscuits rise by beating them; that's the hard way. Southern labor in field and factory has had its share of that. Now both mills and farms are beginning to feel the effects of something like a store-bought yeast powder; but some people, of course, still say beating is better.

Why Darkies Are Lazy

Are ye not as children of the Ethiopians unto me, O children of Israel? saith the Lord.

Now when all the princes, and all the people, which had entered into the covenant, heard that everyone should let his manservant, and everyone his maidservant, go free, that none should serve themselves of them any more, then they obeyed, and let them go.

But afterward they turned, and caused the servants and the handmaids, whom they had let go free, to return, and brought them into subjection.

Abolition, being wished on the South the way prohibition was wished on New York, took some time to enforce. For a good while after the war, the Civil War, it still wasn't safe for a Negro in the cotton country even to go to law against a white man. But last year, in Mississippi, the state supreme court gave a tenant farmer a judgment of $2279.91 against a landlord on the ground that excessive interest was charged on a cotton-crop loan. The interest was said to be more than twenty percent, which isn't unusual. But the judgment was remarkable for more reasons than that it favored the tenant against the owner, and that the amount involved was large. The really remarkable thing was that the landlord was a white man, and the tenant was colored.

More important for Southern Negroes than an occasional court judgment in their favor is the fact that they are now being allowed to serve on juries. Of course it's because they took a lesson from the Scottsboro trials, and from a Kentucky case where the Supreme Court ruled that a conviction wouldn't hold because Negroes weren't allowed on juries in that county. In Marion, North Carolina, they had a case where feeling was so high that a white man walked into the courtroom during the trial and clouted the prisoner over the head with an iron pipe. The Negro boy's fate was as good as settled, because he had admitted attacking a white girl, but they postponed his trial and kept him safe over in Buncombe county until they could get a Negro drawn on the jury. He was the first to serve in McDowell county in over fifty years.

Of course it will probably take another fifty years before the Negroes they put on juries will vote any way except what the white folks want. Still, it looks better, especially to Northerners.

Scottsboro and Decatur are both in the Valley and they voted to have TVA power, although the president of the Alabama Power company, who lived in Scottsboro himself, warned them that they might be sorry for it. Yankees who go through those towns on the train seem to expect them to be different from other places, the way they felt about Dayton, but they're just ordinary little Southern towns. When the train runs through from Chattanooga to the Shoals, maybe you will notice that, though this is black country, there aren't so many Negroes hanging around the depot as you will see some places; maybe the only Negro in sight is carrying a white man's bag and moving mighty polite, because while the Scottsboro boys weren't hanged they did get a scare.

And it seemed as if they had to have enough boys to make up a ball team before anybody paid any attention, because of course there have been lots of individual cases while the Scottsboro trial was spread all over the papers.

The standard Southern reply to talk about lynching is, of course, to mention the gangs in Yankee cities. They don't know that back in 1741 thirteen Negroes were burned at the stake in New York city. It wasn't a lynching, though; it was perfectly legal.

In the South, as everywhere else, bad Negro housing is behind a lot of other troubles, health and morals and conditions generally. You can't, as one intelligent Negro leader in Alabama remarked, do much about tuberculosis when folks have to live five in a room. Surveys have shown crowding to be worse in the South than in other parts of the country, and worse in Gadsden, Alabama, than in any of a group of cities that size. Where crowding is bad you can be sure the Negroes have to stand more than their fair share. But what about the big cities up North?

Not enough Southerners know there are twice as many Negroes in New York or Philadelphia as white folks in Knoxville. There are more Negroes in Cook county, Illinois, than in the state of Kentucky, and the colored population of Chicago is bigger than the white population of Birmingham and twice that of Chattanooga. In none of these Yankee cities do the Negroes live in decency, according to Southern standards. Northerners worried over rural housing down South don't stop to think that if you must live five in a room without proper plumbing, it's better for the room to be a cabin in a cornfield than a dank basement or the fifth floor rear of an old-law tenement. At least you can stick your head out of the cabin door into light and air.

When New York state appointed a commission to see what was being done to the Negroes, they discovered that Harlem rents were out of all proportion to the rest of Manhattan. Up in well-to-do Westchester they found Negroes living in houses that had been condemned, and people prejudiced against hiring them or paying them fair wages. They found places in the Bronx and Brooklyn where Negro girls needing work would go to be hired at low wages by Yankee housewives driving soft-cushioned cars and hard bargains. Harlem called these places "slave markets."

In the Tennessee Valley, Yankees and Southerners are now seeing the same thing at the same time, for once, so you hear a lot of talking about how to treat Negroes. In the public rooms at Norris dam the drinking fountains are marked, as they usually are in the South, "White" and "Colored." Get a group of TVA men to talking about those fountains, and opinions will split right through the middle like the Mason-Dixon line.

The prize example of Southern viewpoint came from a young

Tennessean who admitted it was a mistake to have two fountains.

"All they needed was one, with no mark on it at all," he said. "Then the niggers would know it was for white folks, and wouldn't touch it."

He was right, because in the courthouse yard in Tupelo, Mississippi, there are two drinking fountains, unmarked, and there is never any confusion. The colored people know that theirs is the one farthest from the sidewalk.

While these distinctions are inconsiderate, it's easy to see how a lot of the Southern notions got started. Take the idea that Negroes were naturally made to do certain kinds of work, and white men other kinds—an idea that lingers in the South as in the British Empire. You'll find it right along with the idea that women weren't meant to have jobs, at least not good jobs, with pay. And just as it was once true that you couldn't find a woman capable of being a good doctor or a lawyer, that was once true of Negroes, and for the same reason—they weren't educated.

Also there was a physical difference that suggested adaptation to different work. The Negroes were brought from a hotter climate and they could stand the heat; nowadays of course you see as many white field hands as colored, but white people did think field work more suitable for those who didn't seem to mind it so much, and anyhow didn't show sunburn. Another simple physical difference that Southerners know, though they may not brag about it, is that Negroes are stronger and capable of physical exertion that most white men can't manage. At least that's true of healthy country Negroes; the legendary John Henry who outdid the trip-hammer went to Birmingham from the cotton country.

Intelligent people can see that these differences, and some others, are not to the discredit of the Negroes. But the poor whites have a fear of Negroes that is partly economic and partly to be explained on less flattering grounds, the sort of fear which brought some Southern men back from the World War worried because the Negroes over there went with French girls. So, instead of being welcomed back as fellow-heroes, the Negro soldiers returned to a revival of the Klan, and war memorials down South list the white boys in one column, the colored in another. In life they were not together, and in death they are divided.

Sometimes, as in the case of schools, this works a hardship on the white folks. A woman dipping snuff on the street in Knoxville asked a direction because she couldn't read; then, making conversation with a stranger, asked if it was true that they let nigger children in school with the whites, up North. Clearly she preferred no schooling to such a relaxation of principle.

Color separations last longer in solemn matters like education than in matters of trade, and some new inventions are helping to make the lines fade out. Jim Crow is dying; he was run over by a bus. Hard-up folks of both colors travel by bus nowadays and you can't run an extra car for the Negroes, though a boy in Mississippi did mutter when the driver stopped to let two colored women on.

It is hard to find an end to the evils that follow when men fall back upon a superiority which they believe must be theirs by right of birth. Intelligent white men who wear mental blinkers to keep them from seeing injustice to black men are apt to keep on the blinkers when nearing injustice elsewhere. More, as Southerners well know, the distinction made between white and colored serves as a safety valve for the "poor whites," to keep them from dwelling on their own woes. The no-'count white man forgets his grievances by beating his wife or kicking a houn' dawg or abusing a darky, and the last, since the darky may well be his physical, mental, and moral superior, gives greatest relief. There may be some significance in the fact that, as lynching in the South decreases, labor agitation increases, and vice versa.

The real interests of the "poor whites" are, of course, identical with the interests of the Negro. The term "poor white" (Negro version: po' white trash) has been variously considered by Southern historians. It may have originated in the feeling that a white man in unfortunate circumstances was entitled to sympathy. It may have been an expression of biological snobbishness—the "poor white" had a poor heredity, which explained his shiftlessness. In this connection it may be mentioned that by most young Southerners the poor whites are understood to be the unlucky descendants of Yankee overseers, or of the carpetbaggers and scalawags of reconstruction. But more and more the term "poor white" has come to mean any white folks without money, because the South today has accepted the Yankee measure of civilization, the gold standard.

From some people, Yankees especially, the Negroes might get more if they asked for more. Not long ago a Negro held up a Southern drug store and told the clerk he wanted six dollars. That's what he got, holding a pistol while the clerk peeled the bills from a roll in the cash register. That sort of moderation is all too rare. Of course some white folks might pay more attention if the Negroes whooped and hollered for things, and advertised themselves more as consumers of goods. One advertising survey of the prosperity years showed that city Negroes bought things of better quality than white people, when they were able to buy at all.

But Southerners figure it's Negro nature to prefer a little money, a little work, and ease of mind to more money, more work, and a lot of worry. And some are beginning to think the Negroes may be right. Anyhow money does you no good if you can't buy what you want with it, and there are a lot of things that Negroes still can't buy in the South. Take the case of Tobe Lawson down in Mississippi.

Everybody said Tobe was a good man and he worked hard and got his own farm, and the last time cotton was scarce and high he cleared several thousand dollars, a heap of money for a colored man. Tobe didn't know what to do with it, but he went to see old Judge Pickens at the bank. The judge always advised about things and advanced money to tide over from one crop to the next. So this time the judge picked out some good safe bonds and salted Tobe's money away for him. Then, lo and behold, next season here came Tobe again, asking for the usual loan. The judge knew those bonds were right in the bank; so he asked what Tobe wanted a loan for, and Tobe told him.

"You see, Judge, it's this way. You know my farm—it's right next to a white man's farm. And you know I got two mules. Well, s'posin' one of those mules gets loose and wanders over to the farm next do', and the white man done tek him up. I needs him to wuk with, but I can't get him back; white man say he done hol' him for trepass.

"Now, Judge, all I kin do is to call you in town. And if I runs the farm on my money, I calls you and you says: 'Why, that's too bad, Tobe. I'll come over and see about it.' And you does, but maybe it's two, th'ee days I can't wuk my mule.

"But I runs the farm on yo' money, and the same thing happen, you says: 'What's that you say? I'll be out there right away,' and you is."

But there has been some progress since the nineties, when 1400 white workers in a Georgia cotton mill went on strike because twenty Negroes were hired; and since 1909, when trainmen on the Central of Georgia railroad objected to working with Negro firemen. After the sharecroppers struck bottom, they started a union without race distinctions, and they've still got it.

There was trouble, of course. Back in 1931 a sheriff broke up a meeting of croppers in a church down in Tallapoosa county, Alabama, for no apparent reason except that in that part of the country most of the croppers are colored. Several Negroes were killed and their cabins shot up, and a posse of 500 men under the sheriffs of four counties went on a hunt for union members. They put a dozen Negroes in jail and even arrested a white man who helped a Negro get away.

Newspapers got hysterical; the Birmingham *Age-Herald* called it a "Race War" and the *News* said: "Further Red Violence Is Threatened." Of course all the violence was on the side of the deputy sheriffs; the croppers had done nothing but meet peaceably and try to get on with their organizing. Later a Negro did shoot birdshot at a sheriff, but it didn't hurt the sheriff except in his dignity, while the Negro got killed.

Anybody can see that, even if you wanted to, you couldn't have a lily-white union of tenants, because the planters would just hire all colored croppers. Some favor Negroes anyhow because they aren't so quick to lose patience and spit on the fire and call the dog and move. But when Negroes and white folks work side by side in the fields and live side by side in the slums, why wouldn't they sit side by side in the union meeting? It's the white folks who invaded the tenant-farming business anyhow.

In the slums white folks are the invaders too. Walk down White-side street in Chattanooga, misnamed, since whites and Negroes are living in the same block, and the white people will tell you the revival under canvas on the corner is a Negro meeting. They don't go, even to hear a preacher called the Black Hawk, said to be able to find lost property and give messages from the dead.

But they can't keep apart when they work. A farm truck going through Knoxville on a hot Sunday afternoon was crammed so tight with people, standing up, that you might have thought it was a picnic. Then you noticed they were both white and colored, so it couldn't be a social occasion. There were men and women too, so it couldn't be a convict work gang. It had to be hands going to a farm, and the man who hired them and loaded them on the truck was doing more to break down racial barriers in the South than a dozen Klans could do to raise them.

When a farmer held a gun on cotton-pickers down in Laurel, Mississippi, to keep them working at his price, of course they were Negroes. But when a pickers' strike ups wages from two bits a hundred, it takes white and black wage hands to do it. They organize together for the same reason that their union affiliates with UCAPAWA, the United Cannery, Agricultural, Packing and Allied Workers of America; the set-up of modern industry demands it.

So far not many mill and factory unions admit both races, because not many mills and factories hire Negroes. But the Bemis Bag company in Tennessee, which used white workers for flour and gunny sacks, had Negroes making baskets. At first not even TWOC thought of signing up the colored workers, and some Negroes were scared by rumors that the CIO was another Klan, out to kill them. Then when the union saw it would have to strike, they organized the Negroes to keep them from being used as scabs.

The Negroes were given the job of picketing the back door, because they didn't want any trouble with the white drivers of supply trucks allowed to pass in front. Then the white pickets let some trucks get by with strikebreakers as extra cargo, and the Negroes begged for a chance to stop that. The Negro that stopped the next truck not only managed without any trouble; he kept his head enough to take a gun away from the driver. He also kept the gun, which had the company's mark on it and came in handy as an exhibit at the hearing.

Of course, you'll find the old ways and the new side by side. Down in Florence, Alabama, a gang of colored road workers sang as they spread asphalt. It was going on the street in front of a big brick house with white columns that looked like an old-time Southern mansion as Yankee imagination pictures it. It had been, once, but now it was just the home of the local department-store owner. The asphalt was new, the house was new-rich, and the only thing that hadn't changed since slavery was the song. It said, in a minor key:

> Done lef' dis worl' behin'. . . .

That was just resignation; the world had left the singers, and when Negroes were left behind in a region that got left too, it put them a long way back. But it was near Florence that one of the most encouraging things to happen in all that country had just occurred. They had appointed a Negro foreman to work for TVA in the slag plant at Pickwick dam.

Why Some Folks Are Shiftless

Strengthen ye the weak hands, and confirm the feeble knees.
Say to them that are of a fearful heart, Be strong, fear not: behold, your God
will come with vengeance, even God with a recompence.

Unions can help only where people have jobs. If there is no work, the government or private charity has to start from scratch.

In some Valley counties there never was any industry to speak of, beyond raising a little corn and Cain, or shooting squirrels and revenue men. What industry came in skinned off the trees or dug out the surface ore and then left people flat, worse off than if they never had been hired. When the Tennessee Valley Authority started to work in 1933, there were several thousand stranded coal-miners in the Valley who, chances were, would never work at that trade again. And there were people who had worked at lumbering, left to sit like the stumps in the cut-over country. These people were worse off than the unemployed in the North, because there was no factory that could be expected to hire them when prosperity came out of hiding. They were not needed for anything. They say there were from five hundred to twenty-five hundred people like that in every county in the Valley.

While the whole payroll for a Southern factory is likely to be less than executive salaries and expenses at the company headquarters up in some Yankee city, you might say that the few dollars a week people could earn were the next thing to actual unemployment; certainly no more than "home relief" elsewhere.

No wonder that, as long as there was hope of work up North, thousands of people moved there every year; in the ten years from 1920 to 1930 nearly two million left the Valley states. And then, in the depression, a million of the movers had to come back home to ma and pa. They say seven hundred families came back to one county in 1932, and it was a county that hadn't had much before, or they never would have left.

They are still moving up or down, hitch-hiking here and there, and just milling around, trying to find out which part of the country is least hard on poor folks. You'll see them on the roadsides, with three to five children and one valise, hoping to thumb a ride; in wagons if they still have mules, or on buses if they have the fare.

Until lately the South didn't know much about organized relief work. When the relief agencies started, some plantation-owners took it for granted they'd feed the tenants in hard times, and couldn't see why not. Others objected to any sort of relief, even the Red Cross, as tending to pauperize people and keep them from working as they should. When they got as far as work relief, and the WPA salaries looked as good or better than what a lot of people were making on their jobs, it was taken for granted that this dispensation of government was intended for white people only. Projects for Negroes lacked local sponsors, and Washington had no way of interfering in such matters. But they do say Negroes weren't so welcome on the WPA rolls up in White Plains, New York.

Town people did better than rural people, usually, in getting work relief, and some people said there were places where the Baptists did better than the Methodists. But of course that depended on the local administrator.

It was the same way in the CCC—at first, in some places, the local people took it for granted that only white boys were wanted. They got that straightened out, but only after the first quotas were filled.

In resettlement it was said that the Negro families often did better, but usually it was the whites who got the chance.

You have to remember that there isn't anything like what New York calls "home relief" in the South, just WPA work and county poor. Negroes that go on the county in some places have to live on as little as $1.50 a month, and the whites get from $3 to $5. You don't live long on that, which may be what they expect. But the papers say that up in Cleveland and Cincinnati, and in parts of New Jersey, they didn't do so much for relief people either.

A natural result of this anywhere is that you have a lot of beggars. In Florence, Alabama, they still do things in the picturesque old-

time way, so there a woolly-headed old Negro man, who must have
been eighty-odd, wearing rags and patches and leaning on two
crooked sticks, hobbled through town asking for his rent money in
nickels, and getting it. The South regards these things as natural,
and it may be that a local character like that enjoys his part of the
show. But in places like Knoxville the begging is serious, and while
they ask for carfare, under the traction-company rate a nickel won't
do. Right in front of the TVA office a middle-aged woman in need
of medical care wheedled not only carfare but an extra nickel for
breakfast, while over on the next street an underfed girl with a
scrawny child in her arms asked for breakfast money, only to be
told by passers-by that they had troubles of their own. On the railroad tracks down under the viaducts are more people scrambling
for bits of coal; some of the Knoxville residents appear surprised,
and more are concerned, when it is pointed out that these people
are not colored but white. Increasing tuberculosis in Tennessee,
which has the highest state record, is blamed by the association
fighting it on hunger; while in Alabama they notice how pellagra
goes up and down with employment.

In the Valley the WPA wages start around $25 a month in the
smaller towns, and don't go over $50 even in the cities. Families
average five but can go to twelve. Not more than one member of a
family can be employed by WPA, although occasionally some child
gets Youth Administration help or a CCC job. The CCC is really
better for the family, because sometimes the boys send more money
home than the WPA wage would be.

States are supposed to do what they can for the WPA program,
but in no case do these states contribute more than a quarter of what
is spent. They pay for materials used, and some supervisory salaries,
but no WPA wages. Yet state agencies do the certifying, and WPA
also leaves it to the states to decide whether social-security benefits
disqualify an applicant for WPA work. In some states these benefits,
again requiring state co-operation, are too low to amount to anything.

The Tennessee Valley Authority is one government agency that spends its own money in its own way. It can show direct results where other government agencies still coax and plead. On the other hand, it is not, primarily, a relief or charitable enterprise.

Take the croppers; so far, the Authority hasn't found any way to do much for them unless they are on reservoir land. Then they have to be moved and usually a move helps them some, but of course you can't turn the whole cotton-raising area of the Valley into lakes.

Since the South is the land of hard physical work, some jobs will be made easier by TVA power. The people in the South who now suffer most from overwork aren't the croppers, or the mill hands, or the Negroes, but the women. Besides working in the fields and in the mills, as the men do, Southern women have the families to look after. And they add to the families, which is still another job, although regarded as bad luck or the Lord's will rather than anything you could do anything about.

Southern women who go out from home to work for money don't complain about this lapse in the chivalrous tradition; if they work in the fields, maybe they say they like to be outdoors, and in the mills they say they'd rather be there than doing field work. But what they want is the pay, if you could call it pay. They take to independence more than do some working women up North. Give a Southern girl a union card and she can show surprising spunk; in one woolen-mill strike in Tennessee and another in North Georgia, they held girls on charges of assault and battery directed, not against each other, but against men strikebreakers.

Life is hardest for those who get married and have to do their hardest work without pay, and try to make a little any way they can. North Georgia is the land of the tufted counterpane, otherwise called the candlewick bedspread. Women make them by hand and hang them on the fences to sell to the tourists, the way they do hooked rugs in the Carolina mountains. It's hard work sewing candlewick, and you'd think nobody would undertake much of it, but the spreads were popular and the women needed the money. They sold their work cheap and the word went North, and first

thing you knew the Yankees were down setting up little factories to
make something similar, chenille spreads, by machinery.

They also put the candlewick industry on a business basis, sending out piecework the way they do with artificial flowers in the
North. So the women out in the country were working for the Yankees although they couldn't get together, as the factory workers did,
and organize. Of course nobody in that country had an easy life;
the men couldn't make off the run-down land, and the state didn't
believe in relief, and if they had a mill or factory strike it was apt to
start with singing and guitar-playing and end with shooting. But
the candlewickers getting a dollar or two for work that sold up
North for several times that, with no factory overhead, were getting
the worst of it.

When the wage-hour law went into effect, there was mention in
the New York papers that the price of bedspreads might go up,
because now the workers might have to be paid 25 cents an hour. But
it turned out that they just closed the factories, and left the piecework
to be done by the women, "as products of family industry not covered by the law." [1]

The candlewickers had just one help. Their part of Georgia, on
the road from Chattanooga to Atlanta, is where farmers had been trying for a long time to get electric light, without any luck until TVA
brought it in. The last straw for women who work all day in the
field or in a mill is to have to come in at night and carry water to
wash and do the housework by lamplight. Some of the bedspread
women chopped cotton during the day and tufted cotton at night;
some thought they were called candlewick spreads because they were
made by candlelight. Actually, of course, they used coal-oil lamps,
until TVA came.

So it's no exaggeration to say that in its least job, running a rural
line, the Authority helped lighten the labors of some of the worst-off
workers in the Valley. Of course, all classes of labor will benefit if
TVA power attracts industries that will pay better wages, and com-

[1] New York *Times,* October 30, 1938.

pete with the low-paying mills until labor isn't so plentiful and so cheap.

But the biggest help to labor has been the TVA policy of paying good wages and adopting fair standards. They say the TVA wage scale even helped raise the WPA scale a little, down in Alabama. It's bound, in time, to improve things for the Negroes, and in fact for workers of all grades. For the TVA idea isn't just that the laborer is worthy of his hire, as the ox of its corn; it is that working people are folks.

6. MEN

Help Wanted, 1933

The sons also of them that afflicted thee shall come bending unto thee.

I will cause them to walk by the rivers of waters in a straight way.

And they that shall be of thee shall build the old waste places . . . thou shalt be called, The repairer of the breach, The restorer of paths to dwell in.

One nice old lady in Knoxville was distressed when her son broke the glad news that he had passed the strenuous examinations and landed a TVA job. Nobody in their family, she said, had ever been on relief.

The fact that TVA was started in days when it could be considered a recovery measure may account for the notion some people have that it is a branch of WPA. Certainly, with everything in the country at a standstill, as it was in 1933, the early jobs at Norris were a godsend for the unemployed; but for that very reason, the people doing the hiring could pick and choose carefully among a hundred thousand applicants.

Fifty thousand signed for and nearly forty thousand took the civil-service examinations they gave job-seekers at the start. The result was a staff that was one of the few things in this world good enough for Mr. Westbrook Pegler. He visited Norris in 1934 and wrote: "The picked men of this community, just on sight, compare with the average gang on a big construction job just as a thoroughbred horse to a plug. They show class, even in the quarries and ditches."

The Authority still hires some new people, taking as "internes" the pick of the college crop, and occasionally holding examinations for applicants over the country. Some new jobs are made at the bottom under an automatic promotion plan that moves you ahead if your work is satisfactory, and gives you a warning jolt if you fail to get a raise. Some vacancies occurred at the top because some men, from necessity or enthusiasm, took TVA jobs paying less than they were used to, and then returned to normalcy; because youngsters trained by TVA got flattering offers; and because of temperamental difficulties.

But Norris veterans are still on the job. At Hiwassee a man who trucked the freight from Turtletown, the rail head, said he had begun at Norris and he had never known but one man working for the Authority who just wouldn't be satisfied, and finally up and quit. He was a Republican.

Since the job is only five years old, most of the veterans are young. You never saw so many nice college boys—tall thin ones with glasses, plump ones with pipes, calm blond ones, quick red-headed ones. In the early days of the Authority an enthusiastic observer wrote of "an almost evangelical, messianic confidence which holds them together in a fellowship of service," an "atmosphere of hope and faith," and "a force of social enthusiasm that is full of promise for all our people." Foreign observers drew parallels with the early days of world-making in Russia. But fortunately for the future of the Authority in a cynical and anti-revolutionary world, some of this has been sloughed off, and now the outstanding impression you get from talking to large numbers of TVA employees is gentle conservatism. Their project may seem radical to reactionaries on the outside; they, themselves, are not.

"We weeded out the radicals," some will tell you. Others say: "They weeded themselves out," got tired when they saw the size of the job. All who remain know the undertaking is a big one and a long one; they don't expect real results inside of twenty-five or maybe fifty years. It appears that when the dreams of Thorstein Veblen and Stuart Chase come true and the world is made over by the engineers, they won't hurry the job.

The business of the Authority, they will tell you, is water control.

This is naturally bound to do some good, but people will have to learn to help themselves. The Authority isn't God. "We can dam the river and we have to try to check erosion to keep from silting up the dams, and we hope to do a few other things. But we can't do everything. We aren't supposed to." They seem to have noticed that their river gets its useful power not by rushing over the Shoals but by being stored up in placid lakes.

They do have more than average social sense because they were hired with that in view. When the ordinary qualifications failed to eliminate all the applicants, TVA added some new ones. The three directors, according to act of Congress, must believe in the "wisdom and feasibility" of the project. So they decided to extend that requirement to the men they hired. They could vote Republican, or for Norman Thomas—some of them did—but they had to be able to look the personnel man in the eye and profess a faith in the future of the Valley.

Then there were some things they must not do; one was to bring a letter from a congressman or a senator. One unquestionably honest congressman thought maybe the Authority leaned backwards in that respect, because other government agencies would at least hire one man out of several recommended. But not TVA.

Other rules are to prevent the nepotism which, TVA Director David Lilienthal once pointed out, now runs through big business. An employee of the Authority can't have a post involving administrative or supervisory relations with his relatives. Married people or kinfolk in the same household can't both work for TVA if either gets over $2000 a year. The act of Congress stipulates that salaries over $1500 a year must be published, and each annual report of the Authority does that.

Some Valley folks think that Valley people should be hired in preference to any other, and for work at the dams they are, but this doesn't apply to office jobs. One Chattanooga man was so disappointed at not getting a TVA job that he took a job with a private power company, and then wrote an article for the *Saturday Evening Post* in which he expressed a fear that TVA competition might take that job away. But they say that when TVA took over such of the Commonwealth and Southern properties as that corporation consented to sell in 1934, most of the people were kept on at better wages.

The report doesn't say where people come from, but among the five thousand or so white-collar workers whom the Authority calls its "annual employees," there are over a thousand Yankees and over a hundred Westerners to trade arguments with natives of the Valley and other sections of the South. In general the Yankees on the job deal best with things, and the Southerners with people. The Yankees can tell you all the book reasons why such-and-such a thing should be so, but the Southerners just naturally know that old man Todhunter, he wouldn't want to do that.

So, working together, the Southerners are bound to learn a little Yankee theory and the Yankees learn a lot about Southern feelings. The Southerners proceed at a restful pace, and the Yankees adjust to it, now. "They went through fast, once," said a Southerner in the vicinity of Shiloh.

When they came in this time, an ex-governor of Tennessee said: "I wouldn't give one Tennessee hill-billy for a ten-acre field full of sociological experts gathered up from other regions and brought into the TVA area to be placed over our local people." So they had to be careful; they explained at the start that TVA would be, in the Valley, merely a "catalytic agent." Later on they learned not to use words like that.

Instead, most TVA men can now talk sensibly about fishing, and the result is that a country never fond of strangers too ignorant to keep out of the tall grass in chigger season is coming to accept them. A good many of them marry local girls, which may be what they mean by showing results in another generation. Tactful members of the staff who go out to work with farmers and families being relocated soon learn to let their cars get dusty instead of keeping them bright and shiny like the other TVA cars, and there was a suggestion that they refrain from sporting class rings; clean fingernails were enough. Let no one think that such trifles do not matter in the sensitive South. A famous French journalist who looked at the TVA with approval is ungratefully remembered in Knoxville, not for her warm sympathy with the economic needs of the Valley, but for a harsh word about Southern cooking.

The Authority is officially so tactful that in their history of navigation on the Tennessee they refer to the Civil War as the War between the States; and some of the Yankees even say it in talking. That is more trouble than folks down South will take. The dam-builders did show good sense when, with some argument over what to call Pickwick Landing dam, they wouldn't listen to the folks who wanted to name it Shiloh. They are there to repair the breach, not to renew unhappy memories.

Now and then, being free citizens, TVA employees do open their mouths, and one of them did tell a Tennessee audience that the state had lost $3,000,000 in 1937 by not passing security legislation. After five years in the Valley, a man should be allowed some voice.

But the most strenuous efforts at improvement are those the Authority directs toward its own staff. They didn't stop with picking their people; they set out to make them better. It was said that Norris was from the first more like a college campus than a construction camp—a technical college, of course, where students work. At Norris the men signed up for classes in everything from woodcraft to social science. Thirty were expected for the first course in mathematics, and three hundred came. The entire machine shop registered for training. In those days they had four shifts and a thirty-three-hour week to spread work, so that left a lot of time for education.

And the education spread. Workers down at Muscle Shoals asked for a general course in the history of public ownership and labor problems in America, and the men in the fertilizer plant started a discussion group. Today they still have the spare-time classes—some technical subjects for the dam-builders; stenography, public speaking, and such for the office workers; and all sorts of reading and discussion and special study groups. Some of these have regular teachers, some have volunteer instructors, and some go ahead under their own power.

For job-training, selected members of the construction crews at

Norris were educated as foremen by being allowed to rotate, every five weeks, for experience in different kinds of work. This idea of rotation has now been extended to the training of the bright college boys whom TVA undertakes to make ready for office jobs. Other job-training efforts are tied in with the apprenticeship programs of the unions.

What they say is that the training program of TVA aims to be "multi-purpose," like the dams. They use their schools for all ages, and the school shops, libraries, playgrounds, and combination auditorium-gym-theaters are open sixteen hours a day. The TVA idea is for the whole family to go to school, or at least stick around the schoolhouse.

Then they think education can be made so catching that it will go from the TVA employee to his family and out into the community. To help that spread, and with their determination to co-operate with other public agencies, they swap schooling and library services with county and state authorities in the neighborhood of the dams.

TVA libraries are astonishing to anybody who wouldn't expect to find late newspapers and magazines in a construction camp miles from a railroad, and books meant to acquaint the young men from up North with the region they have come to, as well as to tell the Southerners how the South got that way. In the Hiwassee area, besides maintaining a good library at the dam and sending out books into the hills, TVA has tied up with the local library in the near-by town of Murphy, with the result that Murphy now has unusually good library service for a town of its size. So, in time, some of the disparagements you hear directed towards Southern schools and lack of libraries will no longer apply to the Valley.

The Authority is movie-conscious too; they show free educational movies, and make educational shorts, and had a hand in Uncle Sam's documentary film *The River,* which everybody liked except Dr. Arthur Morgan. Some educational authorities say that TVA, with its maps and pictures and little model dams, has gone farther with visual education than any other agency. And while WPA has taught more grown people to write, it may be that TVA has done more to establish the idea that your education needn't stop even though you are literate and have a good job.

It's unusual for construction camps to be literary centers; Grand Coulee has been called "the toughest spot in America," and a writer about that dam said you couldn't expect men who had worked eight hours with a jackhammer or a concrete-mixer to go home and read dissertations of a high moral character. They took exception to this in the Valley; there were the class and library records, and there was the fact that in the construction days they didn't even sell beer at Norris. And the milk-drinking popularized at Norris persists at the other dams. Some TVA locations are legally dry, and in others the Authority owns enough of the surrounding country to keep distractions at a distance.

To make up for lack of opportunities for hell-raising even on pay night, TVA employees have good quarters and good food. The camp dormitories even afford some privacy, with rooms instead of bunks in a common hall. There is a community house with comfortable chairs, tables for games, a soft-drink bar, a radio, curtains at the windows, and photographs of the country for wall decoration.

In most construction camps they put everything to eat on the table at once and race through meals. At the TVA cafeterias, only the payment is standardized; you pay a flat 35 cents for all you can eat, or 30 cents if you're a regular boarder; and they consider that pretty high because at Norris, when food costs were lower, it was only a quarter. Dietitians have put fruit and cereals and salads on the menu; you have a choice of Southern hot biscuits or Yankee cracked-wheat bread, and other cooking that represents both sections, with so much to eat at all times that you can be a Yankee and have dinner at night, or a Southerner and have supper in the evening.

Outside the community house are tennis courts, usually in use by the office workers, but the dam-builders play in the softball tournaments. Visitors with old-fashioned ideas of what a construction camp should be are usually startled to learn that there are also tournaments for ping-pong and croquet. At the young Hiwassee dam they are using their second croquet set; they wore the first one out.

Daredevils make dates for what is known at Hiwassee as the "night club," a private enterprise a mile or so down the road and off the reservation. The place is a shack with canned beans for sale, murals by Coca-Cola, and a collection of bats and butterflies competing with a slot machine as entertainment. There are also chairs and tables where hard liquor, brought in, can be mixed and consumed; and there is a ten-foot floor space where a few couples can dance. This, according to an observer from TVA's training division, represents progress because until lately, in these parts, dancing was forbidden and when a dance occurred it ended in a fight. Now they have weekly dances in the community house, ending early because some of the young married couples have to get back to take care of the children and see that they get to Sunday school on time the next morning.

When you watch the Authority's efforts to build model communities, you understand that employee qualification which caused some talk when it was brought out during the congressional investigation: "Is his wife an asset?" Of course that's a question likely to be asked by any big corporation hiring a man it means to keep. And it can be especially important if the employee is to live amidst a small group of people who must not only work together but depend on each other for spare-time entertainment. There are cooking and decorating classes for TVA wives, but it helps if they know in advance how to make the little houses look their best, and—as is required of their husbands—believe in the "feasibility and wisdom" of the job. If more TVA wives had understood the reasons for it, they might have had more support for the co-operative grocery store they used to have at Norris.

Whether you think TVA pampers its employees in the matter of wages and living conditions depends on your general attitude about living standards. If you believe people should be made to work for the least they will take, then Uncle Sam has failed to give his jobs to the lowest bidders. If you want to see government employees, and other people, live decently because the richest country in the world should be able to live that way, you find no fault.

Of course a lot of big corporations coddle their employees, and ask in return a certain social attitude, though they seldom make the requirement openly and in advance of hiring. But it's true enough that all the training and the housing and the general thoughtfulness of TVA as an employer—even the nuisance of red tape—could be found in private employment; and when we find it there we call it paternalism. Only one thing saves TVA from that charge, and that is encouragement of labor unions.

Nearly all the dam-builders are crafts unionists, but the office workers' union has CIO affiliation. When the white-collar people organized they were allowed to meet right in the offices, of course after office hours, and use the office bulletin-boards for their notices. At the start one timid soul asked if everything would be all right with the board of directors and the personnel department, and was answered by a young man in a reassuringly responsible position.

"We don't ask that question here in America," he said. "We feel that as employees we have the right to align ourselves with that organization which best serves our own interests, and leave the citizens of Italy and Germany to ask their superiors what to do."

At first the TVA unions were a little like college debating societies because they had no grievances, but now that the project is five years old and plans for the retirement of TVA workers have to be discussed, some people have complaints to make. As the labor paper in Knoxville put it over a year ago: "It is no news that the number of employees in the Authority who are unhappy over the conditions of their work is increasing. To a large extent this fact merely results from the growing maturity of the Authority and is a reaction from the possibly excessive enthusiasm of the organization days."

But to an outsider the employment policy of the Authority looks very fair. There is no need for wage trouble at any time, because the enabling act provides for "prevailing" wages, with "due regard" for rates secured through collective agreement. The congressional hearings disclosed that TVA had interpreted this clause generously; they even raised wages at one time when the country in general was cutting.

An important clause of the official policy provides against discrimination in occupational status or pay on the basis of sex or race. That women are not better represented in the higher TVA brackets is the fault of general training, which has failed to fit them for good jobs in an engineering project. In the early days the Authority had a woman treasurer; at present the supervisor of libraries, making a notable success of her job, has the most important assignment given a woman employee. Women equipped for library work, teaching, nursing, or general office work are, of course, fortunate in landing TVA jobs. Some sought the jobs from a long way off, and hold them with social enthusiasm; some Southern girls, working from necessity, have to learn to tolerate the occasional Negro in the TVA offices. Many, especially those who go to work at the construction camps, marry young engineers and give the personnel division a chance to hire and train somebody else.

But it is the provision regarding race that counts, in the Valley. Appointing the Negro foreman at Pickwick wouldn't mean anything to people who have lived North all their lives, but any Southerner knows you have to get past a lot of prejudice to make a Negro a boss. There is the feeling of the low-grade white people who can't stand to see a "nigger" getting uppity. And there is the conviction of the upper-class white folks that Negroes won't work for Negroes, and anyhow you can't give a Negro authority because he's sure to abuse it, and be harder on the men under him than a white man would be. But the Authority tried it, more than a year ago, and the man is still foreman with eight or ten workmen under him. They've lately got another colored man as sub-foreman on construction.

Of course they started right out paying the same wages for the same work, without distinction of color. Because TVA wages were higher than most local wages, it meant that some of the colored workers on the dams were making more than white men working for private industries in the same places. That was astounding.

Most of the colored workers are in Alabama because TVA made a rule that they would employ Negroes in proportion to their part in the population. This saved argument and meant that they could use a good many colored men down at Pickwick and in the Shoals phosphate plants, while keeping them out of the hill country, where they are not known and not welcome.

Since the Norris territory is what most visitors see, this accounts for occasional claims that the Authority isn't fair about hiring Negroes. It's true that civil-service examinations disqualified about half the Negroes examined at Norris who were eligible on the population basis, but to balance this hardship the first student internes TVA undertook to train were from the Negro universities.

Of course you can't change everything all at once. One of the TVA men engaged in reservoir relocation said it was harder to shuffle people around at Wheeler and Pickwick because you had both colors, and while a white man could move into a Negro house, a Negro couldn't move into a white man's house. This sounds odd even to a Southerner until you figure out that it's a matter of what the neighbors would say. Similarly, on his own account as well as for the sake of the Authority's friendly relations with white folks in the Valley, they knew better than to send a Negro out in a TVA car. But most colored employees of TVA consider themselves fortunate. Of course they are proud of any desk job, and the hourly wages of 47½ cents to $1.37 are more than colored wage hands used to make in a day. The phosphate plant at Wilson dam is about the least attractive place to work for TVA, and because the brown rock dust that hangs in the air is hard to breathe, you might think the workers would want a short day such as was provided for the cement-mixers at Norris. But the head of the union said no; on the contrary, his men thought so much of that hourly wage they were asking for longer instead of shorter shifts.

You have to understand the position of Southern Negroes, as the Negroes themselves understand it, and the labor situation throughout the Valley to see how important the TVA policies are. There was some basis for a strange story that Dr. Arthur Morgan wanted to keep the real unions out of TVA; he did write a piece for *Antioch Notes* in which he spoke favorably of company unions, considered in the abstract and for what they might be. But later he admitted that in actual practice company unions were undesirable, and said he had changed his mind. That is testimony for TVA's union policy, because Dr. Morgan's mind did not change easily.

He had expressed himself as anxious to save the Valley "from the exploitation of mass production that is in search of cheap labor," and he must have seen that it could be done only by the real unions. The Authority has no say-so about what private industry shall do to labor in the Valley, even industry that takes TVA power. It can influence labor conditions only by setting up a "yardstick" in that field, by paying decent wages and taking the best people, and encouraging self-respect. Then maybe, as Mr. Lilienthal suggested in a Labor Day speech, folks will get "a new concept of the value of organized labor."

Trouble at the Top

And who is a chosen man, that I may appoint . . . ? for who is like me? and who will appoint me the time? and who is that shepherd that will stand before me?

Though these three men, Noah, Daniel, and Job, were in it, they should deliver but their own souls by their righteousness, saith the Lord God.

Last spring they had two earthquake shocks at Knoxville, mild ones doing no damage but making talk. About the same time, people heard rumblings that meant a disturbance in the TVA board of directors, and that made newspaper headlines all over the country.

When Dr. Arthur Morgan stood out against the President and got his wish for a congressional investigation, newspaper readers who didn't know much about TVA found the reports of the hearings that began in Washington and lasted through the hot weather in the Valley almost as complicated as the trials they have in Russia. There were all sorts of charges and counter-charges and accusations of "sabotage." There was even mention in the Northern papers of "another Teapot Dome," though you'd think the Republicans wouldn't want to bring that up.

And there were plenty of complications. Dr. Arthur Morgan seemed determined to bend backwards to be fair to the power companies, but he was pretty hard on other people. The other two directors worried less about the widows and orphans who might own utilities stocks, but were more gentle in their handling of small farmers and even politicians with senate appointments.

People who followed the hearings soon discovered, of course, that there was no ground for scandal, no "conspiracy" for anti-New Dealers to lick their chops over. There was a plain case of incompatibility of temperament, which finally required a divorce. As usual in such cases, nobody was wholly blameless, and nobody was wholly to blame, and the gossip was exaggerated.

As the complainant, Dr. Arthur Morgan had to prove the charges he made, and he couldn't prove them; some fell to pieces and some he withdrew. But he was sincere in making the charges. Dr. Morgan is a remarkable man with a keen and original mind, although it is not a mind adapted to effective dealing with people of the present era. Dr. Morgan was so devoted to the Tennessee Valley Authority that he actually paid out some of his own money, at the start, to foot the project's first little bills. But the other side to that is that he could feel too strong a sense of personal responsibility. Like Moses, he was a good head man until he got mad.

As an engineer Dr. Morgan would presumably go around an obstacle when necessary, but as an administrator he was always for going right ahead in a straight line. This brought him into conflict with other people, and he seemed to have some trouble understanding ordinary folks. He himself could always see what should be done, and in theory at least he was always right, so it was odd that people should oppose him. As one young man who had worked for him put it: "It isn't that he wants yes-men around him. It's only that he can't stand fools."

When you know you are right, and the people who don't agree with you are not fools, you wonder if they could be knaves. This suspicion may grow if you are a shy person yourself, not willing to make the little compromises that good mixers have to make to get along. You are afraid there will be big compromises. And Dr. Arthur Morgan was not one to harbor fear or suspicion in silence.

When the chairman was moved to call his fellow-directors hard names, of course it was pie for all the people fighting TVA. They leaped to make Dr. Arthur Morgan a hero. They took his picture for the newsreels and talked about him on the radio and wrote columns about him. He was a great engineer and some said he was a Quaker, and the New York *Herald Tribune* and the *Saturday Evening Post* were in favor of that combination. A writer in *Liberty* suggested that here might be presidential timber. Then the boom-boom stopped suddenly, and somebody must have read some of the things Dr. Arthur Morgan had said and written, and found out his real views.

In his own way Dr. Arthur Morgan was the most radical-minded of the three directors, and long before he complained of them, his fellow-workers had come to feel that he might be too impractical for this world. His ideas weren't foolish, but sometimes his expression of them was tactless, as when he said people might get stung again if they gambled in Shoals real estate.

He wanted to make the Valley over brand-new and right; some said he even suggested that it might have its own money system. You can see how he thought of that because, with electric power, the Valley could feed and clothe and house itself as well or better than any other part of the country. It's paying out for what they buy from up North, and getting so little for what they raise, that keeps Valley folks poor.

And you have to consider that the South has a separate money system now. What else would you call the wage and freight differentials and the higher interest rate? You could even call a crop lien a kind of labor currency, while the tax-free cotton certificates they traded around under the Bankhead Law got to be a kind of currency based on not working. Then there is the store "furnish" they pay plantation tenants and the "company scrip" of mills and mines. There is a separate coinage in Mississippi and Alabama, where they have one- and five-mill tokens to pay the sales tax.

In pioneer days, different Valley states made a lot of things legal tender—tobacco, cotton, bacon, rice, corn, beaver and otter skins, rye whisky, and peach brandy. Until lately they brought in bunches of galax leaves for store trading in the Carolina mountains, and over in Virginia they run a barter theater. There's no real reason to say that gold, which they used to dig in Georgia and which they now bury in Kentucky, is the true basis for trade, and these other things can't be.

So, while the people who worry about TVA license plates on TVA cars would have had apoplexy, you couldn't say that the idea of making the Valley a totalitarian state was visionary. Maybe it wasn't visionary enough. The idea is to take the South back into the Union, not keep it out; but you have to look way ahead to hope that some day, if you keep on acting as if the United States were just one country, it will be that way.

But there were ways in which Dr. Arthur Morgan was impractical and idealistic. He seemed to be that way about the power business. Generally speaking, he favored public ownership, but he was careful to say that we have in this country "a mixture of despotism, aristocracy, communism, socialism, and democracy." The average American, he pointed out, approved "the economic despotism of Henry Ford," accepted "the oligarchic and aristocratic management of Harvard," heartily believed in American public schools, "a thoroughly communistic institution," and was "loyal to the post office, which is socialistic." The democratic balance, Dr. Morgan felt, should be none of the *"isms* that have become little more than labels or battle slogans," and among the isms he included capitalism.

Dr. Morgan himself moved beyond liberalism to a progressive attitude at times, as when, describing his own experience at Antioch, he wrote: "I have been asking people to give me money made by one economic order in order to build another order. Most people are conservative enough not to be persuaded in that way, and so I have not gotten much money. For the past few years I have been living partly on incomes from foundations. But each of these foundations has accumulated its resources by a social and economic order that will, I hope, pass away." [1] This hope was not one to please some of the people who later expressed their admiration for Dr. Morgan.

[1] *Mountain Life and Work,* Berea, Kentucky, July 1934.

But how did these general views apply, in Dr. Morgan's mind, to the power industry?

In January 1937, Dr. Morgan said: "I have come to believe that the attitude of a ruthless fight to the finish and without quarter against public ownership of power has been a characteristic position of the public utilities. . . . In their fight private utilities have bribed legislation . . . controlled newspapers . . . sought to cripple or destroy educational institutions which dared to be independent.

"I believe, too, that the long fight to limit utility abuses is part of a slow-moving revolution which is striving to free the mass of the people from exploitation.

"Yet, notwithstanding my own experience and what I have learned of utility abuses . . . I believe that the proper attitude . . . is to strive to find a basis of agreement between the Tennessee Valley Authority and private utilities which will protect both private and public investment." [1]

Those who find the conclusion a surprise may find that in 1934 Dr. Morgan had said of the private utility companies: "Personally, I hope they will continue for a considerable time." [2]

Speaking generally of the Valley, Dr. Morgan saw three ways for it—public ownership, co-operatives, and what he liked to call, with Henry Ford, "professional" industry, or industry with the trustee attitude. He believed that for many activities, "private industry conducted in the professional spirit would be better than any alternative." As for power, he felt that events in the Valley should determine whether "government ownership and operation are superior to private, or vice versa."

Now, the trouble with all this well-wishing for private industry amid the general goodwill (you note that, like President Hoover, Dr. Morgan occasionally refers to the private utilities as public utilities) is that people can take it both ways. Dr. Morgan must have known what he meant and presumably he had no intent to deceive. But

[1] New York *Times*.
[2] *Survey Graphic*, March 1934.

when he talked about events determining for or against the yard-stick, public-power people naturally felt that Dr. Morgan was so sure of the outcome that he was willing to make a test case. The utilities people evidently knew him better, and indeed, as Dr. Morgan eventually explained himself, he wouldn't have considered it honest to talk about determining an issue on which he already had settled convictions.

But when he felt in need of further knowledge he was apt to consult, not his fellow-workers in TVA, but people at the top in the private-power industry. Some of these are nice people and they all use a lot of high moral arguments. To hear them tell it, they worry nights over their stockholders, and they consider themselves "oppressed from all sides by political opportunists." Mr. Wendell Willkie, always persuasive, found TVA publicity a "cruel deception" and mourned publicly over the plight of a utility system "broken up" and "dismembered, piece by piece."

It appears that Dr. Morgan, whose basic concern was character in government, couldn't bear to be called a political opportunist or a cruel deceiver, much less the torso murderer of a power company. Maybe he had what you might call a vanity of virtue. At any rate he seemed to take it seriously when lawyers made claims in court and horsepower-traders cried: "Robber!"

Now that Dr. Morgan is no longer chairman of TVA, it might not be important to consider his views except that they are the views of a good many other high-minded people, no less susceptible to institutional advertising and the appealing presentations of a good public-relations counsel. Such people do not see a corporation as a wooden horse with men at work inside; they assume the existence of a corporate mind and heart, a "better nature" to be reasoned with and redeemed.

Dr. Morgan believed, apparently, that TVA could reform the corporations by argument and example, somewhat as Woodrow Wilson hoped to reform the European nations. He took to the Wilsonian method of writing letters. In the *Retail Coalman* for August 1934 is a

long, reasonable communication from Dr. Morgan, offering co-
operation and research to discover what should be done about the
possibility that TVA power would hurt the coal trade. He suggested
an eleven-point program ranging through investigation of "actual
displacement of labor in the coal industry" to "electrification of
mines," and invited representatives of the coal industry to a meeting
at Knoxville. You don't even have to wonder what came of it, because
in the same issue of the trade journal is an editorial denouncing a
socialistic administration and a quotation from the president of
Appalachia Coals, who said at a sales meeting: "We are here for a
common purpose, and because we speak a common language we shall
achieve that purpose, which is to sell a larger percentage of the coal
consumed in our markets at increased aggregate profit." The speaker
spoke and presumably the salesmen understood a language that Dr.
Arthur Morgan had never learned or could not believe.

At the Congressional hearings, Dr. Morgan described the settlement of a price war over cement by what he considered a frank and
friendly agreement with the cement companies. What, apparently,
he did not consider was that in that case TVA was the customer,
able to impose conditions, not the competitor arousing diehard opposition. The customer is always right, the rival is always wrong and
can't settle things so easily over a luncheon table.

And while he was hoping to persuade the utilities to rejoice in
the spoiling of their goods, that they might have in heaven a better
and a more enduring substance, you remember that Dr. Morgan had
a stricter attitude towards the small farmer who plows at an angle
of forty-five degrees and decants his land into the river. Of course
Dr. Morgan was right in principle when he held that "we are not
complete owners of the soil, but only trustees for a generation." He
was right in his general reasoning that "irreplaceable deposits of
natural resources should belong to the public," in order to insure
against "wasteful expenditure and against charges based upon monoply of ownership." There is even material logic in being harder on
the farmer who spends wastefully a soil that is irreplaceable, than on

the power company that charges too much for its monoply but does not destroy a tangible resource. But unless you want a sure enough Red revolution on your hands, you won't start the transition to public ownership with the small farmer.

In some ways, although he came from up North, Dr. Arthur Morgan was more like a conscientious, religious-minded Southerner of the mountain breed than like a Yankee. When he got mad at the other directors, he acted like a Southerner, seceding from the board decisions and opening fire, regardless of consequences.

He was like a Southerner, too, for splitting hairs on points of doctrine. Take the Berry marble case, where the whole question was one of procedure, because Senator Berry's claims to the Norris lake bottom looked ridiculous on their face, and in the end a court threw them out. But Dr. Morgan made it a point of honor; he thought that for a senator to acquire land leases in the area of a government project, and try to cash in on them, was plain crooked.

So he said so, and he added that the other directors had the same evidence of fraud that he had. This was interpreted, up North, to mean that the others were in cahoots with the senator; whereas "the same evidence" meant evidence sufficient to convince Dr. Morgan but not, in the opinion of the other directors, enough to convince a court. They were afraid that Dr. Arthur Morgan's sense of sin had led him to lose the distinction between private thought and public proof.

Instead of condemning either the land or the senator, they favored having the claims appraised by a government commissioner, to be appointed by Secretary Ickes. At the time, Senator Berry seemed important in Tennessee politics, and in one little condemnation suit a local commission had raised a TVA offer of $85 to $850. They couldn't mention the Berry marbles without talking in millions.

A funny thing about the Berry case was that if the Northern papers hadn't been so anxious to present the senator as conspiring with TVA, they might have argued convincingly that he was the victim of conspiracy. For it was proposed that a property-holder, deprived of his property by one New Deal agency, should submit to an appraisal by a commissioner borrowed from another New Deal department.

But when Dr. Arthur Morgan tried to explain to the congressional committee that his biggest evidence of dishonesty on the part of the board was willingness to have a senator's claims appraised by an expert from Washington, he gave himself a hard job. When he tried to show why he felt impelled to interfere in the utilities suit at Chattanooga, they brought in a Republican candidate for the Senate to testify that at Chattanooga Dr. Morgan had worried the lawyers to death. When he tried to explain what he meant by honest administration, they asked him if he meant that the Authority had paid too much for its land; and they hardly knew what to make of it when he said: "In some cases, they paid too little."

In a way it's too bad that the whole thing had to backfire because the character of government administrators is just as important as Dr. Morgan thinks it is. But along with honesty, capability, firmness of purpose, and good intentions, administrators need a lot of horse sense about dealing with people. Dr. Morgan's best friends do not credit him with that. On the other hand, his worst enemies say he used good judgment twice, when he picked the other two TVA directors.

Of course Dr. Morgan changed his mind there, especially about Mr. Lilienthal; but to most people, Mr. Lilienthal does not seem such a complicated character that it would take time to make him out. If you have been around up North, you would expect to find him, at any time, just a jump or two ahead.

In other words Mr. Lilienthal is a smart lawyer. People who say he might have been a lawyer for the utilities, if he hadn't started on the public-power side, are probably wrong because he is smarter than that. Anyhow he did study law under Dr. Felix Frankfurter, and made an early success on the public-utilities commission in Wisconsin.

It seemed to worry Dr. Arthur Morgan that as soon as he suggested doing something, Mr. Lilienthal would have it done. You can see Mr. Lilienthal would be like that from the way he likes to get at things on a long desk by moving his chair; the chair is on easy-turning rollers, and people bothered by quick movement might see something suspicious about that. But in a world that mostly suffers from sleeping sickness you don't need to quarrel with a man for getting action. And you have to move in all directions to get flexibility, that flexibility of the private corporation which the President wanted for TVA.

When Dr. Arthur Morgan talked of "intellectual dishonesty," all it came to was that he and Mr. Lilienthal didn't see eye to eye. An intellectually dishonest person is a person with no convictions that he will fight for, and Mr. Lilienthal is not that way. His convictions about power are stronger than Dr. Arthur Morgan's, although he talks less about public power and more about cheap power. Also his convictions about labor are stronger than Dr. Arthur Morgan's, and clearer. When you talk to him, Mr. Lilienthal is pretty definite on both these subjects, and he says himself that if you know where a man stands on power and labor, these days, you ought to be able to judge his other ideas from that. Besides carrying on the power war on the outside, you have to credit Mr. Lilienthal and Dr. H. A. Morgan, who voted with him, for the Authority's firm stand for the unions.

People in TVA seem to like the whole Lilienthal family, including Mrs. Lilienthal, who was born in Oklahoma, and the two children and David Lilienthal's father, who lived at Norris and made friends with the dam-builders. It might interest Yankees, who seem stirred up over these matters, to know that you can travel through the Valley without hearing any comments on this director's racial background. The Klan used to sound pretty prejudiced, but it's up in New Jersey that little boys carve swastikas on smaller boys. Down South the chosen people are apt to build red-brick colonial synagogues and marry local girls, and mighty few Southerners get excited. If they thought about it in this case, maybe they would have enough sense to remember that a young man named Joseph not only led an upright life but did good work on a flood-control project back in Egypt.

To Dr. Arthur Morgan the fact that Dr. Harcourt Morgan and

Mr. Lilienthal voted the same way came to look like conspiracy, but it looks like a very natural thing to happen when you consider the temperamental differences of the directors. People who noticed that Dr. Arthur Morgan was twenty years older than Mr. Lilienthal often failed to notice that Dr. Harcourt Morgan was ten years older than Dr. Arthur.

Dr. Harcourt Morgan was a university president, just as Dr. Arthur Morgan was a college president, when he was appointed to the board. He was an expert in entomology and farming generally, just as Dr. Arthur Morgan was an expert in engineering. He is not a man you would accuse of personal ambition; he wasn't the sort to want to be chairman himself. But it stands to reason he must have been irritated at times by Dr. Arthur Morgan's assumption that the chairman had extra executive responsibility; was, in fact, set over the other two board members.

In the Valley they consider Dr. H. A., as they call him, one of the family. They've forgotten that he wasn't born in the South, and he's almost forgotten it himself. He's been fifty years in the Valley. But since he did start out in Canada, he must have learned how to make adjustments to environment. In Tennessee he is the member of the board who, they know, understands local conditions. They say TVA took away the best president the University of Tennessee ever had. But Dr. H. A. has managed to tie the university, and the other state universities of the region, into the TVA program. He has also tied in the county agents and the farm organizations and any government bureaus lying around handy. He has done more than anybody to make TVA part of its own region and also part of the government of the United States. In Washington they say he was the President's first choice for Secretary of Agriculture, but he wouldn't leave Tennessee.

Dr. H. A. is as good at getting around people as Mr. Lilienthal is, and Dr. Arthur isn't. They say in North Carolina that the rougher element moved to Tennessee, and they say in Tennessee that the toughs all went to Texas; it was in Texas, years before the New Deal ever thought of paying people not to raise cotton, that Dr. H. A.

undertook to persuade some Sabine river farmers to skip a crop and stop the boll weevil. They met him with squirrel rifles, and people tried to get him to take in a gun himself, but he went in without it and he came out alive. They say Dr. H. A. is a good politician, and no doubt he is. But he never ran for office; he never had to.

Now that Senator Pope of Idaho has been appointed to the board, people are talking of more politics, but you don't have to wait for Senator Pope's work with TVA to see why he was appointed. In the Senate, his pet project had been manufacture of phosphate fertilizer, using the TVA process, on the government lands in Idaho. As a director of TVA, Senator Pope will have a chance to do for the whole country what he hoped to start in his home state.

Building a Civil Service

Your sons and your daughters shall prophesy, your old men shall dream dreams, your young men shall see visions. . . .

I lifted up mine eyes again, and looked, and behold a man with a measuring line in his hand.

While the congressional investigation of TVA could not justify Dr. Arthur Morgan's charges, you can see, now, how it may end by improving administration as he hoped it would. It made everybody in the Valley stop and consider how things were run, and wonder how they ought to be run.

For TVA employees, the first question was whether a man was working for his superior in the Authority, or for the government. That question was important and not as easy to settle as some might think. Nobody could blame individuals for admiring one director above another; it was natural for the Antioch college boys in TVA to look up to Dr. Arthur Morgan, and for the University of Tennessee people to side with Dr. H. A., and for the other young men from Wisconsin to go along with Mr. Lilienthal. During the Knoxville hearings one ardent young partisan from Antioch burst into tears on the witness stand, and his emotion was easier to understand than the detachment of an older man, an engineer who refused to acknowledge any conflict between his personal admiration for Dr. Arthur Morgan and his duty to the Authority. "When I work for somebody, I work for 'em," he told the committee, and you believed him; but it was because he was as solid and dependable-looking as Norris dam.

Private business in general is organized on the plan that one man is responsible to another man, owing him a military or maybe a sentimental loyalty. Government, on the other hand, visible legal government as opposed to an invisible political machine or business, offers its employees an impersonal management. Since most people can't seem to think in impersonal terms, this may account for some inefficiency in public service.

But the Tennessee Valley Authority was supposed to have the efficiency of a business corporation. Was there a chance that it might be at its best with an engineering staff picked by Dr. Arthur Morgan, an agricultural staff picked by Dr. H. A. Morgan, and a law department picked by Mr. Lilienthal? Maybe some people would have argued for that, and in actual fact it's what they had, for a while.

In the very beginning, though, the Authority got going, not by personal leadership, but under the impetus of an idea that attracted intelligent people. Here was Muscle Shoals, wasting its first-rate energies; here were unemployed people, equally first-rate, wasting theirs. Let's put them all to work! Instead of the dull, stodgy routine usually associated with government jobs, here was something big and new and interesting and important. It was as good as a war, without the killing; you might say that the good side of war, the novelty and the planning and the sense of collective effort and the fun, was offered, this time, in the Valley. Of course ten or twenty thousand people aren't many unless you are one of them, but if you are, it seems a sizable army.

An army not meant to kill should be all right, and would be, if you could depend on its management. That means it would be all right, and will be, if you can free it from any devotion to personal leaders and persuade it that, as Mr. Lilienthal said in a Fourth of July speech to TVA employees at Chickamauga dam: "We all have the same bosses, and there are almost a hundred and thirty million of them. . . . We are in the employ of the people of the United States."

Dr. Arthur Morgan was the only one of the three TVA directors who appeared cut out for personal leadership, and if you wanted a leader he was considerably above the average of leaders, these days. But it may be that in this country the day of leaders is over; that even one region like the Valley is now too much for one man to manage.

You can see this if you try to figure what TVA would have done without the three men who started things going. As Dr. Arthur Morgan said, it was an engineering project and he was the only engineer on the board, but you have to credit him with more than dams. He said once that the needed administrative qualities were "common sense and a dash of imagination and courage," and in his own way he gave those to the Authority. Much of the originality and style of the project bear the mark of the first chairman. Maybe a man with more understanding of ordinary human limitations wouldn't have planned so well. He planned well and he preached well when he told TVA employees that the government was building bigger dams than any of theirs, so their only chance for distinction was to do a better job. He preached well and meant well, in his most wrong-headed moments, and it's easy to believe that they needed a God-fearing preacher in the Valley at the start.

But look where they would have been without Mr. Lilienthal to wage the power fight and explain the uses of labor unions.

And time may show that the quietest man on the board, the farm expert testing phosphates, had the biggest influence of all.

You also have to give Mr. Lilienthal and Dr. Harcourt Morgan credit for keeping things running smoothly while the trouble was still under cover. A lot of people working for the Authority never knew of any division in the board until they read about it in the papers; and a man Dr. Arthur Morgan had asked to have put in Mr. Lilienthal's place was left unmolested in his own job, as would not have happened under some managements. Of course the two directors who worked together were not the politicians Dr. Arthur

Morgan thought they were, or they would have managed him; there is some evidence that he could be managed by people smart enough to try, people he trusted.

But there is also evidence that, instead of some of the duplication that went with divided authority, such as two different sets of engineers submitting different reports to the former chairman and to the board, the project needed the undivided attention of at least three directors. It is, as Mr. Lilienthal testified, too big a job for one man. It is possible that the board of five said to be preferred by some government experts would be better. Better still would be a whole staff so well aware of a general policy as to be ready and able to go ahead and do things for its bosses, the people of the United States.

Once you remove the menace of individual leadership, the danger is, of course, that government workers will settle down to roost in their pigeon-holes in nests of red tape. But TVA still has young men capable of being stirred to protest when they see twenty-eight signatures on one form. It has men who can start driving over the Valley at eight o'clock in the morning, and talk all day and keep on talking at ten o'clock at night, all about how to make money for other people. It has dam-builders who will say earnestly, over Sunday fried chicken, "Your idea about power costs isn't supported by statistics."

Most of the arguments are polite; a discussion between farm experts and engineers on the possibility of a hay crop in a reservoir area is more like a college seminar than anything business would call a conference. Is that because these men, relatively secure in their jobs, are deprived of the violent personal hopes and fears of unrestricted private enterprise? If that is so, maybe it's a good thing. Because they haven't lost interest in what they are discussing merely because the interest isn't personal.

They are so polite to each other, and mostly so young, that often you won't notice who is head man in a group. They don't rub it in. Also, for a construction job, there seems to be remarkably little evidence of a dividing line between the men supposed to use their heads and those who work with their hands. Maybe the unions helped. Maybe the training program did, when it reversed the Antioch college plan of putting students to work, and put the workmen in classrooms.

The whole attitude—consideration for each other and concern for the job—is shown by a letter that one of the electricians at Norris wrote, when they were building the houses there. The workers' council had made suggestions about such practical matters as lockers and tools, and classification of workers, and then they branched out to considerations of safety, not only in their own work, but also in the equipment they were installing. A workman noticed that the first heaters were without screens to keep the childrens' hands out of the fire. He wrote a letter about it which resulted in a change of equipment, and the letter ended: "Please handle this in such a manner that the people responsible for this heater design do not resent having their attention called to this hazard. My reason for calling your attention to this is that if electrical accidents result in electrically heated houses, it will cause the public to be afraid of electric heat. We must encourage the wider use of electricity in order that a market can be found for the kilowatts TVA is going to produce."

Private corporations working hard to inspire their employees with loyalty to the company might well envy Uncle Sam's corporation this kind of help. The Tennessee Electric Power company had some trouble, and its customers had their lights turned off, when lines were dynamited in an American Federation of Labor strike of electrical workers, while the Alabama Power company, in a Labor Board hearing, was accused of fostering a company union.

Could TVA employees get to be too well behaved, and set up a deadly level of bureaucracy? In Knoxville one Republican investigator hinted that they weren't allowed to call their souls their own, while another, from New Jersey, was shocked to hear their radical talk. If they did any radical talking it must have been just to please Representative Wolverton, but they did show their independence by turning out for the committee hearings. Ticklish as the situation was, those for or against the former chairman would say: "I'll be seeing you at the courthouse," and hurry there when the working day was over, for an intensive course in problems of administration.

Most of them were for the directorate that survived, as would happen in any business. But they could give reasons. They said that early methods had been based on enlightenment from the top down, as from parent to child. They said the present administration was more democratic, aiming to help people to help themselves in their own way. They seemed content with the idea of a hundred and thirty million bosses.

When the New Deal was first dealt, visiting Britons remarked that you can't improvise a civil service. But you remember they thought you couldn't raise an expeditionary force and get it overseas. If this country decides that it wants a home service to do the jobs of peace, it may, again, move faster and farther than some folks would expect. They have made a pretty good start in the Valley.

7. GODS

More Light in Mississippi

According to the number of thy cities are thy gods, O Judah.

So I returned, and considered all the oppressions that are done under the sun: and behold the tears of such as were oppressed, and they had no comforter; and on the side of their oppressors there was power.

The little town of Tupelo, Mississippi, got to be famous as the first town in the United States to contract for TVA current. They hadn't been exactly anxious for it; in fact Congressman John Rankin, one of the authors of the TVA bill, had to persuade the people who ran his home town to take the power. But by the time they got it they were enthusiastic enough to have a parade, and Congressman Rankin made a speech at Washington about what a great thing the cheap electricity would be. A little later on, the President came to Tupelo and made another speech; he said: "What you are doing here is going to be copied in every state of the Union."

Folks in Tupelo use a lot of current; they cook and heat with it, so they've even built some houses without chimneys, and they run electric fans all summer. Industry takes the power, too; in fact the TVA power house was located right out by the Frisco tracks next to the cotton mill, and on the other side of the Authority's property was a garment factory. Another garment factory started making what they called TVA-brand shirts—the label reads "True Value Assured," but they print the initials in red, to stand out.

But one group of people in Tupelo were the only people in the whole Valley to lose instead of save money when TVA power was plugged in. They were the people working for the cotton mill.

The mill people lived in company houses, and up to that time their lights had been on the company line, at the industrial rate. So they paid just 50 cents a month. However, for the TVA power they were put on the regular residential rate like other people, and they had to pay the 75-cent minimum, which was lower for everybody else but two bits higher for them.

The mill took TVA power, too, of course, and saved between $17,000 and $18,000 a year on its bill. Early in the history of government power, Norman Thomas wondered out loud if the companies that saved on it would pass on the saving to their workers in higher wages. They got the answer at Tupelo, because just about the time they counted their savings on TVA the Supreme Court invalidated NRA. So instead of raising wages they dropped them.

The mill was supposed to have a $4000 weekly payroll and it had four hundred employees, so you can figure what they made. They worked forty-six hours a week, which wasn't so bad when you figure what they can do; one of the labor laws they had in Mississippi said that you couldn't work women more than sixty hours a week, except in case of emergency.

But they got the spunk somehow to start a sit-down strike, in the spring of 1937, when everybody was doing it. Jimmy Cox, a Tupelo boy who had been a machinist in the mill for seven years, was the leader. They asked for a fifteen percent raise in wages and a forty-hour week.

Of course they didn't stand a chance to get it. The mill folks said they were making money for the first time in eighteen years, but they couldn't expect to if they had to pay more money for less work. They offered to compromise on ten percent, but it wasn't to be a raise, it would have to be a bonus at Christmas, eight months off. They wouldn't reduce hours at all. And Jimmy Cox, with a two-to-one vote to back him, stood pat.

So the management said, if the workers were going to be ugly about it, they'd just have to shut down the mill.

To understand the situation you have to see how Tupelo is fixed for industry. Besides the cotton mill, there are some garment factories in Tupelo, all more or less under the same ownership. That is, besides being vice-president of the cotton mill, a Mr. Rex Reed is president of the Tupelo Garment company and of Reed Brothers, another garment plant. In addition to this Mr. Reed is president of the Citizens' Bank of Tupelo, of the Community Federal Savings and Loan Association, of the Tupelo Brick and Tile company, the largest builders' supply company in Northern Mississippi, and he is vice-president of R. W. Reed and Company, the biggest department store in that part of the state. There is a third garment factory, the Milam Manufacturing company, and a Carnation Milk plant, and that is just about all the industry in Tupelo.

While Mr. Reed was busy with these different undertakings, his wife did charitable work; she was Lee county chairman of the Red Cross and also devoted herself to managing the hospital, which was financed partly by outside funds and partly by local contributions. Employees of the Tupelo Cotton Mills contributed, and also got to be Red Cross members, by a payroll check-off. But when the strike came and some of them got sick, and they were evicted from the mill houses and asked the Red Cross for tents, of course they didn't get anywhere. You can see how that would be.

Mr. Reed and his wife naturally objected to the cotton-mill strike because the habit of striking might spread to the other industries, and that's just what happened.

Girls working for the Tupelo Garment company were making the lowest wages in the town, a scale that ranged from five or six to eight or nine dollars a week at the highest reckoning, and though most of them lived at home, they weren't satisfied. They were country girls and they had to pay out some of their money just getting to and from the factory. The company put a loudspeaker in the plant to tell them how well off they were, and how unions were not to be trusted; but they seemed to listen more to an organizer, a Miss Ida Sledge, who came in and talked to them. Miss Sledge was a Southern girl from a good Memphis family, but she had gone up North to school, at Wellesley, and got to talking a little like a Yankee and thinking that way too. Some of the people didn't like her talking to the girls, and she was asked to leave town twice, once by some of the Reed Brothers workers who were too loyal to the company to listen to subversive talk, and once by a committee of local business men. It's embarrassing for Southern menfolks to have to deal with a lady that way, but these times it seems it can't be helped.

Then the Citizens' Committee was organized among some of the best people to try and straighten things out, after the Tupelo Garment company girls had tried their sit-down and seven or eight of them had lost their jobs. The girls appealed to the National Labor Relations Board, and the other factories threatened to shut down, so something had to be done.

Insurance men and lumber men and members of the American Legion, people of that sort, were on the Citizens' Committee, and naturally the Chamber of Commerce was behind it, and the local papers for it. Earlier in the year the editor of the Tupelo *Daily Journal* had a citation from the *Nation* for successfully conducting "a liberal newspaper in the dark regions of Mississippi, where poverty and political dictatorship have produced our first corporative state." But Jimmy Cox said neither paper in the town would print his union announcements, sentiment was so against the strike.

They were needing all the space in the papers for the company advertising, anyhow. The Tupelo Garment company took a page to say that "Co-operation Is the Main Cog in the Wheel of Industrial Success," and to express its confidence that "the employees of our industries are of the highest type. True, red-blooded Americans." Just to make sure that the employees understood what this meant, the Citizens' Committee addressed another advertisement to them; it was a sort of warning:

We may be heading for another depression. . . .
The plants here in Tupelo were not built by making employers mad, but by co-operation and good relationship between employers and employees. . . .

Still another advertisement was addressed "To the Farmers of This Territory," with the qualification, "If your daughters or any of your relatives work in the garment factories in Tupelo and the other near-by towns." This advertisement pointed out that "cotton and seed are selling mighty low. The market for them is not as high as it was a year ago. This probably means that you will not have as much money this winter as you had last winter. This condition will not be helped any if our factories close down on account of labor troubles." Then, explaining that outsiders were attempting to organize the workers, the advertisement urged the farmers to "stick by the home-folks—they have already stuck by you in one depression. Advise your daughters and relatives to stick to their jobs and beware of outsiders' counsel."

One of the papers gave to the paid advertising no more support than a publicity story about Mr. Reed, described as chairman of the state board of public welfare, president of the Boy Scouts in thirteen counties, a charter member and past president of the Tupelo Rotary club, and superintendent of the Christian church Sunday school. Mr. Reed said that the road to success was service. The other paper gnashed its teeth at the "CIO agitators" and the National Labor Relations Board. It declared the necessity for "keeping the virgin Southland free at the present from a communistic organization. . . . There is no place in this fair Dixie of ours for labor agitators." As for the government, "We dare one of those Labor Board representatives to go out and tell a farmer how long he can work in his fields. He'll get his communistic head shot off."

The mayor of Tupelo, the same one who had testified to the advantages of TVA power, issued a statement against agitators and said: "It is our purpose to protect Tupelo's industries from outsiders." This resolution was echoed by the sheriff.

The mayor also made a speech at a barbecue tendered the loyal employees of the Reed Brothers factory, who had never had so much social recognition in their lives. The Tupelo *News* said: "Girls, we're proud of you," and the Citizens' Committee gave them a dinner at the Hotel Tupelo that cost seventy-five cents a plate.

The Citizens' Committee also investigated and reported that wages were better in Tupelo than in lots of places in Mississippi. This was true, because in some Mississippi mills and factories they were paying as little as three or four dollars for a fifty-hour week. Industrial Commissioner Harry O. Hoffman said: "We have comparatively little labor trouble in the state and union activity is light." You can see how, if it took an unfriendly attitude towards the factories it already had, Tupelo would be out of step with all the rest of Mississippi.

In fact, Tupelo's face was already red because of comment from outside the state. Florence, Alabama, was right there watching, and headlines in the Florence *Herald* read:

TUPELO BEING RUINED
BY OUTSIDE AGITATORS

HIGH HOPES OF BIG
BENEFITS FROM
TVA GONE

Then, with almost too much neighborly sympathy, the paper went on to say: "The fine little city of Tupelo, Mississippi, so full of hope and enthusiasm only about three years ago, when it signed up for TVA power and became the 'pet' of that government agency, is now fighting bravely for its industrial existence." The trouble was explained as an "influx of CIO agitators," which had kept out new industry and "lost forever" the Tupelo Cotton Mills.

A year after that, young Jimmy Cox was walking along the street in Tupelo, which was his home town just as it is Congressman Rankin's; his wife and two small children lived there too, and he was first on the list of substitutes to be taken on at the post office. With the cotton mills in receivership, nobody could have been planning another strike.

But as Jimmy Cox walked along the street, a car drove up and a man told him to get in. There was another car full of men, twelve in all, and there wasn't much use arguing. They took Jimmy twenty miles out in the country, into Union county, and tied a rope around his neck and told him they were going to tie the other end to the rear axle of the first car. He doesn't know for sure whether he talked them out of that or whether they were just trying to scare him, but instead they took his clothes off and stretched him over a log, and beat him with their belts. He lost count of how much or how long.

When he got away he walked to Pontotoc—another place that has TVA power—and telephoned for help; and he was in such bad shape that they were afraid not to treat him at the Tupelo hospital. It's hard to see just what they were trying to accomplish, because they didn't actually kill Jimmy, and they didn't change his mind. They told him never to show his face in Tupelo again, but he was back that night.

On a Saturday afternoon last summer, the Tombigbee Electric Power Association, the co-operative distribution agency for TVA power to which Lee county belongs, was having its annual meeting in the Tupelo courthouse under a clock stopped permanently at noon. Over in the Jeff Davis hotel, from which Miss Ida Sledge was removed by the gentlemen of the Citizens' Committee, a lawyer assembled evidence to be presented to the National Labor Relations Board.

Look over his shoulder at one of the depositions, written in pencil at the Holiness church. The union witness is reporting a conversation with one of the loyalists, who said: "I just got started to work good when that old union had us to stop." Asked how she knew the union was to blame for the factory's closing, the loyal worker admitted hearing this news from a forelady: "She said the superintendent said that he would close down till the first of April and that old sorry union would be died down." The superintendent also was authority for the idea that the organizers "was old sorry people," and the loyalist opined that Jimmy Cox must be "or he would not took what we called him and that old girl the sorry thing that was with him. We called them everything we could think of. . . . Mr. Fields [the superintendent, part owner with Mr. Reed] told us to run them out of town. . . . Then another bunch of girls sued Mr. Fields but he said they wouldn't get any money, for us to say he fired them for bad work. The other day we met and he made a little talk to us. Told us if we would tell it for him we had a job. And we are going to tell it."

You might talk to one of the prospective witnesses, who was an expert at her job of inspecting finished shirts; before she joined the ILGWU and got fired from the Tupelo Garment factory she had, she says, been offered a job by both of the other factories. Afterwards, of course, neither would hire her. It is obvious that she feels not only indignation at the company methods but a sense that the work denied her still belongs to her. In the feudal state, the serf had few rights but among them was the right to feel aggrieved if the overlord failed to play fair according to the rules. And though the lord owned the soil, while the serf was bound to it, the binding gave, also, a sense of possession; this explains the surprise and indignation felt by Southern strikers evicted from company houses. Realistic Northern workers expect such treatment as a matter of course; to the romantic Southern employee, full of faith in the good intentions of the boss, it still comes as a shock.

But they are learning. The news now spreads that the NLRB hearing will not be held in Tupelo after all, but in Aberdeen, the next county seat. The government board has been denied the use of the Tupelo courthouse; instead, a nice malice has suggested, the hearings might be held in the big cutting room of the idle garment factory.

A farmer, husband of one of the witnesses, sums this up briefly: "Tupelo don't want no riff-raff in its courthouse."

Aberdeen is a peaceful old town that hasn't gone in for modern industry much, or cut its fine old trees. Years ago the Creeks had what they called "white towns," for peace, and "red towns," for war. Aberdeen is a town of peace; not only did it welcome the hearing, it was celebrating, at the moment, the arrival of other company. The streets were draped with flags and bunting for the state convention of the Sons and Daughters of the Confederacy, and the Stars and Bars hung out bravely between the oaks and magnolias.

Of course there was nothing like the threat of violence, at Tupelo, that they had up in Ohio, when they had to move a hearing to Pittsburgh to keep the steel-company people from taking it over bodily. Company sympathizers chartered school buses and came over to

Aberdeen, but they were just girl members of the company union, shepherded by their foreladies—you don't call them forewomen down South. So many came over that, as one man said, it was too bad they didn't have the machinery to put them to work. They had been promised that, if they were good girls, loyal to the company, they would have jobs as soon as the garment plant opened.

In spite of the starvation wages, if you expect to see distress among these maidens come as willing sacrifices to the Lions, or the Kiwanis, you must look again. You must look closely, indeed, to see what makes them different from a group of working girls or high-school girls in any other part of the country. It's certainly not their clothes. They may take snuff, a habit carried straight over from the eighteenth century, but their dresses are what Paris ordered and the garment trade copied in rayon. If a good many of them wear a version of grandmother's poke bonnet, that's because a hat designer thought the fashion amusing to revive.

But there is something about them that goes with the flags on the street below, and reminds you of the picture of grandmother on her wedding day. Maybe it's only that their faces are the pure English or pure Celt which people call wholesome American. Or is it that they show an endurance, an acquiescence, that in most parts of the country has come to be a thing of the past?

It takes a certain polite endurance to survive the speech of their lawyer, now addressing the court. If you wonder why he should pour upon the Labor Board examiner such a flood of jury-box oratory, the answer is that he is mentioned as a possible candidate for governor of Mississippi.

One of several fat men at the table up in front, men with greedy mouths like the later Romans and waistline bulges built for togas, must be Mr. Rex Reed. But none of the girls will identify the boss for a stranger. They say they don't know him by sight, which is odd when you consider what the advertisements said about friendly relations.

However, everybody on both sides is watching Ida Sledge, the girl with the intelligent face and the engaging, confident grin who sits

at the union end of the long table. The girls who have come to
be witnesses take comfort from seeing her there. If they have to tell
about being fired for having union cards, she will tell how the town
merchants drove her out on the Pontotoc road, past Mr. Reed's big
white modernistic mansion mirrored in a lake, and left her on a
railway platform at sundown when they knew there would be no
train till morning. Of course she didn't want a train; like Jimmy Cox,
she was back in Tupelo the same night. And she looks as if she
wouldn't be a bit scared to testify.

Scared, not scared—that, now, is the difference between the two
groups of girls in the courtroom. The loyalists are in the majority;
their lawyer says so, endlessly. But they themselves are afraid to talk.
The girls who joined the real union may be afraid too, but they don't
show it. Their faces have the grim determination of those of our
grandmothers who were pioneers.

As it happens, nobody has a chance to testify; one of the garment
companies has a lawyer from New York, and he advises settling the
case. The other companies are finally persuaded to settle, too, and the
girls discharged for union activities are all to be reinstated with
back pay. The company unions are to be dissolved. The company
last to give in is warned about unfair practices, and there are to be
no more threats or penalties for organization.

Outside in Aberdeen, the Daughters acknowledged an earlier union
victory with a new cedar wreath on the Confederate monument.
Back in Tupelo, there was some confusion and the courthouse clock
marked a different hour on each of its four faces, while county authorities concerned themselves with disposing of forty-five gallons
of captured corn. The Tupelo *Journal,* announcing the order to disband the company union, headlined its story: "NLRB Turns Down
Garment Workers' Plea," and quoted local opinions that the board
was "under the thumb of John L. Lewis and his CIO unions and it
was useless to expect any just verdict." The *News* managed to make
the decision sound favorable to the factories. There was some precedent for this misunderstanding; when they fought a small engage-
ment near Tupelo during the war, they say the Union general won

but even he wasn't sure of it, and went off and left his wounded on the field.

There were casualties now. The girls who wore the ILGWU buttons had that payment of back wages, amounting in some cases to as much as two hundred dollars, and the promise that they might be allowed to sew more TVA-brand shirts. But the real question was, would the garment company, warned about its unfair practices, open up and run? There was talk that a Yankee company had bought it and meant to run it, but was that true?

Some said one thing, some another, so it was never clear just how long the Tupelo Cotton Mills and the Tupelo Garment company might have run had there been no labor troubles at all. The big boss had got mad once and said he could afford to pay the girls fifteen a week, but he wasn't going to do it unless the government made him. But afterwards he denied it, so maybe he was just bragging. His machinery was old, and the management, some said, out of date. The plants could turn out cotton goods and shirts, yes, enough to cover all the ragged people in the state of Mississippi. But maybe they couldn't do it in competition with more modern plants, and show a profit, unless they worked people for nothing.

What was plain was that the people needing work were willing to accept next to nothing, as Yankees count wages, and that those who held out for the union did so not so much in hope of more money as to save their souls. Her girls were jubilant in victory, but Ida Sledge worried over one extra-efficient worker and ILGWU member who could make as much as twelve or thirteen dollars a week. She had her job back, and back pay, but even that wouldn't go too far because she was supporting six people.

And what good will reinstatement in a job do you, if your fellow-workers and the foreladies are against you? The Board said "without prejudice," but you can't expect miracles.

As for the cotton mill out across the tracks, the building with the tall square tower and the smokestack just a little lower than the smokestack of the TVA, it is still unoccupied. Southern workers do not break windows, so the glass is there. And the Southern rains have not washed off the trademark of Tupelo Cheviots, "Look for the Blue Bird." But scarlet trumpet vines are covering the place, and on the door is a card that reads

THIS PROPERTY
IS NOW IN THE
HANDS OF THE RECEIVER
APPOINTED BY THE
CHANCERY COURT
OF LEE CO., MISS.

Beyond the mill buildings, the streets of mill cottages wear the same placards. People are living in them; when they tried evictions, three of the houses caught fire and burned to the ground. But what are they living on? There is no "home relief," as Northerners know it, in Mississippi.

Some of the cottages have garden patches, and some have cows, for the real farming country—corn and cotton, cotton and corn— begins where the mill houses end and the Rotary club sign hangs. It was just an irresponsible child, they think, or maybe a tramp, that set the houses afire—the mill folks themselves are as patient as share-croppers in time of trouble. Three tow-headed children play on the sidewalk in front of one cottage, and their father, in the doorway, tells them to mend their manners: "Whyn't you get out of the way? You oughtn't to set there and let folks walk round you." But sometimes, for young and old, there is nothing to do but set.

It's hard on an ambitious town like Tupelo that wants to get ahead. A lot of Tupelo folks will think that if it weren't for Jimmy Cox and John L. Lewis, and the National Labor Relations Board, and now this newfangled wage-hour law, the mills might be running and paying a Christmas bonus, or anyhow giving a sack of candy to such of the children as would know better than to play with fire, and had come regularly to Sunday school.

Alabama Stays Dark

They shall impoverish thy fenced cities, wherein thou trustedst.

The cities of the south shall be shut up, and none shall open them.

Rain fell on Alabama. The low hills along the horizon were laven-
der instead of blue, and the sensitive Southern ground had darkened
to keep in harmony; it was purplish crimson instead of the bright
orange-scarlet of red clay in the sun. But it wasn't a blinding rain,
yet; it was more like one of those English showers with a light streak
of sky still showing under the cloud.

It would have looked like English country, too, say the pretty
part of Devon, if they had grown a patchwork of different crops
instead of just cotton. But Madison county is the biggest cotton county
in the state.

Huntsville is an old town; for a while it was the capital of Alabama,
and a D.A.R. tablet marks the spot where Alabama entered the
Union in 1819. There is a rumor that Huntsville could have been a
sort of capital again, had it chosen to co-operate with the national
government more than a century later; they say that Huntsville, instead of Tupelo, might have been the first city to have TVA power,
and that, being close to the Shoals, it might have had some of the
administrative offices that are in Knoxville. But it would have had to
have a different attitude towards TVA.

Back in the sixties Huntsville folks were opposed to secession,
doing most of their business with borderline Tennessee. But now
Huntsville is a Southern town. The Confederate monument in the
courthouse square isn't one of those ordinary concrete soldiers with
a knapsack; he's an officer, with a goatee like Beauregard's, and carved
out of real marble. Out in the better residence district, under old
trees or behind high hedges of blooming crape myrtle, are old red
brick houses that escaped burning because they didn't fight here.
One, of brick painted white, is marked to show that a local poet
lived there. It's quiet and peaceful on the better streets.

Northern Alabama is headquarters for trouble in the textile industry, and in Huntsville alone three big mills have been idle for months. They said no orders, and at the same time they managed to blame the unions. Anyhow the Huntsville mills were shut down, and it wasn't a strike. The big ones, their names show, are Northern-owned; Lincoln Mills is a queer name to do business under, in Alabama. But you expect Yankees to be tactless that way.

More people live in the Lincoln and Merrimack and Dallas mill villages than in the town of Huntsville; the town has a population of 11,000 and the mill towns count 15,000. Alabama Power company buses run between them, and Huntsville, in the polite phrase, polices its neighbors; it's against the state law of Alabama to picket, and there are special city ordinances about loitering or talking in groups, and claiming the right of entry and search. Mill people, however, can't vote in the Huntsville elections.

Town folks feel that the mill people should be contented because most of them are better off than mill people in other places, and there is some truth to that. The houses look better than the average in mill villages. At the Lincoln Mills they are stucco, and falling apart as cheap stucco always does in a damp climate. But the Merrimack Mills built white-painted frame houses, some good big ones, with yards, although they are for two families. They have a nice red brick school with white colonial pillars, and two white-painted churches. Of course it's all behind that galvanized wire fencing, with strands of barbed wire on top at the strategic points; and this does look queer. The people who live there are conscious of it—ask a direction and they'll tell you to watch for the fence.

Right now the mill towns are quiet too. It's been three months since the representative people of Huntsville drove to Montgomery to appeal to the governor on "Save Huntsville Day," but the mills aren't open yet.

They had been closed for five or six months when the townspeople undertook to save Huntsville, and it was said that the Dallas Mill would go out of business. The publishers of Huntsville's daily paper, owned in Birmingham, got excited over the loss of what it called a $2,000,000 industry. They printed a series of front-page editorials about it. They lamented the certainty that Dallas Mills would be left just "a deserted village and the memory of what was once a happy community." They said that one person out of five in Madison county was out of work, that only one applicant out of ten could get a WPA job, that unemployment insurance might stop at any time. They said the outside labor leaders were as bad "as anything they ever had in Chicago gangs," and warned members of the CIO union: "You will be BLACKLISTED until your dying day! If you turn back to the farm there is no hope for you."

The Dallas Mills had been running with a CIO contract, but they closed down when it expired and proposed to reopen with fewer people, and an "independent," that is company, union. It was thought they might even tolerate A. F. of L. affiliation, but they would have no dealings with the CIO.

Huntsville citizens then had the bright idea of going to Montgomery to ask the governor to "co-operate" in reopening the mill. By this they meant promise to send the national guard, the way they used to down South, to keep it running in case of a strike.

Plans for "Save Huntsville Day," April 20, 1938, were made by a committee composed of the mayor and the city and county officials. The mayor said: "Huntsville and Madison county are confronted with the most serious and tragic situation that has ever existed in our history." They decided to close the school, and the courthouse, and the banks, and the wholesale houses, and the cotton warehouse, and the *Times* agreed to suspend publication for that day, so that everybody could join the "motorcade" driving to Montgomery. That is, everybody except the mill people.

About a thousand Huntsvillians went, driving over two hundred miles in the rain. They saw the governor, but it didn't do much good; Governor Graves seemed to be siding with the unions. He said the union had agreed to arbitration, and he invited the mill to sit in. That wasn't what the Huntsville people had come for, so they booed the governor and the motorcade drove home. It was still raining.

It was raining in August, and Huntsville had not changed its mind. Anybody could find out by asking, because the rain fell in such sheets that you had to stop in somewhere if you tried to cross the square. The hardware store is handy.

Yes, the rain is bad but it's all right for the cotton, and the town isn't doing any business anyhow. If they could just open the mills —but it's no use with those foreign agitators in town. They ruin everything. Of course it started with the NRA, when Washington first undertook to tell a man how to run his business, and got the mill people used to high wages.

The TVA? The hardware man figures the government coming in and underselling the Alabama Power company is just like a chain store coming in and competing with a local store. It's not fair. Besides, he's heard the government is slow to make repairs when anything goes wrong with a line; they have to wait to report to Washington.

Around the square, you'll hear variations of the same thing. Another version of TVA inefficiency is that the government current is too strong—right down there at Sheffield, it blows out the radio tubes. As for the mills, they've made the town—treated their folks well, as far as anybody heard, until these agitators came in. Built 'em a good hospital, and paid for two months' more school than they'd have had otherwise—paid preachers too, for the mill churches. Have an influence on what the preachers preached? Why, they could say anything they liked as long as they stuck to religion.

Trouble was, the mill people just weren't satisfied; they hated to be called mill people. Of course there was a difference and you couldn't deny it—most of them were shiftless and ignorant, or they wouldn't fall for the agitators' talk.

The shopkeepers and the shop loungers keep dry, but over in the courthouse the common folks, crowding in out of the rain, are wet and miserable. One woman with a nursing baby and a skirt-clutching older child could be photographed as a refugee, but what is she refugeeing from? You can't ask her; talking to some of these folks about their troubles is like asking at a funeral what caused the death.

You can see for yourself the woman hasn't anything you could call shoes, or any teeth, and the children haven't had enough to eat. Of course they're shiftless and ignorant, and probably hoping for some sort of relief. But the men aren't talking about the extra allotment of WPA jobs mentioned in the Memphis paper. One is saying, hopefully: "I heard the Lincoln mill was going to reopen."

These aren't mill folks, though, they are from the country—farm tenants, probably. And what is the farm situation? Ask the county agent. His office is full of busy people, and it's plain that he is an important man, but maybe he can spare you a minute. Yes, the TVA fertilizers are fine. Of course you can't use them on row crops, and this is a cotton county. Always will be—you can't change it. No, of course, they don't just grow cotton—one farm he could show you canned six hundred quarts of fruit. Big farm? Well, yes, of course. But it's not true that tenants aren't encouraged to raise garden stuff because they want the land for cotton. That's just a story you must have heard up North.

Truth is, tenants are shiftless or they wouldn't be tenants. You could divide up everything today and in no time it would be right back where it is now, with the enterprising people on top. You can't help those that won't help themselves. Rural electrification? Well, the Alabama Power company has done a lot to develop this country and they're building new rural lines, right now. The agent doubts if TVA could do any better. But the free phosphates are all right.

Around the square is a little news stand, and the proprietor, with an interest rare in the South, is listening to a news broadcast. Looks like there might be a war. No, nobody around here pays much attention to what they do over there—and they ought to, too, because the warehouses are stuffed full of last year's cotton, and a war's about the only way they could get rid of it. Had to turn one of the old mills that had closed into a warehouse, and they're building a new one, and growing more cotton. The mill trouble and the CIO? If you want to know about that you won't need a paper—just go across the street to the headquarters.

There is no sign, but the CIO office—TWOC, to be exact—is upstairs. Three men are there, two from the local mills and one an "outside agitator," meaning that he comes from another part of Alabama.

If you ask them how it was they stirred up these happy and contented workers, with better houses than they sometimes have, they'll tell you it all started awhile back. You should have seen the housing then, at the three old mills that closed down back in the depression. And it wasn't only the housing, says one of the local men—a young man, embarrassed at what he has to say. "All the conditions were bad. Excuse me, but if the foreman wanted to date a girl, why, she had no choice about it."

There were other requirements of a strict moral nature; if a man and his wife wanted to separate, they couldn't do it and live in a mill house. The young man is still indignant about these things, but the older of the two local men has come to take them philosophically; he talks about books. And weren't you out at the Merrimack Mills last night?

Less than twenty-four hours in town, a trip to the mill village after dusk in a vacant bus—but that's it, they explain. Don't many people come out to the mills from town.

There is a clear division, it seems, between mill towns and Huntsville; and the "outside organizer," himself as Southern as sweet potatoes, explains this later. Huntsville had its first experience of union organizing years ago, and it began the way it always does, with kidnaping the organizer. John Dean—he's dead now—was kidnaped from that hotel right over there. Trouble was, two women organizers were there when it happened and they recognized the kidnapers, one of them a Chamber of Commerce man. The women were reliable witnesses; one of them is in the state department of labor now. So they didn't do anything to Dean, just took him over the line into Tennessee. But it made considerable feeling among the mill people, and strengthened the union.

CIO organizers don't expect you to take their word about what is going on; they all keep scrapbooks of newspaper clippings, which may be useful in Labor Board hearings. The Huntsville news stories were all violently opposed to the union, of course, but the organizer offered no comment except about an account of the speech made under the auspices of Huntsville's better business group—a nonpartisan speech, it was called, although it was made by the brother of an Alabama Power company attorney. The speaker had said that Huntsville industry should not be required to submit to a dictatorship from Washington.

"Talkin' against the government," said the CIO man softly.

The union, as the scrapbook shows, had to have circulars printed to tell the people of Huntsville about the Wagner Act. But the most interesting exhibit in the scrapbook is not printed matter; it is two lines typewritten on a piece of cheap white paper: *"You and your kind are not wanted in Huntsville. We advise you to get out at once."*

"Oh, that," said the organizer. "We get lots of those."

The office is busy; negotiations are under way just in case the mill does reopen. The best local news is that one mill is running now—did you know that?—with a TWOC contract. Forty-hour week, check-off, and everything. Getting along fine, but of course it's a small mill, locally owned.

The wage scale is low but that, the organizer explains, isn't what they're fighting about in Huntsville. The people were tickled to get twelve a week under NRA and they'd be happy with less, maybe, if they had a union contract. It's the idea of cutting down the help, putting in the stretchout, that you have to look out for. The mills answered NRA by bringing in efficiency experts to speed up the work, and people couldn't stand it.

It wouldn't be etiquette to ask the organizers what will happen if they try to open the big mill without a contract. But everybody in town is talking about it; at the little café they say: "Are they going back to work?" And the proprietor answers: "Some of 'em are. This ain't the Nawth." That afternoon the union office is padlocked and the office typewriter established in the organizer's hotel room. Just elementary precaution, he says.

You can meet another kind of caution by calling on the editor of the weekly paper, which is relatively independent; the editor used to be mayor of Huntsville and he says some things the daily wouldn't say. He wouldn't be for the unions, but he does mention them without sputtering; he doesn't come right out for TVA, but he is willing to discuss the possibility that public power might be a good thing. But after you've talked to him a few minutes you begin to notice that, although he is polite, he isn't any too anxious to have a conference with you in his office right behind the plate-glass windows which open on the street. He wouldn't think of saying that, but you somehow gather it, and you learn why when he tells you that, since you were seen to climb the stairs to the union headquarters, people in town think you're another organizer.

This time it has taken less than six hours for news of your whereabouts to spread. Now you can feel yourself under surveillance as you walk around the square.

The courthouse clock strikes all night, and at two o'clock, safe in your own hotel room, you hear a disturbance outside. Cars are rushing around the corner, somewhere a bell rings—you go to the window. There are shouts in the alley—was that a shot?—and more cars. It wouldn't mean a thing in New York, but this isn't New York, and the little girl typing for the union said there might be violence. Then you hear a man laugh, an African laugh, hearty but soft, and you go back to sleep because, if there was trouble, no Negro would be laughing. It must be lodge night and you were a fool to get all wrought up, like a Yankee, over Alabama.

Come daylight, you must see what the mill operators say for themselves. Of course they probably won't talk; up North, the Berkshire Mills refused information to Princeton university.

The Dallas Mills are the pet of Huntsville because they have some local stockholders, although directors' meetings are held in New York. The mill buildings are deserted, but two cars are parked in front of the office, and inside, two elderly office workers are coping with printed forms and adding machines. But they can't give you any information; the only man who could is out of town. They can't say when he'll be back, or how he can be reached. As you go out past the barbed wire, through another office window you see another man and realize that the boss was there all along.

At the Lincoln Mills they don't stop with barbed wire; they have a moat, full of water because it is still raining. But they are franker about the boss—he's in conference; and more like a Yankee corporation, willing to talk without saying anything. Are they going to open? They hope so, for a while. No, they don't look for any labor trouble; there's never been any—just a case of no orders. Their workers are perfectly contented, glad to come back. Of course, since they haven't enough orders to run full force, they'll take only the best people. Wages? That is one of those tactless questions; the superintendent looks annoyed. "Better than a lot of mills pay up North," he says.

Questions about TVA power are also unwelcome, though the superintendent says he doesn't see what the state will do if it loses the taxes Alabama Power pays. As for the mill's taking TVA current, that would be for the directors up in Boston to decide. But you can take it that they're going to run if the orders justify it; it's just been a case of too many mills making duck. Yes, duck for tents—oh, yes, a war would fix everything all right.

Down the road a piece is the mill you really want to see, the one that is running, with machines purring contentedly and girls moving behind its windows. And there is no barbed wire here; now why is that?

Another difference is that the owner will talk to you. First of all, how come he is running when the other mills aren't? Well, he figures he's got extra good people, intelligent people. Intelligent enough to hold out for a CIO contract? Well, maybe, if you want to put it that way.

It's an experiment, he admits, in how long he can make both ends meet with competition from mills paying lower wages. He marks on a pad—suppose you pay eleven dollars a week, and another mill, we'll say, pays eight or nine. Say it costs $1.87 a dozen for you to make men's knit undershirts, and the other mill, with lower labor costs, makes 'em for proportionately less. That's the whole trouble.

On the other hand, he figures, keep everybody everywhere under-paid and who's going to buy the shirts? There was some sense to NRA.

There's a picture of the President on the office wall, the first one you've seen in Huntsville. On the desk, a boy's picture shows a like-ness to the mill owner.

"Yes, that's my son, and he belongs to the musicians' union up in New York. I've got 'em in the family."

"So you're scabbing on the capital strike?"

The mill-owner laughs. He doesn't, he says, know what the other people are doing—they hoe their own row and he sticks to his knit-ting. They may not have any orders, but he has plenty to run on.

He is no sentimentalist about the union—he's heard they didn't do right over at the Dallas Mills, and he isn't sure he approves of the check-off, but if his people want it, that's their business. The forty-hour week's all right if they work when they're working, don't leave a thousand-dollar machine to go hogwild while they sneak a smoke in the boiler room. His people don't do things like that; they're good people, with sense. No, he doesn't build houses for 'em. Of course this is a small mill compared to the others.

Lincoln mill houses line U. S. 241, the road back to town, and men talk in front of the company store. But with the mills shut down they do their buying at the union co-op, on credit. Better not try to talk to anybody here; if they think you're an organizer, you'd just get somebody in trouble. But you have to ask one question—you want to know who lives in that big befo'-de-wah red-brick house across the road, in the beautiful grounds. A barefoot girl on the porch of one of the mill houses tells you; it's the superintendent, the big boss, the one that was in conference.

Maybe that explains something, because his place is so much more expensive-looking than the neat white frame house, in town, where the owner of the small mill lives. The big mill has to pay its super-intendent a good salary and then make money for the stockholders up North, while the owner of the little mill just has to make a living for himself, down here.

A man in a soft-drinks store, on the unfenced side of the road, wonders if the union will hold out. Unlike the storekeepers in town, he isn't against it, or against TVA either. But this is hostile territory here, he warns you. He wishes they would bring in TVA power—sure would make a difference when you run a big refrigerator. Alabama Power charges you so much extra for every outlet. No, that's not a sensible way to charge, but they do it.

He isn't a native of Huntsville; his arm is tattooed from wrist to shoulder with the names of countries he's seen, since he joined the navy during the World War. Kept moving till he got a look at Germany and Italy under the dictators.

"And then you settled down here, across from that fence?"

He grins. It's a pretty country.

Yes, it's a pretty country. Now the rain has stopped and the sunset is red as fire. But they used to call this place Shotgun Valley.

Between the cotton-growing and the cotton mills, it seems a pretty cussed place—worse than Tupelo, because it's older and set in its sins. But maybe you aren't being fair.

When the Lincoln Mills do reopen, instead of a strike they have Labor Board elections, with TWOC ahead. The Dallas Mills start up with a TWOC contract. The Merrimack Mills evict people from the white frame houses, but the union starts a co-operative housing project and they end with another contract there. Maybe the wage-hour law helped.

And maybe you judged Huntsville harshly for a special reason. No use getting mad because, twice in two days, they accused you of being a Yankee. You never told them your great-grandfather was born in Madison county.

Model Town in Tennessee

For the king of the north shall return . . . after certain years with a great army and with much riches. . . .
Also the robbers of thy people shall exalt themselves to establish the vision.

Envy thou not the oppressor, and choose none of his ways.

Northern Alabama always was hard up, and the Yankee mills in Huntsville did the town no good, but why not look at a place industry has made, and made right? The town that was planned just to show what private enterprise can do when it is well intentioned and willing to spend money?

Right in the Valley, that place exists. It is Kingsport, Tennessee.

Industry in Kingsport has just come of age, and the stories of how it all began are very affecting. It seems that the scout for one big Eastern industry was taken to a little school in the hills and there, to the assembled Anglo-Saxon children, it was explained that this great man from the East had it in his mind maybe to build a big factory that would bring the blessings of prosperity to Kingsport. And a little boy stood up and said: "Please, mister, build your plant here." This plea so melted the heart of the scout that he turned in a favorable report.

Another story also tells how a visiting financier was taken up into the hills. In this case, the visitor chivalrously lifted his hat to two sunbonneted women walking on the road, and asked how the hill folks made a living. The local informant admitted this was a problem, and the financier asked what could they do. The local man said they might learn to make hosiery; whereupon "the financier was silent for a time, studying. Then the gracious, big-hearted man replied 'Meet me at eight o' clock in the morning and we will select the site for the hosiery mill.' "

The end of the story is in quotation marks because you can read it, and the other one too, in a book called *Kingsport, A Romance of Industry,* published back in 1928. The story about the little boy was repeated only last summer, in an article in the *Saturday Evening Post;*

so it must be true, although it was added that when grown to man-hood the hero of the tale failed wholly to recall the incident.

It's all in how you look at it, because while you may not believe that Yankee industries ever flew South on the rosy wings of charity, it's true enough that they came to Kingsport because of eager, tow-headed boys and women willing to work. Or, in the words of a Labor Board report, "One of the chief inducements held out . . . in se-curing these industries was the plentiful supply of cheap labor."

You might think that Kingsport would have been entitled to some consideration in its own right, as one of the first places in Tennessee to show evidence of enterprise. The town is right where the two forks of the Holston join, to make what was officially designated by the legislature as the beginning of the Tennessee river. Kingsport had the first iron furnace in Tennessee, and was a boat-building center back at the time of the Revolution; it was in the Kingsport boatyard that the Donelsons, Andrew Jackson's in-laws, fitted out the flotilla of flatboats they took over the Shoals.

Before then there had been the usual fighting to take the land away from the Indians, the Chickamaugas holding hard to Long island, at the forks of the river. They liked to use the island for powwows and councils; it was like the Smokies and the Shoals, one of the pieces of land they thought most of and wanted to keep. But according to the treaty they made there with the white men, they had to give it up.

During the Civil War the only fighting was when thirty-nine Con-federates, hiding in the bushes, held off five thousand Yankees at this same fork of the river. These odds were a little heavy and in time they had to give in, so of course the one big house in the district was burned. That was Rotherwood, a mansion elegant enough to be named out of *Ivanhoe,* built by a gentleman from Virginia. This gentleman's taste ran to marble balustrades and formal gardens and "the most splendid carriage of that day, Napoleonic in style, with gray silk upholstery and finished trappings of pure silver." He had, of course, a large number of slaves, "both house servants and farm hands, all willing and anxious to attend their master's slightest

whim." But those too old or feeble to work, he freed, for he was a
minister of the gospel, serving "without recompense," and also
owning Kingsport's first cotton mill.

That mill ended by losing instead of making money, and for a
time industry in Kingsport appeared to languish. In fact, Kingsport slept for half a century or so, until the charitable capitalists came
down to build a new Kingsport that was, as the book says, "deliberately planned for a city of industrial efficiency, civic beauty, and
human happiness."

Yes, sirree, they planned Kingsport—planning is all right, you
understand, if the right people do it. *The Nation's Business* published
an article explaining in detail how Kingsport was an example of good
planning, by private enterprise, while Norris was an example of bad
planning, by the government. In the words of the Labor Board
report, "Kingsport is what might be called a 'ready-made' city," and
the report goes on to say why it was made:

A certain New York banker named Dennis, with railroad and other
interests in northeast Tennessee, conceived the idea of building an industrial city in this section of the country. He enlisted the services of one
J. Fred Johnson, then a small merchant in Kingsport which was at that
time but a hamlet. Johnson turned out to be a man of unusual vision and
salesmanship and soon became and still remains a kind of patron saint
of the community.

Dennis, Johnson and associates formed a corporation called the Kingsport Improvement Company, which purchased practically all the land in
what is now the incorporated limits of the city; and beginning in the
year 1917, started a real estate development which resulted in attracting
several large manufacturing establishments from the North.

But who would read a report when you could say, instead, that at
the birth of the fortunate little city all the good fairies of industry
presided? The happy parents were the Clinchfield railroad and the
land company; the fairy godparents were the Eastman company, the
Corning Glass company, and the Kingsport Press, all of New York;
the Borden and the Holliston Mills, of Massachusetts; the Mead

Fibre company of Ohio, and the Pennsylvania-Dixie Cement Corporation.

Deliberate planning for industrial efficiency meant that these industries were hitched together. The books turned out by the Kingsport Press are printed on paper and bound in cloth manufactured in Kingsport; the paper mill gets its wood pulp from the Eastman plant, and so on. For the industries, the convenience is obvious. For the town, the idea is that there shall be no dependence on one employer, as at Tupelo, or even one industry, as at Huntsville.

As for civic beauty, by a coincidence one of the men who curved the Kingsport streets was later the planner at Norris. As far as bricks and stones and cement go, it makes no difference who does the planning and it may even be that the private planners will have more money to spend. The architects had fun, at Kingsport; the common is a piece of old New England or Virginia set down on the Boone trail. There are red brick colonial churches reminiscent of New Haven; there is a handsome real-estate office and a matching building for Kingsport Utilities, one of the fourteen companies suing TVA.

Civic administration was likewise carefully planned, under a charter examined and amended by the Bureau of Municipal Research of the Rockefeller Foundation. Could anything more be thought of to insure that third consideration of the planners, human happiness?

You might not think so to read the books or even to look at beautiful Kingsport, if you didn't get too far from the colonial brick filling station and the Kingsport Inn. You might even conclude that whatever might be wrong with Kingsport is no fault of the planning, but rather that the overwhelming success of the plan brought over-rapid expansion.

That there is something wrong with Kingsport, however, is plain if you so much as walk around the place, off the common or Watauga street, where the well-to-do people live.

The book will tell you that Kingsport industries were careful to build model houses for their employees; there is, for example, a Borden mill village where the houses have bathtubs. According to the book there were also, in 1928, two Eastman villages with a total of 62 houses, but at that time there were only 422 employees in the Eastman plant. Now there are ten times that many—with no proportionate increase in housing.

Where do people live? That, in theory, is the real beauty of Kingsport. What makes the city a paradise combining the best features of rural and city life is that its workers are healthfully established all over the neighboring countryside, on their own little farms, from which they drive in to work in their own cars.

One of the troubles with this theory is Long island, which the early settlers foolishly took away from the Indians. No self-respecting Indian would live there now.

Plenty of Kingsport workers do, though, because it's within sight of the big beautiful Eastman plant—a ten-story modern building covering a big acreage, all lit up like a Christmas tree with colored lights at night, and looking in general like a Hollywood dream of the future. Long island has this inspiring view, the way you can look at the Empire State building from Queens, but when you look the other way it's different. Long island itself is not anything the Kingsport Improvement company cares to show.

It's built up with shacks that would do no credit to a cotton plantation, although they rent for ten dollars a month. They are worse than plantation shacks to live in, because they are jammed so close together, and there are no sewers on the island. Actually, the combination of rural and industrial life in this part of Kingsport means that you have rural sanitation with city crowding. The real miracle of Kingsport is that there has been no typhoid epidemic.

Long island folks are not pampered with fancy schools and churches, either. You'd understand that the beautiful brick churches on the common are for the folks who live on Watauga street; and there is a neat little church in the mill village, to which the mill workers contribute by a check-off; but the Long island people will have to build their own church if they are to have one. Their school is a little shack so crowded that the children attend in three shifts.

What's wrong with the Long island people? Nothing, nothing at

all. They work in the mill, or in the Eastman plant, or in one of the
other industries of which Kingsport is so proud. But you remember
that low wages was one of the industrial attractions. If you ask about
wages in Kingsport, chances are they will tell you about the Kingsport
Press, which has to have skilled workmen and pay them relatively
well, though not, of course, the way printers are paid up North. Or
you may hear about the average at the Eastman plant, which has to
have technicians for the various *Ersatz* articles it makes out of wood
pulp (it began as a wood-alcohol plant and moved on to rayon and
the plastics). But the cotton mill had been paying the usual $5 to $15
a week, and of course plenty of the people in the other industries are
on that same wage level. At that level you don't pay much over ten
dollars a month for a house.

You don't have much luck buying your own little home, either.
This is encouraged in Kingsport; with the real-estate company right
behind the town, and lumber and cement and brick among the local
industrial products, you can understand that they'd like to see the
workers invest. So they arrange loans and mortgages and all that,
but somehow it always seems to work out that the families that try
to buy end by losing their houses. Some of them are sold several times.
It's too bad, but you have to remember that Southern workers are
liable to be shiftless and improvident, and of course even in Kingsport
employment is irregular. While the Eastman plant, for example, hires
ten times as many people as they had ten years ago, they have just
lately figured out new efficiency methods that enabled them to fire
twice as many people as they started with.

But don't the Eastman employees sign a contract saying they won't
do this or that—won't claim any invention made while they work
for the company, won't go to work for any other company in a similar
line of business, in this country or abroad, for two years after quit-
ting, and things like that? Yes, but you see that contract works just
one way; it doesn't keep the company from firing you. A company
that has all sorts of secret processes, some of them maybe important
to the country in time of war, naturally has to take precautions. That's
why they have to have guards at the plant, not only at the entrances,

to inspect those passes the workers have to carry, with their pictures on them, but also between the various departments. Maybe that sort of gives you the creeps, but on the other hand everybody admits the Eastman cafeteria is the best place to eat in Kingsport.

You can't expect to take the blessings of industry and reject any little discomforts that come too, such as the pall of cement dust that hangs over that part of Kingsport lying within a wide radius of the cement works, or the fact that chemicals dumped by the Eastman plant dirty the river. These things are part of being what the Labor Board report calls "perhaps the most completely integrated industrial community in America."

If you wonder how there came to be a Labor Board report on this paradise of contented workers and thoughtful management, it must be whispered that they actually had a strike in Kingsport two years ago, in the silk mill that's closed now; and last year the TWOC raised its ugly head in the cotton mill. So they had a hearing, which brought out mostly the usual things—intimidation of workers joining the CIO, and the firing of a few of them; encouragement of a company union, and so on. But the NLRB report is interesting because it considers that some of the peculiarities of Kingsport had a bearing on the case. For example, the examiner wrote:

The city is also unique in that there is an almost complete absence of party politics. But the business of governing Kingsport is not as Utopian as the absence of the familiar political bosses might suggest. The power usually wielded by such is exercised instead by an oligarchy composed of the "founding fathers," to wit, Messrs. Dennis, Johnson and associates.

Practically all real estate has been sold by the Kingsport Improvement Company, with suitable restrictions and strict selection to preserve unity and co-operation in the industrial development conceived by the "founding fathers" aforesaid, so that the latter have exercised at all times, and continue to exercise by this and other means, a very real, if not apparent, control of the government and its affairs. By reason of the extraordinary success of the plan, the principles and methods that are believed to have contributed to that success are, therefore, the object of jealous regard by all of the merchants and industrialists in the community.

To show how this works out, the mayor of the city, at the time of the hearing, was plant superintendent at the cotton mill; while an insurance lawyer who organized the company union was later the recipient of a city job. This is the sort of thing that goes on everywhere, of course, but it appears that the careful industrial planning in Kingsport makes it easier. It's true that when the Labor Board examiner wanted to look at the charter obtained with so much forethought from the Rockefeller Foundation, nobody could find it and they had to send to Nashville for a copy; but that just shows how smoothly things were going before the federal government undertook to interfere.

Now, you have to be fair to Kingsport. It's no worse than most other industrial towns over the country; and if, say, one-third of its people are badly housed, that's true of the nation as a whole. The reason you see all the faults of the place is that it brags on itself so as a beautiful, beatified business Utopia, the ideal of industry, the happy example of what a city can be if willing and obedient.

Will it continue to be obedient? Well, the CIO organizer is still on the job, finding his best arguments in the publicity put out by the town management, which comes as a shock to ordinary people living there. And last election they had a little upset politically. It seems some odd things can happen about taxes in Kingsport—you can see how it would be, with the land company owning everything; sometimes you might get mixed up and count a vacant lot grown up with clover and daisies as a park, and then maybe the land company would have a good offer for it and sell it, and you wouldn't expect to go back and tax it as commercial property, would you? Nobody expects to straighten things like that out in Kingsport, but they did get to watching poll taxes pretty close; reformers do that down South the way the federal government now and then catches folks on the income tax. Sure enough, in the last election one of the local lawyers that didn't get along with the city administration—didn't co-operate, as they say in Kingsport—dug up some things he thought pertinent and got some time on a radio station over in the next town, in order to tell about them. So they up and elected a sheriff that didn't belong, a small independent merchant instead of a paper-mill man. They could use a little reform in the sheriff's office; they'd had seventy-eight deputies in there at one time.

But it's going to take more than one small election victory to change Kingsport. With everything owned up North the way it is, you might say the only thing likely to make a change would be some national interference with the big industries that have made the town.

Or have they done so much, after all? It's true that more people live there; in fact you might say that the big Eastman plant, and Long island facing it, are just a piece of the crowded industrial North slapped down in Tennessee. But go out along the Lee highway, and you come to old Kingsport, which the builders neglected and which is now outside the city limits. There's not much to it, although the old inn where three Presidents slept is still standing, and the D.A.R. has put up a marker on the road. Because it's outside the city limits, like Long island, more of the little sanitationless squatters' shanties have been built along the river—shanties where the people who work in the model city have to live. You can look at them and wonder if the slave labor they used back before the war was any worse off.

Then, going on a little farther, you come to another industrial miracle—colonial Rotherwood, rebuilt and refurbished, still over-looking the river although it is now across the road from where it used to be. But that, surely, is a detail; and so is the fact that in place of the kind master of many black slaves willing and anxious to attend his every whim, Rotherwood today is owned by the New York banker who also owns most of the Clinchfield railroad and the Kingsport Improvement company.

Speaking at a company-union rally to fight the CIO, a Kingsport lawyer said: "Our town is the greatest in the South, but it will not be if you let this foreign element in." And even a mill employee got up to say they must act for the "protection of future posterity in Kingsport." But maybe the best prescription for Kingsport was on a tent in one of the poor sections, where they were having a revival. There a sign read: YE MUST BE BORNED AGAIN.

Religion Takes Sides

I will also leave in the midst of thee an afflicted and poor people, and they shall trust in the name of the Lord.

A wonderful and horrible thing is committed in the land;
The prophets prophesy falsely, and the priests bear rule by their means; and my people love to have it so: and what will ye do in the end thereof?

People who don't live in the religious-minded South don't realize how much courage it takes to go against religion and join a union.

Tourists going by train towards Blowing Rock or Grandfather Mountain have to change cars at Marion, North Carolina, and while you wait at the little Clinchfield station you can read pink and green tracts from the rack on the wall. But religion took its firmest stand in Marion when they had a cotton-mill strike several years ago. It was during the prosperity era up North, and Southern mill hands were making around ten dollars a week, that is, if they were grown workers. Of course they didn't pay the learners, fourteen- and fifteen-year-old girls, more than five.

They worked a twelve-hour shift, with no stop for lunch, and they were trying to put in a stretchout. People lived in company houses, and they complained some about the roofs and the privies; they might have fixed those things themselves but you don't have much time if you work from six to six.

Well, they went on strike, and they went out before their union— an A. F. of L. affiliate—was ready, but they just couldn't stand it and they were being fired for joining up. They were chock-full of spirit at first, and there was a lot of singing, but it's hard to keep that up with nothing to live on and evictions going on. Then the troops came in and were housed in the company YMCA. They broke the picket lines and kept the strikers from getting their mail at the post office. But it was the sheriff and some deputies that went out to the mill gates with tear gas, early one morning, and shot and killed six pickets after they'd started to run from the gas. One of them they killed was a man sixty-five years old, whom they had already handcuffed.

That did seem unnecessary, but some said the deputies had maybe had too much to drink the night before. The mill-owner said they were "damned good marksmen," anyhow. Of course they had to be arrested, but nothing was done with them and the sheriff was re-elected the next time he ran.

So about all the strikers could do was go back to work, if they could get taken back; the others went to making hooked rugs, or their wives did, or just gave up and moved away. Some went to work on the road gang, for moving furniture out of a strikebreaker's house. But first they buried the six men who were killed, in a mass funeral. There wasn't a preacher in Marion who would conduct the service, but a foreigner from the Federal Council of Churches of Christ in America did it. And a mountain preacher, Cicero Queens, said a prayer: "I trust, O God, that these friends will go to a place better than this mill village or any other place in Carolina."

Maybe you'd have to know the mountain people to understand what a queer thing that was to say. Because it is pretty country around Marion and the people think a heap of it, and it would take consid-erable hell on earth to make them suppose there could be a better place than Carolina.

After the strike was over, the mill-owners did what they could to improve things. They built a sewer and put bathrooms in the Bald-win mill houses, and they raised wages at the Clinchfield mills.

So maybe they just agreed, all along, with another mill-owner who said that shorter hours and higher wages might be practical enough from a purely business standpoint, but he was afraid of the moral effect on his people. After they had the strike licked, they didn't have to be afraid. You've seen a man punish a child for disobedience and then give him candy after the child cried and admitted papa was right; it's what they call breaking their spirit.

Also it's the thing some folks call Christian humility, so that may explain the attitude of the preachers in Marion and in some other Southern towns. The mill-owners and the churches see eye to eye about the Christian virtues, as they have about most things since that famous announcement made by a Southern evangelist back in the eighties: "Next to the grace of God what Salisbury needs is a cotton mill."

As late as 1924, a South Carolina pastor was assuring readers of the *Manufacturers' Record* that Southern industry was "a spiritual movement, creating a new people."

So there was no reason why Mr. Rex Reed, of Tupelo, shouldn't be a Sunday-school superintendent. He wasn't working at the job the week of the Labor Board hearing, but the first hymn was:

> He walks with me,
> And He talks with me,
> And He tells me I am His own.

The lesson was on Ruth and Naomi, but the preacher's wife, teaching an adult class of seven, got away from it as soon as she could in order to talk about the need for true faith in our lives today. Our great mistake, she said, was to think we could substitute what was called social service for that faith. Some churches made that mistake, and our President was making it, too, when he made so much of regulating wages and hours of work. We must realize that the need for God in our hearts came first. God raised up governments, and if they departed from right principles—by such things as repudiating the gold standard, or when a President so far forgot the dignity of his office as to interfere in state elections—God would make them fall.

Of course Tupelo people know what an act of God can do. In 1936 a tornado struck the town, killing more than two hundred people; you can still trace its path by the twisted trees and the gaps where one house was taken, another left. There was no sense to the way it struck, because it left the mill houses but took a lot of good ones. The *Sewanee Review* published a satiric poem suggesting that divine wrath might be due a city given over to such strange gods as TVA; but if that was it, why did the storm break on a Sunday night, and flatten four churches?

Up North most people aren't religious any more, but the churches have more influence down South than people realize. People down

South still want to be good. The big trouble with sharecroppers and mill hands and other hard-working folks isn't that they're low and ornery, it's that they're too well behaved to make enough of a fuss to better themselves. They think their trouble must be due to original sin, so only the Lord can help them.

So it isn't true that they build churches in the mill villages just to furnish diversion, the way the Harlan mine-owners were said to put on strip-tease shows on union nights. The mill workers want churches, and in the places where they weren't provided they've saved money to build for themselves. But naturally, when the mill-owner is generous enough to build a church and a school, and pay preachers' and teachers' salaries, he has an interest in what his people are taught.

Mill-church sermons are interesting, and if you go to hear one they won't know how to put you out, though they won't know what to do with you either, and won't crowd around to ask where you're from and extend the hand of fellowship the way they would in a regular town church.

In the Merrimack mill village at Huntsville, the Baptist church members were given a dose of old-fashioned doctrine by a fervid young man in his early twenties. God demanded, the young man said, that you acknowledge him. This meant keeping yourself away from bad company, even though you might be forced to work with people who were unbelievers. The masses, as they called themselves, might be godless. But remember the martyrs, who stood against the masses. Remember Samson, who got into bad company and pulled down the whole house and committed suicide. Remember that when Jesus met a wild man, a man everybody was afraid of, he cast the devil out of him. Those of us who are saved must set an example of duty and obedience for other people to follow; we must be witnesses, we must remember our obligations to God, particularly in a time of summer vacation, which was apt to be a testing time. This vacation reference was a particularly happy way to get around the fact that the mill was closed down in an effort to wear out the union.

The tow-headed youngsters and elderly women who made up the congregation may have missed any subtle intention to identify the CIO organizers with Delilah and the epileptic. But the service did stand, soothingly, for authority. God's demands were somehow to be identified with the demands of the mill; the cross of Jesus was the cross of the loyal worker; and when a quartet had sung "Where He Leads Me, I Will Follow," only a stubborn heretic could have objected to going home peaceably to live behind the barbedwire fence.

At Kingsport, it wasn't necessary to go to church to find out the connection between local theology and local industry. The union people had got tired of contributing to a mill church, and brought the matter of anti-union sermons into the Labor Board hearing. When they asked a deacon just what the preacher had said, the only way he could get out of testifying was to say he had been asleep in church.

This is another situation not peculiar to the South; just lately an Ohio preacher told the Senate Civil Liberties Committee that you couldn't take a stand for the union and against the steel company, in Ohio. In the Valley you can see some progress when you consider that it hasn't been ten years since the preachers were against even the A. F. of L.; you can now find some sympathetic to the sharecroppers and the mill hands and even the Negroes, and beginning to be tolerant of union organization. Last year in Cleveland, Tennessee, they had a field day when rival preachers came right out and argued about it. Inside the courthouse, at a company-union rally, a preacher said it wasn't true that the CIO came from communistic Russia; it was straight from hell. Outside in the courthouse yard, another preacher thumped a Bible and said he couldn't find a word in it against the CIO.

Since they work up a religious horror against the CIO, it is plain that the union could be given a religious appeal too, if the organizers were willing to work that way. But they aren't, maybe because they think that folks have heard enough preaching.

The real problem is theological, though. Everybody knows the South is a hard place for croppers and mill folks and Negroes and women; in other words, that it's a hard place for poor folks, which is true of almost any place. But if you are poor white, or colored, or female, you were born that way, and some think the Lord must have meant you to suffer this curse or he wouldn't have wished it on you. If you or the unions or the government should try to change things, it would be going against the Lord's will.

Besides this fundamental problem of doctrine, they've got another religious conflict to work out down South. They were a little late hearing about it, but a lot of Southern people, especially city folks, have now got converted to a religion that started up North a good while back. Up there they call it the religion of success.

What They Pray For

The rich man's wealth is his strong city: the destruction of the poor is their poverty.

They sold the righteous for silver, and the poor for a pair of shoes.

Stand on Lookout Mountain, looking down at Moccasin Bend, and they'll tell you that you can see clear to Chickamauga dam on the days when there isn't too much factory smoke over the river. That there could be too much factory smoke for the good of a city is an idea that has yet to gain acceptance in the Southern civic mind.

In the South, they're just a little late getting the chimneys. They've waited a long time, and now you ask them to restrain industry, conserve resources, interfere with overdue development? Shucks, that's just an idea of some Northerners jealous of money coming South at last.

In order to get money the Southerners long ago adopted Yankee methods, and the only reason they were not successful was that they started too late. The corporations which rule America today were already established, with headquarters in Delaware.

This did not keep hopeful Southern Chambers of Commerce from beating the drum, printing glossy literature, shushing all critics, and offering subsidies to manufacturers, any manufacturers who would condescend to come and build some factories. A new industry might be owned by foreign capitalists, like some of the rayon mills in Tennessee; it might pay starvation wages, like the cotton mills and the mines; it might pollute the streams or fill the air with smoke and noxious gas, or strip the woodland—what did that matter? It meant money coming to town: deposits for the banks, customers for the stores, advertising for the paper, a new dress for the wife, and shoes for the baby. Welcome to our city!

There was, in the average Southern mind, no question as to where Northern business methods were leading. They appeared to be doing well. Most Southerners would admit that the Yankees were always better traders; it was, therefore, not extraordinary that Yankee attention to business should have been rewarded first. But surely the Southerner, once he put his mind on it, would be equally successful?

There was no criticism, from an ethical standpoint, of *laissez-faire*. The Southern country was still full of natural blessings for those who would work—trees for the cutting, fruits and nuts for the gathering, fish for those who would dig bait. Why was it not true that money was for those who tended to business?

There was no notion that the prosperity of one could depend on the prosperity of all. Had not the North, devastating the South, greatly enriched itself?

While it was a New Orleans court that decided you couldn't deport a man for being a Communist, they don't know enough about Marx down South to tell you that they haven't yet gone through the stage of capitalist expansion, and please let them be until they have. But when they open a new chain cafeteria just off Cotton Row in Memphis, with big white pillars in front like an old plantation house, air-cooled as the old plantation wasn't, and serving a good Southern dinner for forty or fifty cents, everybody welcomes it; and private enterprise did it. The South likes it and wants more. The main question is how to get the capital.

After selling off the trees and skinning off the soil, the South wasted a good deal of time trying to interest Yankee capitalists in the "layer cake of valuable minerals" said to underlie the Southern mountains.

It took a good while to discover that the Yankees were more interested in cheap labor and power sites, and just as this lesson was
learned, the government started interfering with both.

What if, as the President told Southern congressmen, money saved
by paying low wages does not stay in the section where the wages are
paid? Some Southerners are grateful just for seeing it pass, like a
fast train to New York. As for conservation of power resources, the
Chamber of Commerce attitude is expressed in a phrase of pre-war
slang: "I should worry a dam site and build a mill."

In fact the Southern attitude is that the South has just as much
right to sweat its people and sell out its power sites as the North
had, so there. It's the way the Yankees prospered, isn't it?

This may help to make clear Southern opposition to government
spending; accompanying government interference may antagonize
a more powerful, and very jealous, ruler. In some sections of the
South the big corporations loom larger than Uncle Sam; how can
they know in Carolina that the Duke Power company, lasting
through several administrations, will not be at Buzzard's Roost long
after the New Deal dams are gone? If they were so sure this dam-
building was a good thing, why didn't they do more of it on Northern rivers?

Back in the sixties Southerners undertook to establish a government opposed to Yankee capital, and it didn't work, and so Southern realists consider the matter settled. You've got to remember that
no federal government has meant anything but business, Yankee
business, to the South since '65. To say "Alabama Power is a private
monopoly; TVA will be a public monopoly; a public monopoly is
better than a private one because you have a vote to control it" makes
no sense if you haven't paid your poll tax or know that, however you
vote, the Yankees will manage.

As for considering that submission to the will of a private corporation or an individual capitalist is somehow dishonorable, while government is the power of the people, that is the idea of a few young
radicals up North but not of responsible people anywhere. To say
that one man practically owns the town of Tupelo, that the mills and

HARD WORK, BUT TVA PAYS WHITE MAN'S WAGES

MUSCLE SHOALS CAN MAKE PLANT FOOD, OR POISON GAS

THE MILL GOT TVA POWER. THE GIRLS GOT A WAGE CUT

Alabama Power own Huntsville, that the group of balanced industries owns Kingsport, does not seem to fill the residents of these
places with shame and distress. Why should it? You can say with
equal truth that Niagara Power and Remington-Rand and allied
industries own Buffalo, or Ford owns Detroit, or rubber owns
Akron.

Intelligent Yankees may feel that their own smoky towns belong
to the bicycle era, and that if they were starting now they'd do differently. They think the South, just starting her industrialism, should
learn from past mistakes; but maybe it's like expecting the Fascist
nations to learn from the past imperialism of the democracies, anything except to go and do likewise.

Of course you can't generalize too much; there are plenty of folks
down South who hate even to see turkey-wing fans replaced by the
electric kind. But most of the opposition to industrialization is sentimental and apologetic instead of reasoned and firm, and there is not
much hope of controlling industry or of discrimination between industrial gains and industrial evils.

You expect the bigger business men to stand together, as when a
mill lost its blue eagle in one Tennessee town during the NRA days,
and all the town merchants took down their eagles too. You can
understand how small business follows that lead, so that a blacksmith in another Tennessee town seemed unduly bitter about a textile strike until you found that the mill foremen gave him work on
their cars. But it's more surprising that people who don't have to will
trade at company stores, that even the Negroes in a mill town will be
against the union if there is "trouble," and that many of the white
workers are willing to put up with so much. That is, it's surprising
until you consider their situation.

Last spring there was an unusual advertisement in the New York
Times. It wasn't a very big advertisement, but it was big enough to
be headed by a picture of a girl fastening a garter, and the slogan:

MISSISSIPPI
RAPIDLY BECOMES
A SILK STOCKING STATE

This didn't mean that the people of Mississippi were going to wear silk stockings, as those with old-fashioned ideas of Southern luxury and idleness might suppose. It just meant that the "friendly and intelligent workers" mentioned among the assets of the state were willing to work "long hours of daylight and sunshine" in "communities that co-operate with industry" and under "state laws favorable to sound industrial investment." To be sure that the idea got across, they mentioned the friendly people and the favorable laws twice, and said that inquiries would be considered confidential.

If this seems shocking to the new economic morality up North, look at the income sources of Mississippi in comparison with other states. In 1936 Mississippi made a measly thirty-two millions from manufacturing, while Pennsylvania was making a billion and a half, Ohio a billion, New York two billions. Even for the South, Mississippi was low. And yet in the years from 1933 to 1935 Mississippi was the second state in the Union in new industrial establishments—new, that is, to Mississippi. Runaway mills were coming down from the North, to be welcomed as warmly as Yankees once welcomed the runaway slaves.

And Mississippi's governor thought they might come down even faster if towns offered to donate mills and factories, as well as allow a five-year tax exemption to industries moving in. In a way, the governor's wish to balance agriculture with industry in his state was what TVA had in mind for the whole Valley, but he went at it in a very different way, and they say it was the Mississippi Power company instead of TVA that helped him.

Going from stockings to shoes, there were Tennessee towns that competed for the privilege of building free shoe factories. They're tired of hearing about how the South needs shoes, from Yankees who start wearing openwork sandals as soon as they try living in a warm climate.

Up North they criticize the subsidies and tax holidays the Southern states offer to manufacturers, but don't the Yankees do the same thing when they see themselves slipping? Before they gave up and rented rooms in the Amoskeag Mills to the WPA, Manchester, New Hampshire, reduced taxes and got local people to put up money for reopening part of the plant. Now they say up in New England that their hope is for small industries and tourists—a hope that makes Southerners smile because they've heard that one for so long. It's all right if you can't do any better.

But if you get a big industry, as the South has discovered by watching the North, you can cover up its evils by what it makes. Pulp your pines and maybe you can afford to set out sycamores in a park. Poison your rivers and build a swimming pool. Use up the natural things and you get to where you can afford the made things that most people prefer.

They prefer them because advertising has taught them to, so you'd better scrape up money for an advertising appropriation, too. Last year Tennessee undertook to hire an ex-ambassador and spend $200,-000 on advertising to let the tourist trade know "that we have attractions other than monkey trials and child marriages." Virginia had gone in for advertising before that, and so had the cities of Atlanta and Asheville. Even Harlan, Kentucky, bought newspaper space to explain itself as "one of the wealthiest and most progressive cities of U.S. of its size."

Of course they want to make some rebuttal of all the unfavorable publicity the South gets up North. Everybody up there has heard of Georgia chain gangs, and Georgia got so mad she changed her penal system, though she thought it couldn't be much worse than moldering in a cold Yankee jail. She hadn't even thought of such a horror as scalding men with live steam, the way they did in Philadelphia.

But when the intelligent people get to holding Southern policy conventions, as they have of recent years, they can't do much except say how things ought to be. The big decisions which throw Southern people out of work or keep the wage level down are made in the North, where the property is owned. Southern representatives of the absentee landlords are not the college professors who write about wages, but the Chamber of Commerce crowd. And the Chamber of

Commerce mind has not changed much since the old-time Southern conventions when they argued for forced labor, and how to turn non-slaveholders into slave-buyers by bringing in factories.

As the reception committee for new industries, the Chambers of Commerce first looked askance at TVA and greeted it with sickly smiles, if it was determined to come in. Now, in some places, they are reconciled or even friendly; at Chattanooga the Chamber of Commerce passed a resolution against the Norris bill for seven "little TVA's." That wasn't because they wanted to save the rest of the country but because, having discovered they had a good thing, they wanted to keep it for Chattanooga. But elsewhere in the Valley there is still a fear that government interference will drive away other industry.

The Authority, of course, disclaims any effort to lure industry into the Valley from other parts of the country. But the private power companies brag on themselves for doing that; Alabama Power, for instance, took credit years ago for being the electromagnet that attracted steel to Gadsden.

Now, all over the piney-woods parts of the South, they are praying for paper mills to chew up the last of the pines. The companies are supposed to replant what they cut, but they refused WPA help in developing their new pine-paper industry; didn't want government interference. They are hoping to compete with Sweden, where you have to have government permission to cut a tree.

But most people down South didn't see *The River,* and if they had, the refrain:

> We built a hundred cities and a thousand towns,
> But at what a cost!

wouldn't have made sense. Up North, where they've got the towns and cities, they can cry over split timber. Down South, where all they've got is the cut-over land, they aren't crying for the trees they lost as much as for the cities they didn't get.

In one old Southern city, when they got their precious paper plant, the Yankees who built it expected to pay wages of thirty-five or forty cents an hour. But a committee of local business men called to ask them not to do that—said it would disrupt the local wage scale. So the company obliged by paying fifteen cents.

8. LIGHTNING

Land Was Wealth

And I looked, and, behold, a whirlwind came out of the north, a great cloud, and a fire infolding itself, and a brightness. . . .
Also out of the midst thereof came the likeness of four living creatures. And this was their appearance; they had the likeness of a man. . . .
And they had the hands of a man under their wings on their four sides; and they four had their faces and their wings.
Their wings were joined one to another. . . .
As for the likeness of the living creatures, their appearance was like burning coals of fire, and like the appearance of lamps: it went up and down among the living creatures; and the fire was bright, and out of the fire went forth lightning. . . .

And as for their appearances, they four had one likeness, as if a wheel had been in the midst of a wheel. . . .

And the living creatures ran and returned as the appearance of a flash of lightning.

In this age of machinery and power most folks never heard much about the Yazoo land frauds, but they were a right big thing in their day.

The Yazoo river isn't part of the Tennessee system; it flows down into the Mississippi. But in the early days they didn't know just how the land lay, and what they called the Yazoo country was considered to extend way up into the Tennessee Valley, through Alabama and Mississippi and the Lord knows where.

Land was the main thing in those days, so you might think they would have been mighty careful who got hold of it, but they weren't.

Of course the first thing was to take it away from the Indians. But different Indian chiefs would give different titles, and after that there were state claims and federal-government claims, to say nothing of the French and Spanish. Naturally there was a lot of wildcat speculation.

Soon after the Revolution, one set of speculators went to work on the Georgia legislature and got through a bill of sale for more than fifteen million acres of land on the Tennessee river, stretching clear to Muscle Shoals. Of course Georgia didn't have any right to dispose of the country that way, and President Washington issued a proclamation saying so. The Tennessee Yazoo company, as they called themselves, paid no attention to the President, but the Indians drove them off when they got to the Shoals.

Then four companies got together in a combination. They were determined to hold on because, if and when the Spanish claims were settled by the government, land was bound to go up. They knew about these foreign matters in Philadelphia and New York and Boston, where the money was, before anybody could hear about it in the South. All the news they got down South in those days and for long after that had to come over the post road through Knoxville, which is why they didn't know the War of 1812 was over before Jackson and his Tennesseans fought the battle of New Orleans.

So the four companies that divided up the territory kept right after the Georgia legislature. These four companies called themselves the Georgia Yazoo company, the Georgia-Mississippi Yazoo company, the Upper Mississippi Yazoo company, and the Tennessee company. One of them would have been the Alabama company if they'd got the names right. As for the money from up North, that came through what they called the New England Mississippi Land company, what you might call a holding company.

Well, in 1795, when Washington was in his second term, the land companies put another deal through the Georgia legislature, and this time they paid half a million dollars for what was said to be about twenty million acres of land. Actually it was nearer twice that, and most of Alabama and Mississippi went for a cent and a half an acre.

The legislature was said to have had a better offer, but the people
that made it didn't have a powerful enough lobby.

In fact all but one of the legislators had shares in the companies.
But a whole lot of prominent people were in the thing: John Sevier,
the first governor of Tennessee, had been in it, and Patrick Henry of
Virginia. They both got out, but plenty more got in. Before it was all
over they had involved a judge of the superior court in Georgia, and
a United States district attorney, and a United States district judge,
as well as one justice of the Supreme Court who had been one of the
signers of the Declaration of Independence. Then of course there
were congressmen, and there was Senator Gunn of Georgia, who had
been a captain of dragoons in the Revolution. They did say his war
record included a dispute over the ownership of a horse.

But mostly they were solid, respectable people. A man in Georgia
put in a book that, considering the "imposing array of talent, character and influence, and especially what a strong Law Staff the Yazooists boasted," it was no wonder that "by the combined efforts of so
many such men, with abundant pecuniary means at their command
and no scruples or restraints of principle in their way, surrounded and
reinforced, as they were besides, by a numerous phalanx of active
subalterns, and co-laborers, our raw, petty, unschooled Legislature
should have been jostled from its propriety." It took him a lot of
words, but you see what he was driving at. The same man went on
to say: "It was the North, then as now the home of monied capital
and of an intense adventurous love of gain, that was chiefly the
buyer." [1] One of the Yankees behind it all was Robert Morris—you
might call him the Morgan of his day.

And although they were speculating on the government's clearing
the Spanish titles, at one time they wrote to the conspirator Wil-
kinson and to Miro, the Spanish governor at New Orleans. One
company with land in Alabama wrote a letter saying that they considered their interests and those of the Spanish as "intimately connected and inseparable." Maybe it was just a natural sympathy, the

[1] *Miscellanies of Georgia,* Absalom H. Chappell.

same thing that made them lay out a section they called Bourbon county.

But there were some people who didn't admire Bourbons, and besides Senator Gunn there was another Georgia senator, General James Jackson, who got fighting mad over the whole thing. He left the Senate and went back to Georgia to raise hell. He couldn't get results right away because, as the book said, "What was most desirable for the Yazooists was plenty of time for their vast and scattered operations." But the legislature did repeal the act of sale, and Jackson had the fun of burning it in the State House square. He used a sun glass, so as to call down fire from heaven, and he must have had as good a time as Senator Norris had at Norris dam.

However, that wasn't the end. Georgia tried to get out of the whole thing by ceding the lands to the federal government, but that just transferred the claims. You see, a lot of money had changed hands, and now all the lands had gone to the second holders, or to people even farther removed. People way up in Boston had put their life savings into the company that was up there; they were just ordinary working people, mechanics and such, but they paid in two million dollars all told. That was four times what the companies had paid for the land. These people had all bought in good faith and naturally they wanted to sue, but their titles weren't guaranteed—the speculators were too smart for that.

Madison was President by then, and he appointed a commission to settle the claims. The commission said the titles were no earthly good, but they recommended a compromise payment as "expedient."

John Randolph of Virginia and some others opposed that, and it pretty near split the Democratic party. President Jefferson inherited the fight, and while he was busy keeping out of war with Napoleon, Congress was being sought after by what was called "the ablest and most influential lobby that had up to that time ever invested Congress, sustained by a powerful Northern advocacy on the floor." Next thing, they got up a case and took it to the Supreme Court, with John Quincy Adams to represent the Yankee holding company.

And blamed if the court didn't sustain the claims. It was four years more before Congress paid anything, but in 1814 they forked over five million dollars of the public funds to the people that were company stockholders at that time. Five million was a lot of money in those days, more like what five hundred million would be now. And it was just nineteen years since the four companies had paid a tenth of that for the land. But of course they'd had to spend a lot on lawyers and lobbying and such. It was probably worth it to be rid of the claims. Because, of course, nobody would want four big private companies and a Yankee holding company to own the Valley land.

Since to most folks power franchises are just paper and modern corporations a mystery, nobody thought much of the fact that when the Tennessee Valley Authority was established in 1933, there were four big electric power companies in the Valley. They were the Alabama Power company, the Tennessee Electric Power company, the Georgia Power company, and the Mississippi Power company. Leaving out the wheels within wheels, these four companies were subsidiaries of a holding company, Commonwealth and Southern, with headquarters up North.

Power Is Wealth

The lightnings lightened the world.

How hast thou helped him that is without power?

Dutch farms are said to be a hundred percent electrified; German farms ninety percent; Swedish farms fifty percent; farms in the United States, only ten percent. When they say that electric horsepower is the best index of wealth, and that this country leads in it, they are talking of other industries than farming.

But his position in farm power does help explain the troubles of the Southern farmer. Before TVA went to work in the Valley, in a list of states ranked according to the number of farms having electric light, Tennessee was number forty-one, Georgia forty-four, Alabama forty-six, and Mississippi forty-eight. Fewer than three out of a hundred farms in Georgia, Alabama, and Mississippi had lights, and fewer than five had them in Tennessee. In none of the four states did one farm out of a hundred have any other electrical equipment.

The big companies weren't doing anything about it. They said that the use of electricity in the Valley had reached the saturation point. By this they meant that it wouldn't pay to furnish any more; nobody but Uncle Sam would run a mile of wire so a farmer could screw in a twenty-five watt bulb. Mr. Wendell Willkie, president of Commonwealth and Southern, said that the four cities of Knoxville, Chattanooga, Memphis, and Nashville took sixty percent of the power sold by his Tennessee company.

It's true that taking power to farms is like delivering mail, it just wouldn't pay cash dividends right away. Farmers wanting lights were told they would have to pay the cost of line construction, usually five hundred to a thousand dollars. At best they got an extra "line charge" of two or three dollars a month added to the bill.

So when the Tennessee Valley Authority proposed to sell power to farmers, it was easy to ask if it expected to be paid by tenants and croppers who didn't know where the next meal would come from, or to "become a permanent social missionary by supplying mountain cabins with electric lights, even before they have moved up from the pine knot and tallow dip stage to that of the kerosene lantern."

TVA had an answer for that one, and if they can make it stick, it may turn out to be pretty important. Director David Lilienthal said: "The rate charged for electricity, within wide limits, determines its cost."

Of course that's just the Ford idea applied to utilities, but one of the odd things about this country is that, in spite of the success of Ford and the ten-cent stores, so many business people still think you've got to lower the price after you make the big sales, instead of before.

Naturally if you started out to lower the price first, people could say—and they did—that your rate schedule was "pure guesswork, based upon a development of the electric power business which has never been reached, and which there is no indication will be reached for many years to come, if ever." They said pretty much the same thing about Henry Ford and motor cars.

But if you took a dozen American cities and put them in order according to the home use of electricity in 1933, with Tacoma and Seattle, Washington, which used the most, at the top, and Boston and New York and Toledo, Ohio, down near the bottom, you couldn't help noticing that the use went down as the price went up, or vice versa. The Western cities, where power was cheap, used the most and spent the least. You could argue all day about which came first, the rate or the sale; the power companies would always say it had to be the sale, and ordinary people would always say it had to be the rate. But the power companies weren't really arguing. They just weren't taking any risks with their stockholders' money.

To set new rates and expect to get enough new trade to justify them, you've got to take risks and you've also got to do some figuring that is bound to be, in one sense, guesswork. But it can be good guesswork.

You know to begin with that if the local rate is ten cents a kilowatt-hour, that is too high for a lot of people, presumably all the people that aren't taking the power. So you have to choose between making a drastic reduction that will increase sales a whole lot, and a little reduction that will increase them a little. You have nothing to guide you except what people can afford to pay, and what your lowest cost of production will be; and that will vary with how much you sell.

When TVA made its minimum rate to farmers seventy-five cents a month, it was observed that the average farmer paid just about that much for coal oil to put in lamps, so they could have got the figure that way. But as a matter of fact TVA had cost figures of its own to go on because Uncle Sam had been in the power business for over ten years.

Since the papers were full of discussion and doubt as to whether the government had any right to sell electricity at all, most people didn't realize that the government had been selling power from Wilson dam ever since the dam was finished. There was a provision in the

Muscle Shoals Act that would seem to an ordinary person to be
against it, but they were selling it just the same, beginning in the
Harding administration. The usual customer was the Alabama Power
company, and maybe they felt some obligation because the company
had sold the government the dam site for a dollar, back during the
war. But in 1921 they relayed power all the way from Muscle Shoals
to North Carolina, to make up a shortage that resulted from a drought
in the Duke power preserve.

And what was the regular price to the Alabama Power company?
Two mills, a fifth of a cent, a kilowatt-hour, wholesale; then the company resold the same power right across the river, to its retail customers, at ten cents.

So the quarrel was not over whether the government could sell the
electricity generated at the dam, but whether it should sell to a private
company or to the public, and thereby set retail prices. As long as it
did only the first, nobody started any lawsuits.

There was that rate precedent to go on, then, when TVA made its
rate base. The rates they announced were higher than the rate they
charged the power company, because it is easier to sell electricity right
at the dam than to take it to a city, just as it is easier to take it to
the city than to sell it out among retail customers. So, announcing a
rate schedule for cities and rural co-operatives, TVA raised the Muscle
Shoals scale to seven mills a kilowatt-hour on the average load.

Then, not selling retail at all, TVA went on to say what retail
prices should be charged by the cities and co-operatives reselling its
power. They said the customer should have it at three cents a
kilowatt-hour, minimum use, going on down to four mills a kilowatt-
hour for maximum use.

Just as its own price to cities was three and a half times the previ-
ously established price to the power company, this retail rate began at
a little more than four times the average wholesale rate the cities
were to pay. The mark-up didn't represent any profit, but the cost of
distributing the current. The rates were similar to those of Ontario
Hydro, and to those of the exceptional city plant at Tacoma.

But when they got the news in New York, utilities stocks took a drop in the market, and all the utilities experts started explaining how the rates were ridiculous. Why, one expert said, the companies were paying two cents a kilowatt-hour now just in taxes. Of course that was a little exaggerated, in the first place; and in the second place the taxes were proportioned to sales. But experts often speak impulsively that way.

On the other hand Mr. Samuel Ferguson, president of the Hartford Electric Light company, said that a completely electrified house should be able to buy current at two cents or less, for light, refrigeration, water-heating, and cooking. He added that there was much more profit in the all-electric house, even at a rate as low as 1.7 cents a kilowatt-hour, than in the average house using less electricity and paying 4.5 cents, or the minimum user paying eight cents.

Still, the papers and magazines went on talking about TVA's "dream rates," and down in the Valley they had their own troubles understanding how it worked. Maybe the Authority was a little tactless in establishing an average rate for its sale to cities, and then setting retail rates for quantity use that could go below that. It's all right when you study it out, but at first glance it did look funny.

But anybody could understand that the highest retail rate, for minimum use, was less than a third of what people had been paying. That was news. Of course the only towns that could do anything about it right away were the ones that had their own distributing systems. After Tupelo, Mississippi, Athens, Alabama, and Pulaski, Tennessee, came along as soon as they could. Then TVA began selling to rural co-operatives, which was the only way they could reach the farmer.

In Tupelo they got the final bills at the old rate in March, and with so much talk of the whole thing being a mistake, everybody watched for the new bills to see if there was some April Fool trick being played. But the bills were what they said they'd be and after they came in there were a lot of new customers.

One man who had been paying $2.30 for his home lights found he

came under the TVA minimum charge of seventy-five cents. A department store had its bill cut from $65.14 for 966 kilowatt-hours to
$23.69 for 952 kilowatt-hours. The Tupelo *Journal* paid $18.94 instead
of $41.38. The Lyric theater paid $29 instead of $94.

So even the old customers began using more electricity, just as TVA
had figured they would. Woolworth's store had paid $65.22 for 968
kilowatt-hours, on its last bill under the old rates. Its first month at
the new rate it used only 746 kilowatt-hours but it paid only $19.16.
So the store turned on more light. In January 1934 they had used 876
kilowatt-hours, at $61.54. In January 1935 they had increased the use
to 2054, for which they had to pay only $36.22.

In four months the home use of electricity in Tupelo increased
seventy-five percent, and in twenty-two months it had gone up 267
percent. Right away the objectors began to discover that Tupelo was
an exception to the general rule; they said Tupelo's municipal system had been badly managed and they had an extra high rate there.
In fact Mr. Wendell Willkie, in a speech to the American Statisticians'
Association in New York, said that the Tupelo rate had been "one
and a half times to twice as high as the rates charged by privately
operated public utility companies in the same area." That sounded
fine until you discovered that they had paid ten cents a kilowatt-
hour in Tupelo just as they paid the private companies in nearby
Mississippi and Alabama towns. They're still paying a dime in a
lot of places over the country, including the North Carolina mountains where TVA is building a dam but hasn't yet sold current.

Athens, Alabama, went to work and used more current than Tupelo, and Alcorn and Pontotoc counties in Mississippi started to run
up records. Over in Tennessee, Dayton—yes, that Dayton—decided to
believe in electricity.

Next thing, you heard that towns using TVA power would go
broke because they were losing tax revenue. They said that about
Tupelo and about Athens, and somebody paid good money to have
printed and circulated in the Valley an anonymous circular that said
dire things about public power in Pulaski. Eventually, the Federal

Power Commission made a special study to show that tax receipts in
TVA territory were all right, but the town officials had already said
so at the time.

In January 1935 the mayor of Tupelo issued a formal statement:

> One year ago we were buying power from the Mississippi Power Com-
> pany at 17 mills per kilowatt hour. It is now costing us about 5½ mills
> per kilowatt hour.
>
> We own our distribution system and re-sell it under TVA rates. Before
> we contracted with the Tennessee Valley Authority for electricity our
> rates were lower than the average in Mississippi and lower than the Mis-
> sissippi Power Company retail rates.
>
> Our residential consumption has more than doubled since we con-
> tracted with the TVA. The community consumption has almost doubled,
> and we have had a large increase in industrial consumption, due, how-
> ever, to some extent, to our taking over some industrial customers who
> were formerly served by the Mississippi Power Company.
>
> We are delighted with our TVA contract.
>
> J. P. NANNEY, Mayor.

At Pulaski, they replied to the circular by reporting that the use of
power per residential customer had doubled, and the average saving
per customer was $18.50. Pulaski had dealt with anonymous warn-
ings before; it's the town where the Klan was started—the old Klan,
in 1866.

The Rate Determines the Cost

He hath shewed his people the power of his works.

Unto the upright there ariseth light in the darkness.

The actual procedure for a city taking TVA power was all set forth
so there wasn't much chance to go wrong. First of all, the city fathers had to keep separate books on the power business. They had to
appraise their distributing system, figuring it at what it cost new, less
depreciation. They had to agree to take not more than a six percent
return on the investment.

GEORGIA FARMERS TOOK TO SPECS, WAITING FOR LIGHTS

A COMMUNITY REFRIGERATOR MEANS BETTER EATING

From the reserves, they must pay into the general funds of the city an amount equivalent to the regular tax—a tax on the whole value of the property, not written down. Then they were to set aside funds for replacement, and after that they could, if they liked, redeem their bonds before maturity. Any remaining surplus was to reduce the rate to consumers. Some would prefer to reduce taxes, but TVA points out that that puts a sales tax on electricity.

What happens is that when the town first starts taking TVA power and cutting rates, its revenues slump, and TVA has to hold its hand and explain the rate-determines-use idea. As the use increases the revenues rise again, and at the end of a year they are back to covering the costs. After that there may be a surplus.

As polite as the post office, TVA makes no differences, or practically none, between rural and city rates. The average minimum rate was set at seventy-five cents, assuming there were five to ten users a mile. For two to five users it went up to $1.20, for over ten it dropped to sixty cents.

Farm users found they could have an electric water pump for $1.50 a month, and like the town folks they could have a refrigerator and cook with electricity for around five dollars. They could run a little motor by paying as much as eight dollars, and for ten dollars a month they could supply the light and power for a thirty-cow dairy.

The rural co-operatives had the same arrangement for lowering rates as use increased, and in Alcorn county, Mississippi, where they started paying 5.37 cents a kilowatt-hour for 49.4 kilowatts a month in 1934, they worked up to 138.7 kilowatts and a rate of only 1.82 cents an hour. That is more than twice the electricity and less than half the rate given for the average residential consumer in the United States.

Corinth, Mississippi, took the unusual step of helping finance the county co-operative because the increased use decreased the town rate. But the usual procedure was to sell rural co-op memberships at a hundred dollars apiece, and TVA didn't expect to collect all that at once. A man could pay ten dollars down and as little as twenty-five cents a month, the same quarter he saved on a minimum bill.

It's odd how much more important the country market became after

TVA entered the field. Take the case of Rhea county, Tennessee. Up there a man who owned a poultry farm had tried to get lights, and he remembered that the company had wanted five hundred dollars to build a line. They also wanted him to buy a refrigerator. Naturally he didn't do anything about it. But after TVA came in, blessed if the company didn't offer to build at its own expense. The government men, they explained, were just a bunch of Yankees who would talk a lot but not do anything. The company men rushed all around, making hook-ups with Delco lights and working their installation people overtime, though they didn't pay them any union wages.

Over in Coffee county a little town called Beech Grove had wanted power for a long time; three years before, according to a Beech Grove preacher, they had gone so far as to offer to pay the company $1500 to come in. Nothing came of it; but when they planned to start a co-operative with Bedford county, to buy TVA power, the workmen came in a big hurry. The very day before the meeting they put up poles, and strung wire from a farmer's 32-volt plant in his hogpen, and hung up a street light.

It was the same way over in Catoosa county, Georgia, where they started building what the people called "spite lines," hurried-up construction to get ahead of TVA, and some didn't take it any too kindly. You might say there was a little trouble in Catoosa, because one woman got so mad she stood off the company pole-setters with a shotgun. Mr. Preston Arkwright, president of the Georgia Power company, said he found it "particularly gratifying . . . that the agitation in Northwest Georgia attracted little or no attention outside of the comparatively small area," but he spoke too soon; the Federal Theatre play *Power* put it on the New York stage.

All this rural-line controversy was trifling except to the people who lived in the country and wanted lights. But the lawyers in a suit brought by the Alabama Power company against the co-operative in Cullman county, Alabama, wrote a brief that said one funny thing. After charging that TVA had actually gone into areas which the company served or intended to serve, and complaining of the "ruthless competition" of a "powerful adversary," the brief said the company was "forced to appeal to the courts for the protection of the property of the company and its markets." You see they just took it for granted that the company owned the county as a market.

While it was outside TVA territory, some people using electricity up in Toecane, North Carolina, undertook to prove they wouldn't stand for that sort of market division. They were customers of a company that charged $1.50 for seventeen kilowatt-hours, while over in the next company territory the rate was twenty kilowatt hours for a dollar. The companies weren't fighting each other because they understood that they each owned their markets. But the Toecane people got up their own petition; it read:

We, the undersigned, agree to have our lights cut off until the Northwest Carolina Utilities Company meets the price rate of the Carolina Power and Light Company.

The Baptist church signed first, agreeing to stop its night services, and everybody else in Toecane went back to kerosene except one family that was paying for an electric icebox and another that had a baby. You notice the rate they asked for was still considerably higher than the TVA rate.

In TVA territory the companies have had to come way down on their rates but they are still building rural lines. In its annual report for 1936–37, the Authority noted as an "encouraging sign of progress" that the Alabama Power company, which built only 55 miles of rural lines in 1934, built 285 miles in 1935 and 1300 in 1936. The Georgia Power company was credited with a similar expansion; after it had built three million dollars' worth of rural lines the president of the company said: "I won't be so foolish as to say our action was not influenced by the TVA lines, because it was."

Actual rate reductions in the Valley to meet the TVA challenge have amounted to thirty-one percent for the Alabama Power company, thirty-five percent for the Georgia Power company, and forty-six percent for the Tennessee Electric Power company. Increased residential use corresponds to these reductions: the Alabama Power company had an increase of forty-four percent, the Georgia Power company forty-seven percent, and the Tennessee Electric Power company ninety-two percent. Notice that the order is the same, but the increased use keeps a little ahead of the decreased price; also, when you lower the price more, you get a much bigger jump in use.

Since the Tennessee company made the biggest cut and had the biggest increase, it is interesting to note that back in 1933 the company told the legislature that a cut of twenty percent in rates would mean blue ruin. Nobody denies that the companies reduced their rates because the Authority forced them to do it. Besides competing, TVA sold power to the companies, and the act of Congress which governs the Authority provides that requirements as to the rate of resale be made. It was under contract provisions that the Tennessee Electric Power company made its first reductions in 1934 and the Alabama and Mississippi companies came down, while the Georgia public service commission ordered the Georgia Power company to make reductions, and Kentucky joined the procession.

There were also voluntary offers of reductions in certain areas where communities were voting on whether or not to acquire their own distributing systems and plug in TVA power. Most spectacularly, the Memphis Power and Light company cut rates to the TVA level in December 1938, with negotiations for sale of its property to the city under way.

Decisions like these were hard for utility companies to make because they went against their ingrained principles. They hadn't reduced rates during the depression, and they didn't believe in reducing rates. Consider a statement made by Mr. George B. Cortelyou early in 1934; at that time, though worried over increasing taxes and interference of government in industry, Mr. Cortelyou found one ray of hope:

The demand by the public for electric service through the fourth year of a severe economic depression is, in my opinion, an outstanding feature of the electric light and power industry at the present time. That the public highly esteems the use of electricity is very apparent, for in spite of greatly reduced family incomes and the necessity for curtailing expenditures wherever possible, customers generally have continued the

use of electricity. This is striking proof that the electric service is rated
by the consumer to be worth considerably more than he is paying for it.[1]

What Mr. Cortelyou sees as striking proof some people might consider the champion *non sequitur* of all time, because while rate un-
doubtedly determines use in the case of new customers, and of the
amount used by old customers, the family that has got used to electric
light considers it a necessity and does not go back to candles or kerosene. That consumers continued the use of electricity through the depression was no more "proof that the electric service is rated by the
consumer to be worth considerably more than he is paying for it"
than his calling the doctor is proof that he thinks the doctor is under-
paid. Then there was another reason for not lowering rates, discovered
by another writer who put it this way:

> If we acknowledge the secondary interest of vicarious investors, such
> as policy holders and savings depositors whose funds have been invested
> in part in the securities of their companies, it is safe to say that those
> with a proprietary stake in the utilities exceed those who consume the
> services of the utilities.[2]

This is pretty complicated but if you work it out you will discover
that he means to say the utilities have more stockholders than customers. In that case, and if the Yankees are right in saying the pre-
ponderance of officers over privates in the Confederate army helped
lose the Civil War, the utilities industry is in worse shape than anybody thought.

Whether or not you agree with the logic of these gentlemen, it is
clear that, left to itself, their school of thought would not have cut
down the light bill. TVA forced a reduction in rates in the Valley,
and something—perhaps all the talk of government competition in
the air—brought rates down all over the country. To understand how
far the Tupelo candlepower threw its beam, you have to look at what
people were paying for electricity at the time TVA began.

On the day that Tupelo celebrated, Congressman Rankin of Mis-

[1] In *Public Service Magazine*, February 1934.
[2] Joseph Stagg Lawrence, in *Review of Reviews*, January 1934.

sissippi read into the *Record* a report of what 350 kilowatt-hours would cost in various parts of the country. He picked that amount because Canadian consumers were using that much, and in Winnipeg they could get it for $3.08. In Tupelo it would cost $6. But in Baton Rouge, Congressman Rankin found, it would cost $33; and in Bangor, Maine, $31.50. Miami would have to pay $29.90, and Meridian, Mississippi, in the same state with Tupelo, $27.10. Boston would pay $26.25, and Fort Smith $24.75. The price in Asbury Park, New Jersey, would be $19.75, but Denver would get off with $18.10.

Rate news travels slowly, and people in Detroit seemed to think nothing of paying $11.80 for current that would cost only $4.26 across the river in Canada. But the Tupelo rates got a lot of attention, and women keeping house up in the Bronx wouldn't be happy to hear that they were paying as much for lights, and a toaster and a percolator and a vacuum cleaner, as Tupelo citizens paid for all these plus electric cooking and refrigeration. It was possible that they would take notice even in Westchester, which boasted the highest rate in the country.

Down in the Valley a maximum rate of three cents instead of ten cents a kilowatt-hour for the light in the kitchen was what everybody noticed, and over the country the minimum charge was seldom under $1.50—twice the TVA minimum. When you started adding gadgets, Tupelo could have the ordinary amount of them and still pay no more than the minimum for lights in other places. Tupelo could cook and heat water for what other people paid for just a refrigerator, and so on. Tacoma was the only other place that could do anything like as well.

Or suppose you had some sort of little business and could afford to use 850 kilowatt-hours a month. In Tupelo you'd pay $8.50, where it would have cost $58.60 before. Go as high as 4000 kilowatt-hours and you'd pay $20.90 in Tupelo and about ten times that over the country.

With rates gone down a quarter to a third since TVA started, towns taking TVA power don't get the big reductions they used to, but it can still be estimated that the average citizen in Tupelo pays less than half the national average.

Appliance prices were still high, so for a while the Authority under-

took to arrange for cheaper stoves and refrigerators, to be sold on
time. This job was done through the Electric Home and Farm Authority, now a Washington agency, which started in the Valley in
1934. While the manufacturers had to be cajoled into making the
low-priced models, half the established price was plenty for most
Valley folks to pay. But given a chance, they set themselves up in
gadgets at a great rate. In 1934, thanks to EHFA, Tennessee and
Georgia were first and second among the states in sales of electric
ranges and refrigerators. In 1935 the town of Tupelo established a
national record.

Naturally, since private companies were still selling most of the
power in the Valley, the campaign helped them. In 1934 the Tennessee
Electric Power company reported the greatest percentage of increase
in use of residential power of any company in the country, with a
volume of appliance sales three times that of 1933; and won a prize
at the utilities convention in Atlantic City for outstanding business
growth and record appliance sales. The Alabama Power company reported a consumption increase of 19.5 percent, with appliance sales
doubled.

Mr. G. C. Estell, president and general manager of the Florida
Power and Light company, told the Edison Electric Institute that,
thanks to TVA, "large use of electric service is more definitely planted
in the minds of our customers than ever before in the history of our
country." An appliance manufacturer assured the editor of a woman's
magazine that "the TVA is the grandest piece of promotion that has
ever broken for the electrical industry. Imagine the President of the
United States standing up and saying that every house in America
ought to be completely electrified!"

While Mr. Ford in person or even as a corporate person didn't get
the Shoals, it was just applying the Ford idea to sell electric refrigerators to that eighty-five percent of the population which didn't have
them and which, by a coincidence, had an income under two thousand
dollars a year. You could say that TVA and EHFA were trying to
prove that even electrical workers should be able to afford electric
gadgets, because the big sales in Lauderdale county, Alabama, were

partly due to employing a lot of people around there to build Wheeler dam.

Some sales efforts in the lower brackets had been successful before; up in Hartford they rented electric ranges at thirty cents a week, and out on the Coast the Pacific Gas and Electric company offered unlimited electricity for two months at the cost of last month's bill, to get people used to using more. Up in Canada the public-power people installed both ranges and heaters rent-free, regarding them as outlets, at a time when the Alabama Power company was charging extra for an ordinary outlet in the wall.

They couldn't very well overlook what happened in the Valley, so the Northern companies of Commonwealth and Southern got busy with a campaign of their own, and in 1937 Mr. Wendell Willkie was able to report the happy results of "an aggressive, uniform merchandising policy" in the North. But Mr. Willkie did not give any credit to TVA. He complained, instead, that in 1936 more gadgets were sold by his Northern companies than by his Southern companies, and he said: "The difference reflects in part the retarding effect which the Tennessee Valley Authority has had on the development of private enterprise in the South."

You see, Mr. Willkie just had a short memory. He had forgotten in 1937 that the sales of appliances in the South had done their doubling and tripling between 1933 and 1936, and that you can't sell people new refrigerators every year. It was one of those times when the South got ahead of the North but didn't get any credit.

An even stranger reaction to the EHFA campaign in the Valley was that of Dr. Arthur Morgan, who made it the basis for his widely headlined charge of a "hidden subsidy" in the TVA yardstick. He thought too much had been spent for publicity, which should have been charged to the city plants instead of to the Authority. Among the unreported publicity assets Dr. Morgan mentioned the President's speech at Tupelo. But how would you charge that? Moreover, good advertisement as it was, it is possible that the speech, by focusing opposition upon the Valley, made the immediate job of the Authority more difficult.

Dr. Morgan then went on to mention, as another "hidden asset," the low wages paid employees of municipal distributing systems in the South. Unfortunately those low wages are as much a part of the Southern light plant set-up as the icebox where they keep the watermelons. But you can't have it both ways. The campaign of "education" was necessary because of peculiar local conditions; demonstrations of stoves and washers and refrigerators had to be made because here were customers who hadn't seen the advertisements in the magazines. That ignorance was a local handicap which cost money; low wages are a local handicap which saved money. You can let these handicaps cancel each other, because there will be local variations everywhere, but why penalize yourself twice?

How Corporate Persons Fight

Behold now behemoth, which I made with thee. . . .
His bones are as strong pieces of brass; his bones are like bars of iron. . . .
Behold, he drinketh up a river, and hasteth not: he trusteth that he can draw up Jordan into his mouth.

He is the chief of the ways of God: he that made him can make his sword to approach unto him.

When the Tennessee Valley Authority began to function in the spring of 1933 there was no more opposition than there was at that time to other energetic recovery measures. The utilities did not fight the power provisions of the TVA because it was assumed that the power produced would be sold them without strings attached to the resale. In the words of Dr. Arthur Morgan, "In its manner of selling power to private utilities . . . an administration inclined to do so might almost contribute to the exploitation of the region by utility companies at public expense." [1]

Even after the government had gone into the public-power business, in what *Public Utilities Fortnightly* called the "Truce in the Tennessee Valley," the Commonwealth and Southern Corporation signed

[1] *New Republic*, January 6, 1937.

over to TVA some $2,900,000 worth of transmission and distribution facilities in Mississippi, Alabama, and Tennessee. The districts included Knoxville and Pulaski, Tennessee, and the "Tri-Cities" at Muscle Shoals—Florence, Sheffield, and Tuscumbia—as well as Decatur, Alabama. The power company was praised by the Washington *Post* for its "fine spirit of co-operation," and *Barron's* said: "It could be worse."

Knoxville also arranged to buy its city plant from the Tennessee Public Service company, a relative, through National Power and Light, of Electric Bond and Share. It looked as if the Southern power companies were like the farmers in the reservoir area, glad to sell out at a fair price.

But it is one thing to sign a contract with a corporation, which is a person for purposes of court decision under the fourteenth amendment, and another thing to carry out that contract when the corporate body changes its mind and the real persons who own its stock agree to pull its chestnuts out of the fire. Some years before, when the Alabama Power company was trying to buy everything at Muscle Shoals, an army major testified that the government was morally obligated to live up to a contract giving the company an option on the Gorgas plant, though the judge advocate general held the contract was null and void. And the company got the plant; but that time, it was the government's obligation.

In November 1934 thirteen coal- and ice-dealers, non-residents of Knoxville, won a court ruling in Tennessee which killed the city's agreement with the Tennessee Public Service Corporation. This ruling was annoying in several ways. Ninety percent of the company stockholders, it was generally admitted, were satisfied with the sale. Knoxville was satisfied with the plan to buy. But the court ruling gave the plaintiffs ninety days to prepare evidence, which was just long enough for the agreement to expire.

Over in Alabama, thirteen minority stockholders of the Alabama Power company prevented the sale of TVA power to fourteen towns. Among these towns were the "Tri-Cities," where Shoals power is generated, and where retail customers were charged thirty to forty times its cost. More suits then tied up the PWA funds that had been allocated for purchase of company plants. Legal measures against a law are an old Alabama custom; the state undertook to test the thirteenth amendment that way.

The suits were to go on and on, but what was clear from the start was that the utilities industry, in the headlines of its own organs, had declared war on TVA. What was the cause of this breaking of the "truce"? Maybe a smarter question would be: "Why did the power companies ever agree to sell anything?" They had good lawyers. They could have fought right from the start, tooth and nail.

What actually happened nobody will ever know, maybe, who didn't hide out in the offices of Electric Bond and Share and Commonwealth and Southern. But you might make a guess just by putting yourself in the place of the power people and their smart lawyers. Here you are with power companies all over the country, including a stretch of it that you haven't given much thought to because you never expected it to pay anything. Here comes the government proposing to develop its own power, and offering to buy your transmission lines. You aren't much concerned over this part of the country, but suppose the thing spreads? Common sense tells you the time to stop it is now.

But a new President has just been elected and people are for him. This is his plan, part of his popular New Deal. The thing hasn't been tried and it doesn't sound well, but a lot of money is going to be spent and nobody knows yet who will get it. This is no time to antagonize the spenders, or the misguided public that elected them.

Down in the Valley the local people are all excited over the money coming in, and it won't help public relations any if a big corporation from up North openly opposes the whole plan. In fact the less said about Northern control the better; most of the people don't even realize that the home address of their light company is 15 Exchange Place, Jersey City, or suspect that the company is just a midget in the Morgan lap. If you could arrange it so local people did the objecting . . .

Local people owning stock were hard to find, and some of the misguided Southern stockholders thought it might be a good thing to sell out to Uncle Sam. They thought his price offers fair and they never had been sure that these Northern holding companies were running things right. They paid their officers mighty high salaries, and there were such a lot of vice-presidents and directors and such, and there was that man named Insull; look what he did.

But the coal- and ice-dealers who eventually brought suit at Knox- ville and Birmingham saw which side their bread was buttered on, and from as far away as New York they looked like local people. And the beauty of a stockholders' suit was that the company could go ahead and sell, as disinterested and unselfish as you please, with only a few tears for the sacrificially low price. When the sale was blocked, it would not only look better but it would create delays, during which it might be possible to get things straightened out with those crazy New Dealers in Washington.

Nobody knows if this was an actual plan. But it worked, at least as far as the delay. And it is plain to see that the regional planning of the power companies could, from the first, be summed up in two words: divide and delay. City against city, county against county, one group of politicians against another, one state against another, one region against the rest of the country, and idealists against realists even among the government planners—these made the divisions. Court injunctions and long-drawn-out trials made the delay.

The delays worked so well, indeed, that after 1934 it was unnecessary to cede any more territory, and the companies sat tight on what came to be called their "Hindenburg line." Their lawyers did the work. Suits by minority stockholders to break contracts, suits to enjoin the use of PWA funds to build municipal plants in sixty-one towns, suits challenging the legality of farmers' co-operatives, suits charging con- spiracy by the government of the United States—they have all been tried, and they have all been successful in causing delays. The two suits that got as far as the Supreme Court, so causing the most satisfactory delay, questioned the right of the government, through the Tennes- see Valley Authority, to sell power—a right which the government first assumed at Muscle Shoals in 1921.

Whether eventual court decisions were for or against, the power of injunction was worth trying whenever it caused delay, because any action postponing construction or sale of power from the dams would hurt the project. If you could prevent any big sales of power, it would be possible to show such a loss as must have resulted if, after expensive search and equipment produced the first Model V Ford, the Ford Motor company had been enjoined from selling cars. As long as citizens of Chattanooga, Memphis, Knoxville, and the "Tri-Cities" could be kept from buying TVA current, taxpayers' investment in the dams could be kept from showing any real return.

Then it was wearisome, and even embarrassing, for Knoxville—TVA headquarters—not to have TVA power. It was disappointing to Chattanooga and Memphis, which had voted for it, not to have it. And it seemed unreasonable that the little Shoals cities, which had been disappointed so often, couldn't buy the current that was generated right there. In Sheffield it was still so dark that the train conductor held down a lantern to guide the traveler, and candles in the hotel rooms bore testimony to the unreliability of the company service. In Florence the hospital was unable to install a new sterilizer because the power lines were overloaded, and new consumers were not served unless they were willing to pay cash for the installation, just like the farmers.

But the South is used to waiting, and it's just possible that in trying to tie things up the smart lawyers over-reached themselves and succeeded too well. While the courts granted injunctions, TVA went ahead building dams. There is a certain amount of persuasion about a big, expensive structure that just sits and says: "Well, here I am; what are you going to do about me?" It's possible that there never would have been a Tennessee Valley Authority if it hadn't been for Wilson dam, sitting there and saying that at the Shoals.

While the lawyers wrangled, granddaddy longlegs of steel and copper spanned the Valley; and the judges sat at Chattanooga under a mural that pictured a high-power transmission line as part of a rural landscape. It is not suggested that they were influenced by this pretty picture, but it is obvious that the court itself was a different sort of

tribunal from Judge Grubb's court at Birmingham, where the Alabama Power case, known to lawyers as the Ashwander case, was
tried. Judge William I. Grubb of Birmingham, a seventy-two-year-old
corporation lawyer appointed by Taft, held that the government could
not sell power: "If there was a question of doing an illegal business
or letting a product go to waste, as I see it the government would have
to let the product go to waste." His view was reversed by the circuit
court at New Orleans and later by the sound physics of the Supreme
Court in holding that "the power of falling water was an inevitable
incident of the construction of the dam." But the Ashwander decision,
somewhat laboriously catching up with the plans of 1917 and the
practices of 1925, was specifically confined to Wilson dam.

This did not settle the question. As far back as 1934 the Edison
Electric Institute made public a report that TVA was "palpably unconstitutional." Mr. James M. Beck and the late Newton D. Baker
both said so, and were retained as counsel for the nineteen companies
which united to sue TVA on every possible count.

By the time the case was tried at Chattanooga in 1937 it was an
eighteen-power-company suit, Georgia Power being out; and if the
utilities had fifty-two lawyers, TVA had a Buffalo Republican, John
Lord O'Brian, as special counsel. The court was presided over by
Judge Florence Allen. They say a woman named Anna Ella Carroll
was responsible for the success of the Union campaign in Tennessee,
during the war. As the court decision was unanimous, it would be too
much to give Judge Allen entire credit, but she did have a record of
approving social legislation while one of the other judges had granted
some power-company injunctions.

The utilities seemed to consider it very harsh of the court to say
that the government had the right not merely to curtail their business
by competitive sale of power, but to destroy their business if it should
choose to do so. But what is government for if it hasn't got that
right? Back in the days when the infant Alabama Power company
was objecting to taxation instead of bragging about what it paid, they
were saying that "the power to tax is the power to destroy." So it is.
But you have to consider that, as Dr. Arthur Morgan once observed,

the government is asked to create and maintain monopolies by granting franchises. The power that creates and maintains has to be able to destroy.

The Supreme Court decision of January 30, 1939, was no surprise even to the stock market; if the court of 1936 could decide that Wilson dam was legal, it seemed safe to suppose that the court as now constituted would say the same thing of all the dams. It was to be expected that Justice McReynolds, of Tennessee, would dissent. Since the plaintiffs said that Chattanooga snubbed them on the issue of due process, perhaps it was to be regretted that Justice Black of Alabama did not take the opportunity to say once more that the fourteenth amendment applies to people and not to corporations.

At any rate, the three dams at work in the Valley, and the others being built, are still legitimate. It remains only to consider the court costs; in 1936 the Federal Power Commission estimated that 278 injunctions had cost 196 public authorities some $376,233 in actual litigation costs, and nearly twelve millions in indirect expenses. In 1938 TVA estimated that forty-one suits brought by private power companies had cost the Authority nearly six million dollars, $403,642 of this in direct legal expenses; and had cost consumers deprived of cheap power over seven millions more. Of course you have to figure that court costs on the utilities side are always paid by the consumer, who may or may not be a taxpayer contributing to both sides.

Reading in the Dark

Woe unto them . . . that put darkness for light, and light for darkness.

Therefore is judgment far from us, neither doth justice overtake us: we wait for light, but behold obscurity.

Court delays, intended to give the Supreme Court time to have its say about the constitution, went on until public opinion had a say about the court. So it was necessary to see what could be done with public opinion.

Fortunately the power industry was already organized on that

front long before TVA began. The NELA, or the National Electric
Light Association, was not an alphabetic government agency. It was
a publicity organization for the utilities, and perhaps its crowning
achievement was back in the Hoover days when, through a crack press
agent, it induced the United States post office to put pictures of lamps
on stamps.

Some other NELA ideas were to print and provide to kindergartens
a little booklet called *The Ohm Queen.* For older readers they had
what they called "Bruce Barton stuffers," inserts for electric-light
bills. Other educational activities ranged from subsidies to needy
college professors to a present of eighty thousand dollars to the General Federation of Women's Clubs, which investigated the use of
electricity in the home and reported its findings in the slick-paper
magazines.

When the utilities undertook to establish friendly relations with
hard-headed business men, it was found that money need not be
spent, but merely parked. The president of a Philadelphia utilities
company wrote to the president of a company on the Pacific Coast:

> We have at this time accounts with 230 country banks scattered all
> over our territory, and while our policy keeps an average of around a
> million and a half dollars tied up in balances in these country depositories,
> we believe it worth while; first, because the service they render to us is
> worth something; and second, because it cements their friendship and
> co-operation. Incidentally we require no interest on these deposits.

That was the North talking to the West, and it's possible that down
South they never even got a smell of the money. But bankers do tend
to think alike, and the *Southern Banker,* in its "Industrial Recovery
Edition," published in January 1934, spoke kindly of the "magnificent
public work" of the Tennessee Valley Authority, but worried lest the
advantages of "increasing employment, reforestation, etc.," be defeated by the sale of power. "Bankers should throw the full weight of
their influence against this use of untaxed government power in competition with private enterprise and private investment in excess of
$1,150,000,000."

Other business interests such as the life-insurance companies, with utilities stocks, were willing to throw the full weight of their influence in the same direction. Newspapers and magazines were favorable; a report of the NELA press bureau found it "amazing and valuable" that small papers were willing to print publicity releases in their editorial columns. But big papers and magazines that wrote their own editorials came to the same conclusions. The 1929 advertising expenditures of the industry have been estimated to be more than the cost of Norris dam.

As Mr. Merlin H. Aylesworth, at that time manager of NELA, said to a meeting of the southeastern division of NELA at Birmingham in 1924: "Don't be afraid of the expense. The public pays the expense."

They didn't neglect the Valley; one editorial service had its headquarters at Florence, Alabama, and in one year they landed over a thousand of their prepared editorials in Valley papers. In North Carolina the NELA bureau went after "prominent names," and was happy to have articles signed by the attorney-general of North Carolina, the president of the state press association, the secretary of the state merchants' association. With the help of a University of Tennessee professor, the director of publicity of the Alabama Power company was able to supply speech material to the governor of Tennessee; he had already obliged the governor of Georgia.

Eventually, over the protests of what was said to be Washington's most formidable lobby, the Federal Trade Commission investigated. In 1934 a published report covered the activities just touched on and others even more fascinating, with the result that NELA is no more. It was succeeded by the Edison Electric Institute, and nobody has investigated that. The NELA manager, Mr. Aylesworth, had already been nominated by Mr. Owen D. Young to be a director of the NBC radio network. Later Mr. Aylesworth became publisher of the Scripps-Howard papers, which had been inhospitable to NELA releases, but were about to switch from pro- to anti-New Deal.

You might say, though, that NELA did its work so well that some of its efforts survived. Many college professors still oppose public power; only last year a former trustee of the New York state power authority said that every department of electrical engineering in the country was "operated essentially as an adjunct to the private power industry." As for the bankers, the mayor of a Birmingham suburb wanted Congress to investigate "the extent to which private sources of finance have been closed" to cities anxious to buy distributing plants for TVA power. As for the papers, you only have to read them.

But from the first the most valuable work for the utilities was done free, by people honestly convinced that the American standard of living, "already the highest in the world," should not be tampered with; that the constitution was "not to be lightly discarded"; and that the Tennessee Valley was imperiled by "a dangerous venture into Socialism." Back in the NELA days, one of the state bureau directors said that, faced with an argument for public ownership, his idea "would be not to try logic or reason, but to try to pin the Bolshevik idea on my opponent."

Such efforts ranged from the attacks on TVA made over the radio by the Crusaders, in speeches dividing the population into "reds, pinks, yellows" and "true blues," to the announcement in Document 127 of the American Liberty League that the trend towards collectivism in the TVA area constituted a threat to the American system. These glittering generalities were much the safest arguments, because every time the power-company apologists adventured into facts they managed to contradict themselves.

For example, one early propagandist said that TVA would waste the people's money because the three Hell Gate stations of the New York Edison company could generate as much power as the whole Valley. In a little book published by the YMCA, this was discovered to be giving about two million kilowatts too much power to hell. So next thing they started talking about a power surplus.

Mr. Owen D. Young, chairman of the board of General Electric, was one who worried over a possible surplus; he couldn't have known about the appliances his company was selling in the Valley. And Mr. Wendell Willkie accused TVA of overbuilding while he complained that Commonwealth and Southern just couldn't afford construction costs.

But the worst contradiction was between the talk about handing private systems a cup of hemlock juice, and that about the amount of money the power companies were making. According to their arguments, power earnings over the country and especially in the Valley should have gone into a decline when TVA began to sell power. Exactly the opposite happened: power use increased steadily from 1933 on, and in 1935 passed the boom year of 1929. It reached an "all-time high" in 1937 and another in December 1938.

Nor were the sales made at a loss. This was an awkward situation and the New York *Herald Tribune* used lots of semi-colons trying to crow and cry at the same time; a typical headline read:

ELECTRIC BOND AND SHARE HEAD
DECRIES U.S. COMPETITION;
REPORTS INCREASE IN NET

Commonwealth and Southern was embarrassed a great deal by having its earnings rise right up—they netted twenty cents on the common stock in 1937, going up from thirteen cents in 1936 and one cent in 1935. The president of the company hastened to say that the Northern companies were doing better than the Southern ones. Yet all four of the Valley companies showed healthy advances in spite of the dark forebodings broadcast by the parent company in paid and unpaid newspaper space, and in radio addresses by Mr. Willkie. Mr. Willkie is fast on his feet, but he served, so to speak, right into the net. Take the Tennessee Electric Power company; in one of their conversations at the White House, President Roosevelt reminded Mr. Willkie that in the years from 1933 to 1936 the company's production of current had gone up nearly forty-four percent, and its gross income from fifty-four to sixty-seven millions.

By 1938 they were able to announce a decrease in the consolidated earnings of the Commonwealth and Southern subsidiaries, but subsidiary losses were not uniform; the Tennessee Electric Power company made money. The slump in power sales corresponded to the general industrial "recession" but did not extend to home use of electricity.

Paralleling the structure of the four state companies under Commonwealth and Southern is the corporation pyramid made by the city service companies—Memphis Power and Light, Birmingham Power and Light, the Tennessee Public Service Corporation in Knoxville, the West Tennessee Power and Light company in Jackson, and so on. These are little octopus arms of National Power and Light, which in turn is a tentacle of Electric Bond and Share. Or, as the companies prefer to put it, in broad human terms, Electric Bond and Share is the parent company. These children didn't behave any better than the Commonwealth and Southern family, because they all picked the most embarrassing time to show healthy growth.

Today the actual complaint of the companies is not that they aren't making money, plenty of it, but that they can't sell bonds or "refund." When a company makes money, it can make more money by redeeming its high-interest bonds and issuing low-interest ones. The talk about the serious situation of the Southern companies doesn't mean that they aren't making good money, but that they can't trade in their securities. It's too bad.

Mr. Willkie has often sobbed in print over this situation, saying first that the Southern companies couldn't be expected to spend any money on construction while they were in this hazardous situation, and second (the pressure of business apparently becoming too great) that Commonwealth and Southern had actually advanced thirty millions to the Southern companies for construction purposes. In his sorrow Mr. Willkie seemed to forget that one of the reasons holding companies have so far been let live is that they are supposed to render such services to their tentacles, or tots.

As for TVA, its public relations have not suffered so much from contradictions and it has even been able to overcome some of the handicaps of press opposition simply by making news. Let no one overlook the fact that there was plenty of press hostility, even in the Valley; but the Valley was able to set straight some criticism made elsewhere. When the *Magazine of Wall Street* said of TVA payments for grave removal, "apparently they bury them cheap in Tennessee," that wasn't the sort of remark to sit well down South; and some other complaints didn't make sense if you were on the ground. To persuade readers of the *Saturday Evening Post* that TVA employees were irresponsible joyriders on government gasoline, you could take the total amount of gasoline bought by the Authority in a year and divide by the number of gallons it takes to run a car, and prove that they must drive around and around the world every day. But in the Valley, people know that on a big construction job you use gasoline for other engines than those of passenger cars.

Or you see where the Authority paid $4500 for a jack, and you jump to the conclusion that their object was to improve the breed of draft animals on Tennessee Valley farms. You note further that they sold a jackass for $350, and you say these moonstruck theorists must have let the taxpayers in for a whopping loss. Newspapers everywhere print that one, and a congressman from New England reads it into the *Record,* and most of the papers don't have space to follow up with the correction that the jack they paid $4500 for was a mechanical one to use in building dams. The one with long ears that they sold for $350 had cost $290.

In both these cases you see that the tendency is for the cost critics to forget that any construction is going on. They are all ready to believe that TVA spends its money just for fun or to spite the power companies, instead of in building dams.

When they do count the cost of dams, they insist that the only reason for building a dam is to generate power. That may be a power company's only reason, but if you live in a country subject to floods you can think of others without half trying.

Direct argument between the government and the power companies has mostly been over the "yardstick" idea. In his speech at Tupelo the President said: "In spite of fairy tales that have been spread in other parts of the country, your power system is still paying taxes to the municipality." Whereupon Mr. Wendell Willkie hastened to find the most polite words in which to call the President of the United States a liar. In a press release he said that TVA was paying only five percent taxes while the power companies had to pay fifteen or twenty percent; so the President had been "incorrectly advised." Mr. Willkie added that TVA enjoyed other advantages peculiar to government enterprise; it could frank its bills and ship freight at low rates.

Dr. Arthur Morgan took over the job of explaining that the president of Commonwealth and Southern had been incorrectly advised. He explained about the taxes: TVA paid five percent, that being the amount due the states of Alabama and Tennessee under the TVA Act; but it "set aside" in its cost figures 12.5 percent, an amount slightly higher than private utilities were paying in the Valley. It was "pure fiction" about franking bills; not selling to retail purchasers, the Authority sends out no bills. As for the freight saving, careful calculation showed that it would take a consumer more than fifty years to save a dime on what TVA saved by the government rate.

These were just the opening salvos in a long yardstick war. A lot of the arguments consisted in playing with the word "yardstick"; it was "rubber," or "warped," or a "hundred-foot chain." The *Magazine of Wall Street* found it "as crooked as a ram's horn," while the *Gas Age-Record* feared that it was heavy enough to be used as a cudgel against "thrifty investors." It was Dr. Arthur Morgan who, in 1935, insisted it was "a full 36 inches."

They argued over the yardstick as a whole, and they argued more over the adjustment clause inserted to permit a surcharge on industrial and commercial sales, while the city distributing plants got on their feet. One objector said that clause changed the yardstick into a slide rule. On the other hand Mr. Samuel Ferguson of Hartford found that the surcharge changed the whole undertaking from "a fraudulent political yardstick to an honest effort to endeavor to demonstrate the effect of low price on sales volume."

Mr. Ferguson did get the idea. The price-volume test is the important thing, because if the country is to go on or even to keep from slipping back into another slough, it must devise some economy of increasing use. If the TVA can prove that the way to increase consumption is first to reduce prices, we may have an answer that will work for more things than power.

Among all the complaints about the yardstick idea, there seems to be a fundamental mistake: people think that TVA is selling yardsticks.

A yardstick is not a commodity, not even a price, but a unit of measure. There is no need to confuse the TVA yardstick with the rate at which TVA sells electricity to the consumer. There is no indication that there was such confusion in the mind of the government, but there is plenty of it outside.

As far as sales go, the government, not being in business to make a profit, can and should sell electricity for as little as possible. Its rates belong right on the ground level, as long as they will eventually, over a long period, pay for the dams. A yardstick, on the other hand, should show what it costs to produce and sell electricity. On the rate-determines-cost theory, the rate is part of the yardstick, rather than the yardstick part of the rate.

If the costs had to be determined by the government, the companies that drowned out the figures in a flood of water have only themselves to blame. Everybody knows the story of the Yankee company that put down a natural lake on its property at the "reproduction cost" for an artificial one. That was just a sample of the watering done before the Federal Trade Commission reported to the Senate that after several years of looking over the utilities it had found write-ups amounting to nearly a billion and a half dollars in top-holding, sub-holding, and operating companies. So for the Authority to clutter up its demonstrations of actual production costs with "capital charges" equivalent to those of private industry would be silly. The capital charges of different corporations vary, and that's just what we're getting at.

Under the present system, some of those charges are fair. But the power companies don't like to talk about them. They would prefer the consumer to think, as the seller always likes the buyer to think, that this business is done for love and not for money. They do not want to commercialize their art by mention of the ugly word profit. When the holding company structure is revealed, some corporations feel as outraged as do persons of great wealth when confronted by publicity for income-tax returns. Howls of unfairness over the TVA yardstick are due to this rude revelation that not the Ohm Queen but vulgar money makes the horsepower go.

An elementary retort to the yardstick idea is the reiteration that

TVA has its own system of bookkeeping. In 1935 the *Magazine of Wall Street* said that a TVA director "has frankly admitted that TVA could not compete with the private companies if its books were kept by the same standards as the private companies." The nearest thing to such an admission seemed to be the observation that TVA had "no $100,000 a year executives to pay, no million-dollar political lobbies to contribute to, no fake telegrams to be paid for, no dividends to be paid on watered stock."

But there is no doubt whatever that the utilities people adopted their own system of reporting on TVA, including certain basic fallacies which were repeated again and again, in spite of corrections made publicly and privately, and so showing that somebody hoped the constant repetition would make the wishing true. Some of these basic fallacies were:

That the expense of the project would be $1,400,000,000, sometimes referred to in "round numbers" as two billions.
That TVA paid no taxes.
That TVA made no charges for depreciation.
That TVA paid no "capital charges."

The easiest story to trace is the one about the final cost. That goes back to the army report. At the time when President Hoover was commander-in-chief of the army, army engineers made a million-dollar survey and a report on the possibilities of flood control, navigation, and power development on the Tennessee. The engineers differed among themselves but on the whole they were against any such steps, if taken by the government.

Ever since, opponents of the TVA program have been quoting the cost figures in the army report, which actual costs have shown to be hypothetical and in fact too high. They have been quoting the opinion of one group of army engineers, flatly contradicted by another group, that high dams to combine flood control, depth control for navigation, and power production are a mistake. And Mr. Wendell Willkie of Commonwealth and Southern, and General Hugh Johnson of Mr.

Merlin ("The Public Pays") Aylesworth's papers, are still of the opinion that the army engineers are the ablest in the country.

Of course the army engineers are capable, or everybody hopes they are; they have charge of the navigation locks on the Tennessee. But there is some reason for belief that their million-dollar survey for President Hoover showed they didn't know any more about unified river control than army fliers knew about carrying mails. Army men are specialists, not all-round handy men or over-all planners. A young engineer who had worked for both the army engineers and for TVA said the West Point men were fine organizers and disciplinarians and knew their stuff as far as it went, but they made no effort to save money or time or to use the brains of the man down the line. So he had turned down a better-paying army project to stay with TVA, and it was his private opinion that if the army had to tackle some of the problems TVA had in the Valley, they'd be lost like a ball in high grass.

Anyhow, with all their painstaking paper work, the thing they were bound to be wrong about in the prosperity era was costs. Back in war time, when they built Wilson dam, everybody knows they paid two or three times too much for it; and the army figures of the Hoover period were almost as bad.

So whenever anybody quotes $1,400,000,000 as the final cost of all the dam-building in the Valley, you have to remember that is what the army engineers guessed it might cost and not what TVA is spending. So far, TVA has spent only a little over $200,000,000 and the estimate is something like $500,000,000 for the whole job.

The other misstatements about taxes, depreciation, and interest have been set right many times; the last time, officially, was when the allocation of costs made last summer was accompanied by a statement that, allowing for depreciation and three percent interest, normal power revenues from the dams in operation should cover operating costs and return the entire investment for flood control and navigation in thirty years. The TVA act provides for tax payments to the states; the TVA regulations for sale of power to municipalities provide for tax payments to the cities. It is true that TVA does not pay federal taxes, being a federal enterprise.

To hear them tell it, one of the chief reasons for the existence of power companies it that they may contribute to the public welfare by paying taxes; and so it is interesting to discover that as recently as the days of President Wilson the Alabama Power company was threatening to throw down its cards and quit if it had to pay taxes at all. In those days it was just a simple little company owned in Alabama, its organizer and president an individualist named William Patrick Lay. After writing the act of Congress that authorized his Coosa dam, Mr. Lay devoted himself to fighting off the "taxationists" who would demand what he called "government tribute." Mr. Lay fought on strict constitutional grounds, for riparian rights, which he considered as sacred as home and fireside; for states' rights, which, on the power issue, he considered far to outweigh the importance of the slave question; and finally for the corporation interpretation of that fourteenth amendment which his father, a Confederate hero in river fighting along the Tennessee, had fought to keep out of the constitution. In other words Mr. Lay fought as hard, and on the same grounds, as Mr. Wendell Willkie; but he fought to avoid taxes while Mr. Willkie fights for the privilege of paying them.

If you want to be charitable and find some basis for the charge of no depreciation, you can go back to the first year of TVA and find that a United States comptroller doing a last good turn for the Hoover administration chided the Authority for not allowing depreciation on the work under construction, while charging off a good-sized loss against Wilson dam. The latter charge was, of course, no ordinary depreciation; it was an admission that the dam had been built at a time when it cost too much, and there seemed no more reason to carry the original cost figure than to retain an eighteen-dollar price tag on a war-time silk shirt.

While depreciation charges now put down are, no doubt, proper, it is interesting to consider that the Authority is taking extraordinary steps to make its dams last. Their durability does depend on what can be done to stop erosion, but the Authority is better able than most to see that reservoirs do not fill with mud from sources upstream. In twenty-three years, the privately built dam at Hale's Bar, the only

Tennessee dam still functioning under private control, had a third
of its reservoir space silted up. Then the building of Norris dam
doubled the power capacity of Hale's Bar. How was the private company to allocate depreciation and appreciation in that case?

Then, if you want to exercise your mind, you can figure that by
charging for depreciation on the extra money it spends to build for the
ages, a conscientious business makes the whole thing sound crazy.
Puzzling it out will be good practice if you intend to try to find out
what the utilities mean by capital charges.

And all the arguments have served a purpose; as time passed, the
public was bound to get better informed about TVA and the whole
power question. At the start people might have believed such a primitive economic fallacy as, choosing at random from the wealth of such
material published by the *Saturday Evening Post:* "Every time some-
one in Athens, Alabama, or in Dayton, Tennessee, or in Tupelo, Mississippi, switches on his lights or tunes in his radio, each one of us, in
Boston and Peoria and Spokane, has a little more added to his taxes."
The objections now have to be as close to the truth as the comment
of the New York *Times* on the publication of cost allocations and of
the declaration that TVA should be able to pay out the investment for
flood control and navigation in thirty years: "In order to accomplish
such results, utility circles believe, the TVA will have to enlarge the
scope of its operations in the Tennessee Valley through further competition with private companies, unless it buys them."

In other words, it is admitted that the use determines the cost.

What the Public Wants

Multitudes, multitudes in the valley of decision: for the day of the Lord is near in the valley of decision.

And there shall be a very great valley; and half of the mountain shall remove toward the north, and half of it toward the south.
And ye shall flee to the valley of the mountains. . . .
And it shall come to pass in that day, that the light shall not be clear, nor dark. . . .
But it shall come to pass, that at evening time it shall be light.

What the arguments come to is that some people want public power and some want private power, and you can figure on either side.

There is a third possibility, cheap power, without regard to how you get it, and TVA was willing to proceed on the simple theory that it wouldn't matter who provided the power if it was cheap enough. As long as the price was kept low, some people would prefer to buy from private companies; and maybe some would even be willing to pay three or four or six percent extra to retain the privilege of trading with a ruggedly individualistic corporation. Up in the Carolina mountains is a crossroads storekeeper with a conscience like that. He complained because the single droplight in his store, and a waffle iron his wife used, and two ordinary home refrigerators he was using, cost him eleven to sixteen dollars a month. But he wasn't interested in TVA rates; he didn't believe in government in business.

It was no doubt with such consumers in mind that President Roosevelt asked Mr. Wendell Willkie if he would consider, say, seven to eight percent a fair return on utilities stocks. Mr. Willkie, like Dr. Arthur Morgan, did not answer. But writing in the *Atlantic Monthly*,[1] Mr. Willkie had already testified that the Southern companies of Commonwealth and Southern had to pay as much as 39.5 cents out of every dollar for borrowed capital. Admission that the "cost" of private capital is so high is staggering to the ordinary citizen, because what Mr. Willkie sees as a cost must be a profit to somebody,

[1] August 1937.

and certainly it is a loss to the consumer. When private corporations admit the necessity of "capital charges" of this sort, it is true that they cannot hope to compete with a government interest rate of three percent. But do they expect TVA to set down a charge of 39.5 percent to save the face of private management?

Later Mr. Willkie explained in a radio talk that it was necessary to pay so much for money because the small investors were scared. Of course any small investor would be scared to death if offered an investment paying 39.5 percent, and of course no utility stock pays that; it is the holding-company structure that absorbs the money. Back in 1927, a Western power company was found to return 96.8 percent on its common stock, but of course the stock was owned by a holding company and the holding company was affiliated, like some of the Valley companies, with Electric Bond and Share. Those were the days; just the year before, the Alabama Power company and the Georgia Power company went into a merger that brought a revaluation of more than twenty millions to each company, without additional investment, but presumably with "capital charges."

Reversing this process under direction of the SEC, one Eastern power company lately proposed to write down its common stock, owned of course by a holding company, from seven millions to a dollar. A holding company proposed write-downs, throughout its system of affiliates, amounting to $195,000,000. Maybe this sort of thing scares big and little investors as much as does TVA competition. In fact, they might put TVA out of business if they could find a way to harness the falling water in utilities stocks.

The funny thing is the way business itself has spread the scare talk. Anybody could see how reluctant the companies were to follow up the big sales with new construction; with sales up thirty or forty percent, they dropped their line-building appropriations down to a third of what they had been. The explanation offered by a group of utilities executives was that capital was frightened.

Mr. Willkie felt that the utilities had a right to know "what the government plans to do with them." This sounds reasonable until you stop to think that no sooner does the government pass laws to show what it intends to do, than private industry stops everything to "test" the law in the courts.

Maybe the mistake has been in expecting too much courage from capital. There used to be an idea that there were two sorts of investments, risky ones bringing big returns and safe ones bringing much less. One sort was for rugged male capitalists with large mustaches, gold watch chains, and cigars, the other for widows and orphans. If you look into the history of the railroads, you may begin to wonder if even the first sort of capitalist ever took any real risks; he seems, nearly always, to have had or thought he had an inside tip. And his rarity today could be explained by the fact that Uncle Sam, who once financed his business expansion with land grants, has quit making outright gifts to private companies and now asks for a little security.

But the widows and orphans content with a modest income have vanished too. When they talked of a power pool to combine public and private power facilities and give utilities investments the stability of government bonds, the physical problem was simple: it was easy to show a physical likeness between the Valley area and Great Britain, where the Central Electricity Board has been doing a successful job for years. Under the combination of public and private power developments which they call the "Grid" plan, the British government owns transmission lines and makes arrangements for most effective use of the pooled power. The governing board, an independent government agency with a separate budget, separate issuance of securities, and freedom from much red tape, was said to resemble TVA. Mr. Lilienthal made a trip to England to see how it worked, and the same people who thought the Swedish "middle way" might be transplanted to this country were full of hope.

But this country isn't Sweden and it isn't England. At the World Power Conference, American observers noted with some surprise that the foreign delegates were inclined to look on utilities investments much as we look on government bonds, that is, as safe three percent investments. Over here, apparently, since Insull was acquitted, we haven't quit dreaming of big profits—and no risks.

In other words, the big companies want everything; the luxury of 39.5 percent rent on their capital, if they choose to pay it, plus a promise of no interference with their business. As long as they can take this stand, the citizen-consumer should look with disfavor on any pooling of private and public resources. With utility organization "a ninety-six inch dog wagged by a four-inch tail," the tail might be active enough to wag a few government boards.

As for what the public wants, a Harvard professor, writing in the "Voice of Business" section of the New York *Sun,* January 8, 1938, gave it as his opinion "that the people of this country have reached a conclusion about their railroads and public utilities and that its name is government ownership." A Princeton university survey found other authorities willing to prophesy that the change to public power would come within twenty years. If and when that happens, the real fun will come in deciding what to pay for the property of the private companies. You can say that the TVA negotiations, setting precedents in that way, will be as important a yardstick as anything they can prove about power production.

Look at the arguments they have had at Memphis, and all over the Valley. Mr. Willkie's proposal to let SEC fix prices was another idea for delay and division, but they've done well enough at holding up a settlement without that complication. And so far, by holding out, the companies have made money. The second time TVA bought the Knoxville plant, they paid about two million dollars more for it than they had agreed to pay four years before. The company claimed to have spent some $800,000 for improvements, but beyond that it seemed that the city and TVA just thought it would be nice to pay the preferred stockholders $60 instead of $40 a share. The city didn't much care, because the money had to come from RFC if they bought, or from PWA if they built. The opponents of TVA weren't grateful; some papers complained that the "common stockholders" would get nothing, and the *Saturday Evening Post* said they'd be "wiped out," but there were no common stockholders; all the common stock was owned by the holding company.

But it looked as if the government was trying to pay for peace.

There were precedents for that in the Valley; when they named the Free State of Franklin, they wrote to Benjamin Franklin about it, maybe thinking he would do something for his godchild. But all they got was advice; Franklin wrote to Sevier to make treaties instead of encroachments on Indian lands, because "war with them costs more than any possible price they may ask." Of course Franklin went on to say that the Indians "usually give good bargains in the way of purchase." It's not certain what he would have advised if the price of peace had been measured in millions of dollars instead of boatloads of trade goods.

But there was a later, and closer, parallel in the Yazoo case. There the government commission well knew that the claims had no standing in equity, and they were not cheap, but they recommended payment because it was either pay the five million or split the party and the country.

Buying utilities, you do expect to wring some of the water out; estimates of the value of private investments in the Valley, made by the companies themselves or by their spokesmen in print, run all the way from $500,000,000 to two or three times that. Smart people have calculated that if Uncle Sam wanted to act like a regular trader and buy control of the power corporations, instead of buying them outright, he could get hold of all the utilities in the country for $500,000,-000. And he owes it to his stockholders, the American public, not to spend money foolishly.

But so far he has left the trading to the other side. After the Knoxville arrangements were made, there was a postponement while they waited for bonds to be turned in, and the delay wasn't due to hesitation over the price, because the price offered was $975, while the bonds had sold for as little as $572.50 that year. People were trading; in one day, curb sales amounted to seventy thousand dollars and only three thousand dollars' worth of bonds were deposited for sale. It gave Mr. Lilienthal a chance to remark that they couldn't all be owned by widows and orphans.

You want to be fair to bona-fide stockholders, of course. If you pay too little for a power company while leaving, say, an armament manufacturer to do business as usual, you just penalize the man who put his money into kilowatts instead of killing. On the other hand, is it fair for the government to save the power stockholders and leave railroad investors to mourn their losses?

Setting aside ballyhoo, there are three ways to figure what the companies are worth. There is "replacement cost," the companies' own happy invention and a beautiful thing in an era of high prices, though not so good in a slump. There is the "prudent investment" theory, commended by the President. There is the "actual cost plus depreciation," the basis for negotiation picked by Mr. Lilienthal, which has the advantage of demanding a peep at the company books.

And there is a fourth valuation, which maybe only a taxpayer would think of; anyhow, it isn't likely to be used. That is the value at which the property is assessed for taxation.

Since there will be yells of murder no matter what you do, it is well for kind-hearted folks to remember that, as the meaner Indians scalped each other when left to their own savage ways, the private corporations are accustomed to being skinned in their own wars. That is what unrestricted competition means, and they asked for it just as the Cherokees said: "We cannot live without war," and what would be the use of living if they weren't allowed to fight the Tuscaroras?

Of course, to hear them tell it, nobody ever worried over industrial changes before the days of government competition; but you know better if you stop to think. When it came to fighting the government, the coal and ice people joined with the power companies, but that was just like the Chickamaugas joining with the Cherokees; can't you remember when everybody had to feel sorry for the ice man because the electric refrigerator took away his job?

Right in the middle of the power controversy came a little private invention that might make as much difference in the long run as the Rust cotton-picker. Columbia university and several business buildings in greater New York put in power plants using Diesel engines.

When a Brooklyn department store started up its plant in 1936, Mayor La Guardia said that New York now had its own "footstick" for power costs. After two years the store estimated costs to be half the utility rate. Diesels are no answer to the problem of individual house-holders, but they are something for hospitals and theaters and such to consider, and they're using them on the Southern trains between Chattanooga and Tuscumbia.

When private business looks at these hazards it gets frightened and raises its capital charges, but when taxpayers look at them they can figure so much off the real value of utilities property to be purchased. With all these complications, of course the job of buying out the private companies will take a lot longer and be more trouble than building dams, but they are making some progress in the Valley. When they started the suit decided by the Supreme Court in 1939, it was eighteen power companies against TVA, or hydra against hydro. It ended with only fourteen suing; the others had sold out.

9. WIND

Politicians Talk

And, behold, the Lord passed by, and a great and strong wind rent the mountains, and brake in pieces the rocks before the Lord; but the Lord was not in the wind.

They've had strong winds at Tupelo, Mississippi, and orators too. Southerners still remember the mongrel metaphors of Private John Allen, known politically as the ranks of the Confederate army, who hailed from there. But Tupelo's present Congressman John Rankin is something of an orator too.

Congressman Rankin, one of the authors of the TVA Act, is at his best on that subject. He is at his worst on labor, but you have to consider that he represents Tupelo on that. When they were having their trouble with the National Labor Relations Board, they wrote to Washington and asked him to do something quick.

Congressman Rankin said on the House floor that the Labor Board had "deliberately closed" the Tupelo Cotton Mills. He suggested that the Board was "conspiring with Communistic influences to destroy Southern industries" in order to aid Eastern industry. He said: "The ruthless manner in which they helped to destroy and forced the liquidation of the cotton mill in Tupelo, throwing all the employees out of work, and the brutal manner in which they are now trying to destroy the garment factories in that city, is enough to stir the people of my state to revolt." But the congressman felt that he could not withhold his own protest "until the streets of Southern towns are stained with the blood of innocent people as a result of the activities of these irresponsible representatives of the so-called Labor Relations Board."

Not only did Congressman Rankin see the "Communist demon CIO" behind the NLRB; he was confident that the passage of the wage-hour bill would mean "the end of human liberty as we know it." The Tupelo Chamber of Commerce sent him a letter of thanks.

Southerners expect their Washington representatives to make rip-roaring speeches, and some of them seemed to get such a habit of speaking against the government that they didn't know how to stop when the Democrats got in. Of course you could expect them to raise their voices against the wage-hour bill and the anti-lynching bill, both contrary to Southern traditions. You could expect them to oppose court and departmental reorganization, because any efficiency added to the federal government conflicts with the idea of states' rights, and there was too much court-packing in Reconstruction days.

But there was too much spending then too, and some think there is now; anyhow, when a national government undertakes to interfere with business you have to look out for your state. Take North Carolina, where Senator Bailey told the New Deal to keep out. In North Carolina the Duke Power company and the Aluminum company have as good a hold on power resources as Niagara Power has in New York, and expecting all North Carolina to be for TVA is like expecting upstate New York to embrace a public power project.

In Alabama, Oscar W. Underwood had done his best to save the Shoals for private business by opposing the Norris bill of 1924. In those days there was some idea of a lily-white Republican party in Birmingham, while last year the South's first Garner-for-President club was organized in Huntsville. But sensible folks in Alabama are coming to be for the New Deal with an adaptiveness exhibited by General Joe Wheeler, for whom the dam was named. General Wheeler, who led the Alabama infantry at Shiloh and made a famous leap over the Duck river to join Forrest in Tennessee, jumped again to fight with the United States army in the Spanish war; he is credited with taking to Santiago the rebel yell and a cry of "Charge 'em, boys,

the Yankees are runnin'." In Alabama they voted to send young
Lister Hill, for the wage-hour law as well as for TVA, to the Senate
instead of spellbinding Tom Heflin. And they started a state rural
electrification "authority."

But in Kentucky they think of coal. Back in 1933, when President
Roosevelt visited the Shoals, Congressman Andrew J. May of Kentucky was one of those who spoke in favor of federal power. Later
on, Congressman May came to describe the Tennessee Valley Authority as "a stench in the nostrils of those who cherish the ideals of
Thomas Jefferson." It appears that, as the wind changed, what the
congressman actually smelled was coal smoke. So there can be no
doubt that he was sincere in saying that, if only the Supreme Court
would declare the project unconstitutional, he would be "one of the
happiest men in Washington." That way, he would have been saved
deciding between flood control for Paducah and the interests of the
coal operators. In the end, as chairman of the House military affairs
committee, he saw it his duty to oppose the building of the Gilbertsville dam. Last fall Kentucky re-elected Congressman May.

The other Valley states weren't, until lately, bothered much by
business. In Virginia the chief industry is history, so they beat young
Mr. Dodd for Congress because you can't expect Virginians to vote
for any young man even if his daddy was an ambassador. Their
natural instinct is to vote for Washington or Madison, so they compromise on Carter Glass.

Mississippi and Georgia have to choose between private industry
as represented by the little textile mills, and public industry as represented by WPA. Mississippi's Senator Pat Harrison had no trouble
deciding; he was sure, when he considered the movement for higher
wages, that "the workers of the South, as a general rule, are not
interested in this agitation. . . . They are not appealing to Washington for regulation of their wages. They are more interested in holding
their jobs." [1]

At the same time, the senator was reasonably certain that people

[1] *Collier's,* January 22, 1938.

with money were interested in keeping it, and so, on the Senate
finance committee, he did his best to keep the moneyed people from
having to pay taxes.

It was Mississippi that figured out a cute way to use the WPA
when they arranged to build school factories to instruct young ladies
in the fine art of making hosiery for four dollars a week. Two towns
got the buildings and three others asked for appropriations before
Washington caught on, and WPA is still trying to get the money
back. It lost two ways, because the companies that moved down from
Pennsylvania and Indiana presumably left their Yankee workers to
go on WPA up there, and the relief wages are higher in the North.
Mississippi sponsored the plan in all innocence, though, because
Mississippi folks tax themselves to build factories under Governor
White's plan to "Balance Agriculture with Industry."

But look at Georgia—another hard-up state; and they've got an
almost perfect balance between agriculture and industry, not making
a living from either. So Georgia refuses to melt under the smiles of a
distinguished visitor to Warm Springs. When the President came
right out and mentioned poverty, speaking at Gainesville last year,
some of the people on the platform behind him looked like they could
chew nails, because the Georgia idea is that being poor is something
to be seen and not heard about. If they were to talk about their economic troubles they'd have to mention Sherman and that wouldn't
be polite to Yankee company, but you can't convert overnight a state
where Northern economy has been represented by the federal peni-
tentiary in Atlanta and the march to the sea.

Tennessee is the state that looks most complicated to an outsider.
In the first place they've got two parties there, as in North Carolina
and Kentucky, so you have to watch the elections as well as the primaries, and you don't just assume that Rep. is an abbreviation for
reprobate. Then, as regards TVA, they've got a history like Alabama.
Senator McKellar of Tennessee became such a strong supporter of
TVA that there was a proposal to name Pickwick dam for him. But
it's a matter of record that back in 1928 the senator filibustered for
twenty hours against the Norris bill of that year to develop the Shoals.

At that time Senator McKellar was particularly opposed to the building of Cove Creek, later called Norris, dam.

On the other hand ex-Senator Berry apparently looked forward to some development when he bought all those marble leases, and he wouldn't say he was opposed to TVA even when he was suing the Authority. Governor Browning of Tennessee was also in favor of TVA at the time he proposed to the President a plan for state purchase that might, it was thought, help the utilities. You won't find anybody in Tennessee politics who comes out and opposes TVA, not even the Republicans.

In the 1938 election you could say they voted for the people who were most definitely pro-TVA, such as a utilities commissioner running on a TVA platform; and they settled Senator Berry, and the governor. But it was hard to tell how much of the vote against Senator Berry was righteous indignation in the matter of the TVA marbles, and how much was because of his campaign against WPA and his demand for "rigid economy," except where government purchase of mineral rights was concerned; or how much was dislike for the fancy four-color posters he had printed by the pressmen's union. It was hard to tell how much of the vote against Governor Browning was due to his threat to send the 117th infantry to Memphis. Because the real mistake made by the Browning-Berry ticket was opposing Mr. Crump.

Some folks in Tennessee haven't kept track of an eminent Tennessean named Cordell Hull, but if you don't know who Mr. Crump is, you sure enough are an outsider. This year's election, like others before it, showed that the government of Tennessee is located on Adams avenue between Main and November 6th streets in Memphis. That is the office of E. H. Crump and Company, Investment Bankers. Mr. Crump holds no public office, but he was described in election speeches as so enjoying the love and respect of his fellow-townsmen as to be "entrusted with complete civic leadership over a period of twenty-five years." You could say the same of state leadership, because Mr. Crump had been for Governor Browning before and the governor was considered ungrateful for past favors.

Mr. Crump puts on a good show, and Memphis appreciates his provision of free picnics at the fair grounds, including concessions and Coca-Cola, to celebrate an election victory before it is won. Of course Mr. Crump is noted for his ability to forecast election results. Mathematical-minded persons notice the unanimity of election returns in Memphis; there have been cases of, say, exactly 46,363 votes for every Crump candidate from senator to dog-catcher. But that's just because Memphis folks agree with Mr. Crump. If you stand by him, he'll stand by you. So they say the dead will rise from their graves to vote for Mr. Crump's candidates, and Negroes who never get a chance to vote down in Alabama have come all the way to Memphis to be enfranchised.

Besides the threat of troops the loudspeakers made a lot of noise in the last election, including one on the governor's car that played "I Want to Meet the Bully of the Town." That one was said to have been brought up from Louisiana, a relic of the Long regime. But Mr. Crump had no trouble; things were so well under control that they say they gave the other side one of the boxes in the colored district just to prove they were fair. It was all so tame and so open and above-board that a visitor in town less than twenty-four hours was invited to hand out sample ballots at the polls, marked to show which candidates Mr. Crump favored.

Some think Mr. Crump is a little unsubtle. When he said, yes, the city would vote for TVA power, and they asked him by how much— say two to one?—he said he didn't think much of that sort of a vote; how about seventeen and a half to one? And seventeen and a half to one it was. They named November 6th street to celebrate the victory.

If you ask why Mr. Crump is for TVA, it goes back to the one defeat of his life—one time Mr. Crump was mayor of Memphis and they impeached him. The reformers got after him and the power company joined the reformers. Mr. Crump never forgot, and he has favored public power ever since. They say he wanted to build a municipal plant instead of buying out the power company, and you can't blame him for that because it would make more jobs. Jobs are

ALL GOD'S CHILLUN GOT SHOES, SUCH AS THEY ARE

GOING...

GOING...

GONE

BUT SOME FOLKS HAVE GOOD FARMS IN TENNESSEE

Where water runs off a hill farm, the soil goes, too, until there is no living for man or beast. In contrast, see the contented cows in fat, flat, and flourishing Middle Tennessee, where God put plenty of phosphates and they weren't washed away.

NORRIS POWER AND LIGHT ADD TO THE STATURE OF MAN

why, down on Beale street, and in the YWCA, and some say even in the Overton park zoo, Memphis votes for Mr. Crump.

Mr. Crump rides on the merry-go-round with his voters and he bets on the right horses in national politics, so Memphis gets New Deal appropriations and Mr. Crump gets the credit.

So far state legislatures in the Valley have co-operated pretty well with TVA, and the Authority has managed to sidestep control by state commissions. With regard to these commissions, Mr. Lilienthal, who served on one in Wisconsin, remarked at the start that "in effect, the utilities were regulating the regulators." In both Tennessee and Alabama the commissions claimed jurisdiction over TVA, and demanded the filing of schedules; the Authority complied but reserved its independence by doing so as a "courtesy." In the same way Mr. Lilienthal, subpoenaed to appear before the Tennessee commission, appeared as a voluntary witness; and eventually the states enacted legislation exempting federal agencies from regulation by their commissions.

The utilities, discovering states' rights, did hope they could be made as useful as national rivalries have been made in other spheres of trade. It was true that lawyers' briefs which deplored "a revolutionary transition of utility function from state control and personnel to Federal investment and operation or control," and lawyers' speeches objecting to Uncle Sam's "power to level the mountains and fill the valleys of the state of Tennessee, and supplant an industry established under the policies of the State to serve its people," seeing in this Authority no less than "an unprecedented invasion of the states by the Federal government," were pretty sure to be quoted with some approval in the Southern papers.

And it should be clear that you can't get the Valley states together as a region because, first, the Valley doesn't take in all of any of the seven or much of four of them, but also because they don't think alike. When Southern governors meet for regional conferences, it is probably to see who will take credit for getting rid of the freight differential when TVA brings that to pass.

What does seem true is that, after five years, TVA operations have

had some political effect. Tennessee, a border state where the most
has been done, has made up its mind. Kentucky, another border state
where less has been done, is still doubtful, but there is hope for North
Carolina. Alabama is definitely New Deal as a result of its large
TVA present, while Georgia and Mississippi, minor beneficiaries,
remain conservative.

This alignment would seem elemental to any Southerner. It's all
right for candidates to unbutton their collars and thump the table
and drink out of the water pitcher, but everybody knows that's just
talk. Your real Southern politician likes to sit on the gallery and split
hairs, and he can give you good constitutional reasons for the way
he votes. Then sometimes he will surprise you by saying right out,
as they did in the cynical eighteenth century, what the real reasons
are. Up in the Carolina mountains there is a rich man who voted
against the New Deal in 1932, and for it in 1936 because, he saw, the
President had saved capitalism. In the same district a cymling-headed
young theological student said fascism was better than communism
"because it puts our class on top."

As for what some people consider the new social objectives of
government, they wouldn't know about them.

Can They Stop Roosevelt?

*Say not thou, What is the cause that the former days were better than these?
for thou dost not enquire wisely concerning this.*

*For before these days there was no hire for man, nor any hire for beast;
neither was there any peace to him that went out or came in because of the
affliction: for I set all men every one against his neighbour.*

*Then shall stand up in his estate a raiser of taxes in the glory of the king-
dom. . . .*
But tidings out of the east and out of the north shall trouble him.

"Some of those poor whites on the island don't live half as well as
the niggers. You'll see."

The TVA launch landed, and a tramp through the tall grass with
a relocation man who knew the district proved his point.

"Take that shack, now. No fences. No chickens. No screens at the windows. They had a pig last year, but they killed him and didn't ever get another. That isn't a pig there in the dirt under the house, it's the baby. Two-three children are sort of mixed between this family and the next one down the road.

"Nobody home—yes, she is, too. Just shy."

When she opened the door, you could smell the place without going up the battered steps. She was young and still pretty, but embarrassed because her feet were bare as well as dirty, and she had nothing on under her dress.

He was away, but we could come in if we liked. She didn't know when he'd be back. Like to look around? She was sorry she hadn't cleaned up yet.

Yes, they had a radio but it wouldn't work any more. Yes, that was a right nice clock.

It was a large gilt clock, set in a ship's wheel held by a figure that seemed familiar.

"Yes, it's Mr. Roosevelt," she said. "But he's done stopped."

Stopping Mr. Roosevelt is naturally a beautiful dream for people in the North who think the New Deal has separated them from money, or feel afraid that it will. It's harder to see why they should want to stop him down South, where money is being spent. But down South as elsewhere, it's presented as a matter of principle.

Suggesting, back in 1937, that the President should be impeached, a Macon, Georgia, paper said: "It can be done and if our free institutions are further threatened, it must be done." At that time the President hadn't even committed the serious offense of saying what he thought about Georgia elections; the paper was worried about his encouragement of that foreign invader, the CIO. Putting it a little more mildly, the Atlanta *Constitution* urged that the ship of state be steered "away from the shoals of socialistic experimentation."

Down South they could complain, as Ireland once complained, of being governed by a succession of kicks and kindnesses. And they don't always realize that, by and large, they are being treated to an extraordinary amount of kindness after seventy years of kicks.

Instead they object to New Deal advice which comes with the spending, the way good counsel generally accompanies social-service handouts. They don't want to be socially bettered and they think missionary work should be directed towards the heathen in China.

Anyhow they don't see Mr. Roosevelt as a missionary; they see him as a politician. Of course Mr. Roosevelt says he is a politician, and up North some folks consider this a sort of honesty, a step ahead of stuffed-shirt claims to be above it all. They tried out the stuffed shirts up North for a good many years.

But the South, when it voted for Hoover, was just getting to that stage. For years before that, they'd had one-gallused statesmen haranguing farmers at the forks of the creek, and they were working up to the Better Business, starched-collar type of candidate.

Up in New York, last year, they seemed to think it was funny when a Tammany congressman lost out in the Democratic primary but was nominated by the Republicans. Down South, the well-to-do Democrats have been headed that way since the days of Rutherford B. Hayes. It was then that *Harper's Weekly* said: "If this is Southern Democracy, it is wonderfully like the best Northern Republicanism."

The truth is of course that it was a mistake ever to make the Democratic party the Southern party. It's the way it was in Ireland and the way it is in Spain now; the rebels aren't radicals but conservatives. It's embarrassing to Southern Democrats to be mixed up with a party that is supposed to kick over the traces and take in all sorts of radical riff-raff. The only thing the solid South ever had in common with the party was being in the minority, and when the party got to be a majority it was no place for a true Southerner. A majority favoring change is unnatural anyhow, but never at any time was the Southern minority in favor of social reform.

Southern tradition is all the other way. There was some talk about a Scottish girl named Flora Macdonald, who came to Cumberland county in the Piedmont section of North Carolina, after helping Bonnie Prince Charlie escape from Culloden. The Macdonald clan fought in the Revolution, since you can't hope to keep a Mac out of a fight, and you might think they would have fought with the colonists, but they did nothing of the sort. Their clan chief seemed to think that you had to take some sort of royal oath, even to the wrong king, so he fought with the British. You couldn't expect a Mac to admit a mistake, but in her last years they say that Flora Macdonald said: "I have hazarded my life for the house of Stuart, and for the house of Hanover, and I do not see that I am the great gainer by either."

She was buried in a shroud they made out of the sheets that her prince had slept on, and somehow it reminds you of the way that some of the Daughters of the Confederacy, with a sure instinct for a lost cause, transferred their allegiance from Hood to Hoover.

Nor is the spirit confined to females. In the same Carolina mountains where Flora took refuge there lives today a doctor of some local repute who explains his allegiance to the Republican party with no blush for the campaign charge of economic royalism. "My folks were always royalists," he says, and tells of the Tory ancestor in Virginia who went to jail rather than break the king's oath, though he had two hot-headed sons in Washington's army.

A remarkable thing about this settlement of the Southern mountains was that the settlers moved there, not because they were progressive-minded, but because they weren't. They crossed the ocean and came over the hills, not because they were born explorers or radicals wanting to experiment, but because they were too set in their ways to put up with change at home.

Southern governments, state governments, mostly began back when there was no doubt about there being classes, but no consciousness of anything wrong in the idea. The North Carolina "constitutions" were designed for privilege, and the constitution Tennessee finally adopted copied that of North Carolina. Georgia started as a resettlement project managed with a firm hand by a board of governors. Virginia, as all Southerners hear in infancy, was settled by younger sons of the English nobility who were adventurers not because they were eager to establish a new and different civilization, but because they wanted room in which to repeat for themselves the pattern of civilization at home. In the same way Mississippi and Alabama were settled by younger sons from Virginia. That second-generation colonials are more conservative than the home country is a British axiom safely relied upon by reactionary premiers under the statute of Westminster.

So Southern colonists in general asked only to be let alone, that they might hold in peace to their ancient faiths. An extreme interpretation of this in some of the mountain counties made it impolite to interfere in personal killings. Certainly the law, or the government, was not expected to be heard from on any lesser occasion. This was the attitude of the hill people at the time of the Civil War, and it is the attitude of many of them today; they may be starving, but if they are to be helped, they prefer to be helped by direct intervention of the Almighty. For silence and conservatism, for narrow-minded, stubborn, single-track determination, they can be considered the Vermonters of the South. The "Uncle Sam" face, lean and lined but firm of chin, is to be seen more often in the Southern hills today than in any other part of the country.

The mountain folks do believe in letting the other fellow have his opinion, misguided though he may be; that is the philosophy of secession as opposed to invasion. Take the liquor question in Tennessee; the state is dry by vote, although it has over two thousand federally licensed bootleggers. But Tennessee recognizes the right of other states to trade in liquor, and so the state has licensed one distiller. What surprises them is Yankee zeal for uniformity. The North made a fuss when the state of Tennessee objected to the doctrine of evolution, while in Tennessee it was allowed that the Yankees were entitled to claim any family descent they might fancy.

You might say that, what with figuring ways around legislation that was wished on her, the South has had more political experience than the rest of the country. Take the matter of relief. In reconstruction times they had the Freedmen's Bureau, and they had exactly the same troubles then that they're having now, with the local administration. Right in Tennessee they had to warn the bureau employees to keep out of politics. As for the cotton agents they appointed at the same time, to take over the Confederate forfeits, the Secretary of the Treasury said he was sure he had sent some honest cotton agents South, but it looked as if none of them had stayed that way very long.

While they may hesitate, as in Kentucky, between old-age pensions and the WPA, Southern politicians naturally expect to spend federal money in the way that seems best for state, city, or county machines. This attitude is not unknown in other parts of the country. What the South can't understand is the notion of some of the federal administrators that the New Deal projects are to change things around. Take the WPA; as deputy administrator, Mr. Aubrey Williams made two memorable speeches in the Tennessee Valley. In one of them he urged the sharecroppers to organize, and in the other he said that the New Deal had most of its trouble with the moneyed, educated people. Mr. Williams is an Alabama boy, so they let him say it, but was that any way to talk?

Next year Mr. Williams's boss, Mr. Hopkins, made a speech at Memphis that was all sympathy and promises of jobs. But Memphis remained calm, and the Peabody Hotel was so full of a girls' sorority, trailing chiffon dresses and perfumery, that hardly anybody knew Mr. Hopkins was there. The papers published the speech but they didn't give it any bigger display than the papers in New York. They don't like having to take government charity, and they don't really believe that story about the smart Yankee economists wanting to make the South rich enough to buy Yankee goods and so keep the Yankees employed.

As the South still sees it, tax money shouldn't be spent recklessly, in excess of what it takes to get out the vote. Look at those Dixie Homesteads in Memphis—brick cottages for colored people. In Memphis Mr. Crump has always managed to get out the colored vote when he wanted it with nothing more than a truck ride.

As for TVA, it's been just about the biggest possible disappointment to people who expected to see the money spent in normal political ways. From the first the Authority acted as if the regular officials who had been handling roads and schools and post offices for years weren't competent to handle dams. The TVA people didn't understand how to manage contracts, politically, and they declined to co-operate in the matter of jobs for Mattie May's boy or Cousin Sue's husband.

You might say the South has an old, blasé attitude towards political corruption, but a childlike innocence of economics. Down in Florence, Alabama, Uncle Sam's development of the Shoals has so far failed to make them rich that one out of every six persons is on relief. Of course that doesn't mean the luxurious sort of relief they have up North; the director of public welfare for Lauderdale county said he had seven thousand certified and expenditures of over $10,000 a week, which he thought high; but Yankees can figure it's less than two dollars apiece.

Now, Alabama is the state where the mill tokens they collect for the sales tax are stamped "Luxury Tax," although you pay them on a nickel cup of coffee or a ten-cent bar-b-q sandwich. And a banker in Florence said he thought it was a good thing—the fairest form of tax. It taught the reliefers, he said, the value of money.

From a Yankee point of view, some of the other Southern taxes seem almost as ill-advised. Tennessee spends money to advertise the Smokies to the tourist trade, and puts a seven-cent tax on gasoline. All the Valley states grow tobacco with one hand and tax cigarettes with the other. They all tend to tax land and commodities instead of incomes and corporations.

But you might say, first catch your incomes. Go back to the so-called prosperity era, and you find that in 1929 Southern incomes were still so low you couldn't give a thousand-dollar exemption and collect any revenue. Even back then, out of more than five hundred men in the country making incomes of over a million a year, only seven lived in the South, and three of those were in Florida. Last year, down in Mississippi, the average family income was $768, as against $2587 in Ohio. Bank deposits, on demand, averaged $58 as against $675 in New York.

Corporation taxes, as advertised by the chambers of commerce, are low or non-existent; and when the utility companies pay their taxes with a flourish, the states are deeply grateful. They wonder what will happen when they have to do without those taxes, although, with federal tax receipts from Tennessee up a third, or more than thirty millions, in 1938, they may come to see that a bigger general business will more than compensate them for the loss.

But for cash money they still have to have a sales tax, or tax land. Back in 1934, during the worst times, it was figured that a hundred-acre farm in Mississippi assessed at $50 an acre would have to pay $275 in state and county taxes. That is, it would take seven bales of ten-cent cotton for taxes alone, and the state and county wouldn't get much at that. Even the federal government can't get blood out of the Southern turnip; back in the prosperous twenties Uncle Sam was collecting $44.93 from Delaware for every thirty-nine cents he got from Mississippi.

The less you have to pay with, the more it hurts, and every candidate who runs for office down South promises tax reduction. It's as much a part of the campaign as registering in the primary. And maybe they do spend foolishly. Alabama puts three-quarters of the state revenue into roads, and most Southern states are extravagant that way. But expensive as roads are when politicians award contracts, you can argue that they are just a subsidy to the bus companies, the way public lands were to the railroads years ago. Hard-up folks use the buses, and when most of the state revenue comes from a gas tax it's only fair to spend it on roads.

But when it came to state allotments for federal spending, the Southern states found themselves being asked to a party they couldn't afford. Take the last PWA program: Alabama will spend a dollar where Wisconsin spends ten. Georgia puts up $2.20, Minnesota $8.10. Mississippi pays $3.60 and Montana $8.75. Tennessee can't afford more than $3.10, while Illinois and Nebraska both splurge with $14. North Carolina chips in $3.20 and New York planks down $12. And, of course, the federal government comes across in proportion; to him that hath shall be given.

So, it's been figured, in its first four years the New Deal spent $267.17 in Wisconsin to only $160.10 in Georgia, and $1114.12 in

Nevada to $202.48 in Mississippi and $129.34 in Kentucky. Worried as it was about Problem Number One, the administration couldn't get around the handicaps.

But the South isn't sold on this idea of spending, anyhow. Southern instinct is to do without when necessary and above all to let other people do without what they can't afford; an economy of abundance sounds like some smart Yankee selling trick. Up in the Carolina mountains a locally popular doctor had been put in charge of a co-operative cannery that was started as a relief measure. He couldn't see how Uncle Sam expected to get anywhere, because they actually wanted to pay the mountain people two bits for blackberries that could be bought right across the line in Georgia for a dime. Yes, of course the people needed the money; maybe the surveys did show they didn't have more than forty-five dollars a year cash money, and ten of that came from relief funds. Still, you couldn't compete with private enterprise by paying more than twice as much for labor, now could you?

This idea that the standards are set by private enterprise and can't or shouldn't be raised by the government was extended by many people to the operations of the Tennessee Valley Authority. Farmers who sold their land in the reservoir areas for what TVA appraisers considered a fair price said to their neighbors: "I would of took less," in deprecation of government extravagance.

And, no matter how much money TVA brings into the Valley, the Southern taxpayer doesn't forget that the government doesn't have to pay state and county taxes on its property. In Tennessee and North Carolina they resent not being able to tax the land that's gone into national parks and forests, although the forests pay the counties a quarter of what they make from timber sales, and build roads to boot. In the same way people don't give TVA credit for paying state taxes, as it does, on power; they think of the land. A North Carolina native watched the cable car cross and dump its load at Hiwassee dam, then spat disparagingly down the hillside. "The power company would of built that there in time," he said, "and paid taxes to Cherokee county."

Some Folks Vote

Ye have plowed wickedness, ye have reaped iniquity; ye have eaten the fruit
of lies: because thou didst trust in thy way, in the multitude of thy mighty men.

Elections in the Valley states were comparatively quiet in 1938.
In Tennessee, a candidate for the United States Senate was beaten up
so he had to withdraw from the race, and one man was killed in the
primaries, but it wasn't necessary for the governor to send troops to
Memphis as he threatened to, and only two were shot in the fall
elections. In Kentucky, the governor thought he was poisoned while
out on a speaking tour, and had people taste his food, but it was discovered to be from drinking water. Only nine were killed in arguments on election day, four of them in Harlan county.

One reason people get into arguments on election day down South
is that so many of them can't afford the luxury of voting. Poll taxes
of a dollar or two are too much for some to pay. While enough are
paid to help out the state treasuries, they weren't imposed as a financial measure; they began back when the fifteenth amendment forced
the South to apply an idea that some framers of the constitution had,
that voting should be limited to responsible holders of property.

Several of the states had begun with such a qualification; in
Georgia you had to have fifty acres of land or a taxable equivalent,
and in North Carolina you paid a poll tax of sixteen shillings four-
pence, back when they used that currency. Of course a poll tax is a
property tax, considering the amount as the interest on so much
capital.

When the Yankees insisted that the Negroes must vote down South,
although they wouldn't allow it in Connecticut, Wisconsin, Michi-
gan, or Ohio at the time, the Southern states had to find a qualification to take the place of color. New York had a property qualification
for colored voters that didn't apply to whites, and maybe that's where
they got the idea.

With a poll tax, of course you bar the hard-up white people from voting, along with the Negroes. But a lot of folks don't see any harm in that; in New Jersey they've been suggesting that relief votes be barred.

In Tennessee, in 1938, a lady with ideas about good government undertook to run for the legislature on the Republican ticket, and she thought her party ought to start an educational campaign for voters in Knoxville—tell them what they needed to know about registering and paying the poll tax, and generally try to get out the vote. When she suggested this to the campaign manager, she was surprised to have him say that the less said about that the better. It's pretty well known that if you did away with the poll tax you'd have a lot bigger vote in the South, but it would be a vote for the wrong side, maybe. They think of that.

Then you've got to consider that, with a poll tax, you not only keep out votes from people in the lower financial brackets, who might be led astray by radical agitators; you also make it possible for people with money to multiply their influence. Because of course there's no law against paying a poll tax for somebody else if the other person can be relied on to vote right. Sometimes they get a little careless about that; some years ago the Knoxville *News-Sentinel* made a to-do about uncovering what they called blocks of poll-tax receipts, run off in series the way the big companies use stamping machines for their mail. The congressional committee investigating the 1938 elections noticed the same thing, and there's a growing sentiment against doing things like that right out in the open.

But some things are taken honestly for granted. Talking to a stranger on a bus, one man in Tennessee said he'd be glad to see the primaries over. Politics had interfered with his business, bad. He was a painter by trade, and of course times weren't so good; he'd had only eight or nine weeks' work since last March. So he'd been mighty glad to get a job working on a country school, though it meant taking the bus every day because it was over in the next county.

Thing was, he'd been laid off a whole week because he couldn't vote where the job was. In fact he was lucky to lose just a week. They'd raised considerable objection because he wouldn't be able to support the county ticket; some felt he should be laid off altogether, but they'd compromised on letting him go for election week. Thought they could take him back when things cooled down.

Yes, it was too bad, because of course he'd have voted for 'em if he could. It wasn't as if he wouldn't vote with 'em on the state ticket—and here he pulled out of his pocket a letter that he carried around with him, in his wallet right next to his union card. The letter was to tell anyone concerned that the bearer had been a loyal supporter of Senator McKellar in past campaigns.

County politics got to be important down South back when the federal government was out of the question and the carpetbaggers were running the states, and only the counties were left for the home folks. Most folks wish there were more county offices; up in Carter county in East Tennessee there are twenty-four lawyers, and last year twenty-one of them announced for county attorney.

Of course in most counties everything is organized and under control. In the early days of TVA, the Authority made its usual offer, in a North Carolina county, to pay the salary of an assistant county agent to start a soil-conservation and reforestation program in the watershed. The county officials listened and finally said, all right, if they could name the man—and he'd have to be a Republican.

It takes time to educate folks out of ideas like that, and since TVA hasn't been one to compromise, they've had to go slow in some places. There are counties which have made objection to the Authority either independently or as part of a general obstructive scheme; for example, Campbell county, Tennessee, filed a protest against flooding an eleven-mile branch of the Southern railway that was in reservoir territory. As individuals the people of Campbell county appeared to profit from the dam-building, many of them selling unprofitable farms, and others getting jobs; but as a county they figured that, when TVA acquired twelve hundred pieces of real estate, it meant the loss of twenty-two thousand dollars a year in county taxes. In some other counties of the Valley the losses were greater, although there were some gains through reclamation, too.

The losses look bad until you realize that it might be a good idea to do away with the county system. Dr. Arthur Morgan once suggested that reorganization of the county governments could save a third of the taxpayers' money. He wasn't referring to what county officials have been known to get away with in the matter of bond issues, or road work, and such; he meant the legitimate but foolish expense of keeping up the county salaries. He said investigation disclosed that in some counties "the work of an entire week can be done in half a day. In some courthouses the officials are present only on Saturday, yet full-time salaries are paid." It's true enough, because in the Valley they have counties like Van Buren, in Tennessee, with only 3500 people; and when you travel, it may be no more than half an hour on the bus from one county courthouse and Confederate monument to the next. The explanation is that these county seats used to be as hard to get to as the state capital is now.

But to do away with the duplication will do people out of jobs. While it's true that the average county official would be more useful doing road work with the WPA, people are used to hearing him talk about his public service, while they consider WPA a charity. This attitude is not unknown in New York and Boston and Jersey City.

So counties continue to be important politically and something is to be said for the idea that the way to effective political action in the South starts with the counties. If that is so, something significant happened this year in Grundy county, Tennessee.

Grundy is a little lost county up in the Cumberlands. County officials had always been named by the coal company that operated there, and this continued as a matter of course even after the mine shut down and everybody went on relief. Probably nothing would have been done had it not been for a little mountain school near Monteagle. In Tennessee, some say the Highlander Folk School is run by Reds. The head of it did have the honor of being mentioned to the Dies committee, and they have classes for mill workers who go back to be organizers; but they also harbor earnest young girls from Smith and Radcliffe, and young Quakers engaged in welfare work in the mountains, and Southern university professors guilty of bringing their history courses down to date.

The school helped some with union organization in the county, and this year the unions took an interest in the regular Democratic primaries. The result, surprising to nearly everybody, was that they elected a sheriff, a school superintendent, and two road commissioners endorsed by their "labor conference." Announcing a post-primary rally "at the cross tie pile" in Monteagle, the Workers' Alliance could head its multigraphed handbills: "The Working People of Grundy County Have Won a Vital Victory."

This is by no means a common occurrence; in fact there is probably no other county in the Valley's hundred where such a thing could happen, yet. But there are plenty of counties that are like Grundy before it happened. In them, the ruling powers can oppose to any foreign invader—say an agency of the federal government—a network of nuisance. The counties are the first line of opposition to TVA in a policy of delay and division.

Next come the cities, where, as elections were held over the Valley, the TVA issue came to be fought along definite lines. In general, labor organizations endorsed public ownership while commercial associations and large industries opposed it. So-called "citizens' associations" were formed to give this opposition a democratic look, and to circulate appeals based on tax rates. Newspapers frequently mentioned communism, as when the Jackson, Mississippi, *News,* in an editoral headed: "We Are Not Communists," said that, if the vote went wrong, "we may as well disband our Chamber of Commerce, and make no further efforts for the growth or development of our city. Capital seeking investment will shun us like a whole community rotten with bubonic plague." Jackson, headquarters for the Mississippi Power company, had heard that if the election went for public power, the company headquarters would move to Vicksburg.

You would hardly have thought it necessary to hold an election in Knoxville, headquarters of the Authority. Knoxville was flat broke when TVA went to work in 1933. All three national banks had failed and city bonds were selling for seventy cents on the dollar; the city owed back salary to its schoolteachers, firemen, and police, and all it could do was lie flat on its back and kick like those loud-complaining locusts they have there in the summer. The Authority moved in, rented quarters, and spent money, carefully staggering its orders to do as much good as possible. So if the Knoxville folks had been considering only their own selfish interests, they must have voted unanimously.

But there were then, as there are now, rugged individualists in Knoxville to say they never asked for TVA. The usual arguments were used: TVA was a socialistic experiment, taxes would be higher, loss of power-company taxes would cripple the schools, street-car fares would go up. They had an anti-public-power association, headed by a former power executive, to spend two thousand dollars in advertising alone during the last week of the campaign. This was more money than it looks like to a Yankee, because only 2567 people voted against public power. Of course TVA won, but a third of the votes cast were against it.

Birmingham, headquarters for the Alabama Power company, voted against TVA, and they figured the election was cheap enough although it was estimated to have cost anywhere from fifty to a hundred thousand dollars. The newspapers gave full co-operation to the power company, one publisher worrying in print about the menace of communism and in private about a revolt of Northern industry, of which Birmingham has a larger share than most Southern cities can boast. People mostly voted along the lines you'd expect: a white-collar suburb turned down public ownership although its council was said to favor TVA, while the people of Bessemer, the working suburb, decided for TVA as soon as they could persuade the town council to put it to a vote.

Chattanooga, headquarters for the Tennessee Power company, had the funniest election of all. That is, it was funny if you could look at it from the outside, but in the city, at the time, beautiful friendships were broken and relatives stopped speaking. There was even a little feeling left in 1938, when the congressional committee took a few days off to look into what had happened three years before.

The election enrollment back in 1935 was the largest in Chatta-

nooga's history, and more money was spent, they say, than ever
before in a city election. The line-up was what would be supposed—
the labor unions endorsed public ownership, the Chattanooga Manufacturers' Association opposed it. In general the arguments and tactics
used in the open part of the fight repeated those of Knoxville; a body
known as the "Citizens' and Taxpayers' Association" published an
open letter to teachers asserting that salaries would be cut if the bond
issue for a municipal power plant was carried. Another open letter
was sent out by the publisher of the conservative morning paper, who
got worried when he found that his colored cook, Georgia, was mis-
takenly determined to vote for TVA. He wrote that he had reasoned
with Georgia, telling her that such a vote would raise his taxes, but
all she could see was that it would lower her light bill. He therefore
begged all right-thinking people to help him kill Georgia's vote. That
letter was one of the mistakes that Northerners make, because
Southerners who might feel the prejudices he appealed to wouldn't
think a white man should make mention of them, and some folks
laughed because he couldn't seem to manage Georgia.

The evening paper, the *News,* supported TVA, so the morning
Times got all the power-company advertising, and in addition the
power people subsidized another little paper that had hitherto been
given away free to customers of a chain grocery. They also used
billboards and circulars and door-to-door canvassers.

Eleven hundred power-company employees made a formidable
voting bloc in a city the size of Chattanooga, to be balanced only by
the promised employment of even more people in TVA offices and
in building Chickamauga dam, only eight miles away. The *News,*
finding that economic arguments for municipal ownership failed to
register, played up the dam-building and no one seemed to have the
sense to ask if Chickamauga dam wouldn't be built as part of a
regional planning program, even if Chattanooga didn't buy TVA
power.

This lack of gumption on the part of the private-power people was,
they say, what swung the election. Money alone isn't enough; you
have to know how to use it. If you buy Negro votes, for example,

every Southern politician knows you must buy them on election day, not two or three weeks ahead. The Yankees spent some of their money too soon.

Then there was the conspicuous error of the 162 votes on the cow lot. To vote in Chattanooga primaries you have to own property in the city; it's a local provision for disqualifying the undesirables while giving a say-so to the well-to-do people who live up on Lookout Mountain and register as owners of town lots. That's all right, Chattanooga feels, if you're a bona-fide property-owner.

But on the last night for registration a long line of strangers appeared in one district, keeping the regular registrants out; and it was so noticeable that somebody complained. The newcomers were found by a curious coincidence to be power-company employees or executives, or their wives or family connections; and they all registered as owners of the same city property. This property turned out to be a vacant lot down by the river, considered to be worth fifty dollars because, while under water in time of flood, it was otherwise suitable for pasturing a cow. These facts, revealed in the *News* that 162 persons had invested thirty-three cents of their life's savings" in buying the lot shortly before the primary, were considered to affect election returns in a way contrary to that intended. Down South they are used to political finagling but they do like it to be done with some finesse.

In Chattanooga, Knoxville, and the other cities, except maybe Memphis, they said the vote for TVA would have been larger if it hadn't been for the poll tax. Folks sure to vote for TVA power are the ones who would maybe have to choose between paying a poll tax and paying the light bill. They say that when people in Decatur, Alabama, first met to consider taking TVA power the meeting was notable for the absence of all the prominent people in town. In the end they did get action by counting plain, common noses and such poll tax receipts as they had, and it's been the same in other towns.

Public-opinion polls in the Southern states still turn in four-to-one totals for the New Deal, and of course the majority sentiment comes, as elsewhere, from the lower financial brackets. Down South these brackets include more people than they do elsewhere, in proportion, and these people are taking a new interest in national politics. The last time they asked the question: "Are you better off today than you were a year ago?" more people said yes in the Southern states than in any other part of the country. Maybe some of them, in Tennessee, were among the forty-odd thousand who paid income taxes; but more were no doubt among the eighty-odd thousand families given some form of federal aid. First thing you know, some of these people are going to want to vote in regular elections without paying admission.

Lately it's been considered that a national party, by basing the national convention vote on registration, could force the South to do away with poll taxes. It would make a big difference, more than a Yankee would expect, because two Valley states not only have the poll tax; they have restrictions against sudden, upstart voting. In Mississippi you have to show poll-tax receipts for two years back. And in Alabama you must have paid all your back poll taxes from the age of twenty-one.

Outsiders Object

I was a reproach among all mine enemies, but especially among my neighbours. . . .
I am forgotten as a dead man out of mind. . . .
But I trusted in thee, O Lord. . . .
My times are in thy hand: deliver me from the hand of mine enemies.

While Southerners are considering the real reason for political action and the taxes they lose on government land, they might wonder why people in other parts of the country should pay for improvements in the Valley.

You can't very well get around the fact that the Valley is enjoying the TVA at the expense of taxpayers elsewhere. With the 1935 internal-revenue returns as a basis, it was calculated that New York would pay over twenty percent of the cost of the project, while Tennessee would pay less than one percent.

So far New York has not complained of being a sucker, but in 1935 the Ohio Chamber of Commerce published a pamphlet entitled:

"Why Should Ohio Finance an Industrial Rival?" Ohio was paying nearly seven percent of the federal taxes, "whereas the area embraced in the TVA pays a very minor percentage." The Cincinnati *Enquirer* met the menace with an editorial headed: "A Threat to Many Cities," and Chamber of Commerce secretaries over the country exchanged warnings. Mr. Harvey J. Campbell, vice-president and secretary of the Detroit chamber, told the National Association of Commerce Organization Secretaries that TVA was "a cancerous growth on the bosom of the Goddess of Liberty."

The trouble with outside diagnosis of this disease is that the people who object to spending money in the Valley can't agree on whether TVA is a blessing or a curse. The Chicago *Tribune* can say that the project drains forty-eight states for the benefit of seven, and that "the whole Tennessee Valley folly was undertaken to pay a political debt to the solid South at the taxpayers' expense," but the argument is weakened when the *Tribune* goes on to say that the project is terrible. If terrible, it is no benefit, but rather a conspiracy by the Washington politicians to wreck Southern initiative—an idea that has seriously occurred to some folks in the so-called solid South.

Opposition to TVA has less to do with regional geography than with habits of thought about government enterprise. When *Fortune* took its poll on New Deal measures, the opinions ranged from 82.7 percent for TVA in the South to only 53.2 percent for it in the Middle West. But the economic range was wider; that was from 77.9 percent for TVA among the hard-up colored people, to 68.3 percent against it among the rich white folks. They could have split that last percentage some more if they had asked how many people were really against the objectives of TVA, and how many would have been for the whole thing if it could have been built like the Union Pacific railroad, with a new version of the Crédit Mobilier.

Of course, considering that its money comes from all over the country, the Authority is smart to insist that its materials and machinery come from all over, too. Last year they estimated that ninety-five percent of the thirty-five million dollars spent for construction equipment had been spent outside the Valley, and "rather evenly dis-

tributed over various industrial areas of the Nation." This meant
distributing the jobs too; in fact, at the start, they claimed that two
men would go to work in a distant factory for every one on the job
in the Valley. These explanations are a good thing for the country,
though they don't sound any too well to people in Tennessee.

Also the TVA directors not immediately concerned with power
were wise to talk of the Valley as an experimental laboratory for the
whole United States. Every section, Dr. Arthur Morgan said, will
need "patterns and working principles" for regional planning; and
Dr. Harcourt Morgan said that every step taken by TVA, "Every
project set up, every result obtained, is weighed from the point of view
of its possible application to other parts of the country." Mr. Lilienthal
has had less to say along this line because he is having enough trouble
with power interests in the Valley, without emphasizing the idea that
the plan will spread.

So far, if you don't count congressional arguments over appropriations and the speeches of Congressman Bridges of New Hampshire,
who wouldn't like a New Deal measure if it was good, the national
government hasn't interfered much with the Authority. In the early
days Comptroller McCarl, who carried over some ideas from the
Hoover administration, spent some time combing over TVA accounts and objected to the ways they had cut corners and neglected
red tape in getting started. He was for waiting for bids on everything,
the way the government is supposed to, instead of buying where goods
could be had in a hurry, or where they were of better quality, or where,
in the judgment of the Authority, some social purpose could be served
by buying. It's hard to explain social purposes to government auditors;
and Comptroller McCarl couldn't see why they should buy books and
magazines and newspapers for the TVA libraries; but as the Authority had been set up to have the flexibility of a business corporation,
it was finally allowed to use discretion in its purchases.

The congressional investigation of the Authority came about, of
course, through a temporary alliance between Dr. Arthur Morgan and
the Republicans. This alliance was involuntary and even unconscious
on Dr. Morgan's part, but his disgruntlement gave the people who

didn't like TVA a chance. It wasn't much of a chance at that, because with a majority of Democrats voting on party lines, you could pretty well tell in advance what the committee's verdict would be. Back in the seventies a committee went down to investigate the Ku Klux Klan and took twelve volumes of testimony, without even getting to Tennessee, where the Klan was founded; and they voted, in the end, according to party labels. Congressional committees have a habit of doing that.

If you watched the congressional committee inspecting dams in the Valley, or listened to their hearings in Washington and Knoxville, you might get the idea that the whole thing was a little complicated for a congressman. A representative or even a senator doesn't look any bigger than anybody else beside a dam, and when the investigators got to Hiwassee, you couldn't tell, from across the river, that they weren't ordinary tourists. It was possible to think that the Washington autographs on the visitors' register didn't mean any more to the future of TVA than the signatures of the Akinses of Alabama, the Goinses of North Carolina, and a whole clan of young Campbells who also came to look at the dam that day.

It's true that another sort of checking up might have resulted in some interesting discussions of TVA policy. Congressman Maverick of Texas objected to a contract with the Aluminum Company of America, under which the Authority agreed to supply a large amount of power. Mr. Maverick said that the ten-million-dollar art gift made to the nation by the Mellon estate was an inadequate return for more kilowatts of power than could be generated at Norris dam. He said, if the power companies were one monopoly, the Aluminum company was another, or part of the same. Why sell public power to either?

There were reasons. For one thing, the hecklers were complaining that expensive TVA power was going to waste—and so it was, while injunction suits tied up sales to municipalities. Another consideration is that the dams generate two kinds of power, "firm" or continuous, which is the sort you need for lighting the kitchen, and secondary power, which can be used by industries. But industries will not contract for secondary power alone; they must have a certain amount of primary power. The Aluminum company contract sold almost three times as much secondary as primary power, and paid the Authority $1,500,000 a year.

From a business standpoint there was plenty of excuse for the contract because, thanks to the lawsuits, TVA was all dressed up with no place to go, and people were talking, when the Mellons offered a date. The best criticism of the contract is that the date is for too long. But while it is good publicity to talk of a possible power shortage in the Valley, after all the talk about overproduction, it has yet to be proved that there will be any difficulty in meeting municipal demands. Since they took so long to make up their minds, it might not hurt one or two Southern cities to wait awhile.

There is still another consideration. Northerners are quicker than most Southerners to feel that fighting Morgan and dealing with Mellon interests is a case of out of the fire and into the aluminum frying pan; the Yankees know how closely aluminum and power are tied together in New York state. Some of them feel that a corporation that almost quadrupled its net profits while turning guns on Southern workers who asked for the Northern scale is not entitled to share in the benefits of a great national project. They note that, in spite of the beautiful silver-ink advertisements in the magazines, the price of aluminum saucepans is still high; and they do not like the sale of aluminum for war use abroad.

But the South has not arrived at this state of squeamishness. Southerners remember that when TVA came, the Aluminum company was sitting on the western slopes of the Blue Ridge, as Duke Power was on the east. They meant to build another dam of their own on the Little Tennessee, and TVA stopped them only by beating them to the purchase of a thirty-by-fifty foot piece of land at a strategic point. Then they thought of moving over on the Yadkin, and the Federal Power Commission held them up there; and the Charlotte *Observer* felt that was pretty mean: "Instead of showing such an attitude it seems to us that these Federal authorities should be encouraging and helpful to a private enterprise that wants to dump $6,000,000 of the Mellon millions into North Carolina."

Nor was there criticism, in the Valley, of the fact that Alcoa workers
and police were swapping shots at the time the TVA contract was announced. Southern papers referred to the "Deplorable Trouble" at
Alcoa with complete sympathy for the management, and rejoiced at
a restoration of order which involved the death of two strikers. Of
a rumor that the company might increase its force, the Knoxville
Journal said: "Imagine what doubling Alcoa's payrolls will mean. It
will add millions of dollars to the wealth of Tennessee." There was no
suggestion that, had the strike been successful, it might have increased
payrolls by raising wages.

There was further rejoicing when it was announced that the company would build a four-million-dollar plant at Mobile, to employ
maybe two thousand men; and it would have gone hard with TVA
had a refusal to supply the power held up that plan. When Tennessee
heard the rumor of a Fokker plant to be built in convenient proximity
to the aluminum supply, Governor Browning hastened to warn
John L. Lewis that no "labor strife" would be allowed to interfere
with that happy possibility. Of course, if you want to get ready for a
war, you've got to take care of all the war industries.

You can't do everything at once, and TVA is no doubt justified in
declining to assume responsibility for the customers who contract
for its power. What about the little mills, and the hostile papers, and
even the families who buy Maytag washing machines? Maybe it does
look funny for a government agency to be selling cheap power to a
corporation being sued by the government under the anti-trust laws;
but you can say it's up to the Department of Justice to wash the
kitchenware.

The other TVA contract that has been criticized is one made with
the Arkansas Power and Light Corporation. This contract makes no
provision for the rate at which power shall be resold to the consumer,
although the TVA Act says that such provisions shall be made. It was
explained, first, that the amount of power involved was too small to
justify dictation to the Arkansas company, and there was a precedent
because small amounts had been sold to the Valley companies without
the rate provision. Another explanation was that the Authority had

no jurisdiction outside the Valley; but of course Tupelo is outside the watershed, and they didn't hesitate about régulating rates there. It is possible that TVA was not wholly averse to demonstrating, at a safe distance from the Valley, the fact that sale of power to a utility corporation is unlikely to benefit consumers.

It would have been interesting to see a committee dig into these things. But the hearings were a good show, with Dr. Arthur Morgan and Mr. Lilienthal, Attorney Francis Biddle and Mr. Wendell Willkie, playing heroes or villains according to the point of view; and the investigation will no doubt have the effect of a similar investigation of Ontario Hydro—establishment of the enterprise on a sounder basis of public confidence.

10. RAINBOW

Land of Promise

As the appearance of the bow that is in the cloud in the day of rain, so was the appearance of the brightness.

Thus saith the Lord; Refrain thy voice from weeping, and thine eyes from tears: for thy work shall be rewarded, saith the Lord; and they shall come again from the land of the enemy . . .

And it shall come to pass, that like as I have watched over them, to pluck up, and to break down, and to throw down, and to destroy, and to afflict; so will I watch over them, to build, and to plant, saith the Lord.

Heaven-set rainbows often rest their feet in the Valley, stretching easily from the morning mists on the mountains to sun and shadow at the Shoals. Smaller man-made rainbows now play around the dams, wherever water goes over a spillway and dissolves into the air. They must promise something.

They do promise fewer floods, but there is more to them than that. Like the river, the big rainbows lead right out of the Valley and tie onto the rest of the country. The Valley runs east and west, like the railroad lines that cut north and south apart, but the river laces across to pull the gap together and the rainbows arching over do the same. You can't hitch a rainbow even to the highest hill, and you can't consider the future of TVA as bounded by the Valley watershed.

Then you have rainbows when the weather man can't make up his mind between sun and showers. It's that way now, down South, between cheap power and cheap labor, with men wanting both and in need of a sign to say you can't have both. They fought about it once, but as war never decides anything, the issues of the Civil War are still to be determined on the Tennessee. You have slavery and sectionalism on one side, as before; you have the machine age and federal power on the other side. But in place of guns you've got a new trading technique that says, let's swap a wage floor for a freight differential. Instead of talk about conquered provinces, you've got concrete evidence that Uncle Sam means well.

If you are the sort of all-around American that can now be developed in this country by travel South from the North, and travel North from the South, then you are glad to see the family row adjusted. A Southerner usually sticks to his mother country until he goes to work for the Yankees and comes to see some virtue in the sterner parent; the Northerners stay ignorant unless, like President Roosevelt, they spend their winters in a "mother state." Even then it's easy for them to say, as menfolks do, that women are too hard to understand.

Maybe, unless you know her, the South does appear changeable. One time she's a hard-working wife, used to scrimping and saving and bending over the washtub, and hard to sell a vacuum cleaner —where will the money come from? Another time she's a spoiled beauty, getting on in years but still harking back to when she was young, and smirking over the attentions of a villain who will have his way with her only to fling her aside like an old shoe factory.

But on her hard-working side, this female has the "intuition" that is the sound psychological insight of the slave, surprising only because it is accompanied by economic ignorance, and also a religious patience developed only by the put-upon. Even on her vain and flighty side, she has a streak of hard practical sense that goes unrecognized only by men blinded by sentiment.

She needs these qualities for a part of her job that has made her, for some, even less understandable. The South is the part of the country that produces the children, but this fact does not make the region young in the head. Young voters in the South, it has been well explained, are conservatives because they are not merely young people, but young parents. You don't have "youth movements," in the sense of revolutions, among people who get to be grandparents at thirty-five.

Overproduction of population is now coming to be recognized, even in the South, as a fundamental Southern problem; but you can't do much with it because of the fundamentalists. You just rouse opposition, as when a Catholic weekly, attacking TVA, grew fearful lest the "next move may be to let loose a flood of scientists upon these hardy hill people to tell them how many children every home should have, if any." Social workers conversant with hill-billy needs are indeed convinced that some such move might be desirable; groups of Protestant young people, and Southern planning conferences, have actually discussed the possibilities; but maybe this is a reform that can safely be left to economic change. When Southern farm women learn more and have more money to spend, the birth rate will fall fast enough.

Meanwhile, it just isn't sense for the rest of the country not to realize that you can't leave a pore widow woman with seventeen children to starve. The children will grow up and have revenge on you, in one way or another. And if papa has been gadding off to play with foreign markets when he should have been paying attention to hungry consumers nearer home, it will serve him right if they grow up to join the Silver Shirts.

So it's fortunate that the Yankees have now developed an economic philosophy that says you should feed a customer. It's fine to hear that the South could be, not the potential industrial center, but the potential buying center of the country. It will be a big change, because now, if you buy a pair of shoes in the Valley, they are apt to tell you automatically that the price is low "because we know you're having a hard time."

But it's true enough that to keep mass production going you need buyers just as you need raw materials, and in some parts of the country they are beginning to think that people who can use things should be coddled and cosseted. Lincoln said the country could not prosper half slave and half free; experience has added that there is no prosperity when a third of a nation is ill-nourished, ill-clad, ill-housed. A colored employee of the Tennessee Valley Authority managed to combine these discoveries, and a remedy; he said: "My people would be the world's best customers, if they had the money."

Since there is sectionalism on both sides, of course you have people in the North objecting to any program that proposes to help the South, even if the idea is only to fatten it for market. So it isn't enough to say, with Mr. Lilienthal, that TVA is "a challenge and an opportunity to the people of the South." It is also a challenge and an opportunity to the people of the North. When Yankee Professor Tugwell saw the TVA directors as pioneers whose job was "not to conquer the West but to conquer the East, with all that implies," he was confirmed by a Southern professor, who warned that "the war of 1861–65 was a preliminary skirmish," and by a Southern congressman, who noticed that the South had been a colony of New York since the Civil War.

Fortunately, in the case of TVA, the charge of regional discrimination is easy to settle. Not to favor the South, you need only establish more planning regions over the country.

Plan for the Nation

The heavens are thine, the earth also is thine: as for the world and the fulness thereof, thou hast founded them.
The north and the south thou hast created them.

Say to the north, Give up; and to the south, Keep not back.

So far there is only one regional power Authority, and when you come to look at what the other parts of the country are doing about water power you find almost as many approaches to the problem as there are states. As long as you stay inside state boundaries, of course, you don't get very far.

Wisconsin, where Mr. Lilienthal was on the power commission, established a "little TVA" that was declared unconstitutional by the state supreme court, then re-established by the same court in a reversal. But the state authority has advisory capacities only—no money to spend on construction.

Nebraska, Senator Norris's home state, has gone farthest but has not yet got out of the woods. They've spent as much in PWA loans and grants as one or two TVA dams would cost; in fact they've built two dams and planned a third. They've had a lot of argument and some natural difficulties; now they are combining three state projects and buying out the private utilities. But one trouble seemed to be a dispute between Wyoming and Nebraska over the dispensation of water in the Platte river, for of course the headwaters of the river Platte are up in Wyoming and Colorado. So it might have been better if Nebraska could have been part of an interstate region.

Texas, you'd think, is a state big enough to manage by itself, but Texas seemed to need a little outside engineering advice. The trouble at Buchanan dam, chortled over by objectors to public power all over the country, was what Dr. Arthur Morgan always said would happen if you had too small a reservoir for the height of your dam. The danger is not in using flood-control dams for power, but in scrimping on storage space. There is no excuse for that in Texas, where they have plenty of room, but the Buchanan project had begun in the Insull days as a private money-making scheme. The truth is, and a Texan born has a right to say it, that they never did have any sense about dams on the Texas Colorado. Years ago the one at Austin broke because they built it right over the Balcones fault, a crack in the limestone which runs across the state; Texans just won't take water seriously. When the Buchanan dam went wrong, all the Dallas *News* could find to say about it was: "Mr. Roosevelt is trying to put something by the Constitution."

But Yankees needn't think they manage much better. New England was so concerned over the constitution that they didn't do anything about flood control until they had to have help from the WPA instead of the PWA. New York state is so passive in the hands of Niagara Hudson and Consolidated Edison that they couldn't even get a state constitutional convention to let folks vote on a proposal to hang on to what power resources are left.

As long as you stay inside state boundaries, it seems you don't get very far. The big Western dams are more like TVA in that they affect wide areas; and Mr. J. D. Ross, administrator for Bonneville dam, has made proposals to link up public-power projects all over the country.

Of course they managed to kill the bill for "seven TVA's," and from the time they got the power provisions out of it there was no use trying to save it, because it got to be nothing but a pork-barrel measure for spending public money without bringing anything back. But while they were talking the regional bill to death, they did say one or two interesting things; a group of investors worried over this "destructive socialistic adventure" were told by their leader that the bill came in logical sequence to TVA, encouragement of municipal ownership by PWA loans, and the holding-company act. This was true. Maybe it is also true that, as a Niagara Hudson executive told stockholders, "There will be no permanent recovery in this country until the power issue is solved."

The regional bill was a logical development after TVA if you regarded TVA as a test, and a successful one, of regional planning. TVA is still young but it was even younger when the President first observed that they were wanting authorities all over the country. He didn't stop with the states, because they've been trying for some time to get an Authority in Puerto Rico, where some of the TVA phosphate went for tests.

Early TVA experience did teach the lawmakers one valuable lesson: the Norris bill for seven regional authorities carried a provision against sniping by injunction, requiring complainants to put up bonds to pay the government and consumers for court delays. And while utilities watched the regional-planning bill, Senator Barkley and Congressman Rankin, of Mississippi, succeeded in getting some useful power provisions in the amendments to the flood-control bill. It remains to be seen how these provisions will work out, with Vermont dissenting, but the House fight over them was bitter enough to earn a Connecticut congressman a telegram of approval from his governor on his stand for states' rights. Yes, the gentleman from

Connecticut opposed the federal dominance suggested by the gentle-man from Mississippi.

The regional planning bill, it was rumored, was allowed to die on condition that the utilities would start necessary spending for con-struction. Later they were invited to do this as a national-defense measure, perhaps to be helped along by government loans. But so far nothing has happened, and taxpayers have time to ask one ques-tion: "If it is a necessary thing to link the power facilities of the country in time of war, and presumably to operate them under gov-ernment control, why wouldn't that be a good idea in time of peace?"

If you find it hard to take seriously the idea of defending this country from an attacking army, you can still feel interested in keep-ing it up to the mark set by other countries in planning for the public good. Other countries have, from the first, kept an eye on the Tennessee Valley; and their various power developments have been undertaken with the benefit of American experience. Of course the builder of Wilson dam went right off to build the Dnieprostroy dam for the Russians; now the Soviet Union is planning the world's big-gest power station on the lower Volga, and a power program for Siberia is intended to electrify the Trans-Siberian Railway. In France, after journalists repeatedly called attention to the TVA pro-gram, extensive plans for rural electrification are being made, and they have begun to worry because the Garonne river rises in rebel Spain. The British had a similar worry about the source of the Nile, so you have to conclude that, if you left it to the rivers, nations wouldn't fight at all.

While the fight is over power, the more you look at TVA the less important its power features seem and the more you think its real value to the country lies in the other things it is doing in the Valley.

In theory, the advantages of regional planning are a fairly old story, and they had to try it out to find there was no such thing. The more TVA plans for its territory, the plainer it is that, while the valley may be a useful example, or laboratory, or guinea pig, or whatever you choose to call it for the rest of the country, the rest of the country is not only concerned with the verdict, but involved in the progress of the case.

As TVA men have so often said, the Authority is not independent of the people of the Valley, but wholly dependent on their co-operation. And the people of the Valley, whatever they may have preferred to be, or may imagine about themselves, have not been, and are not now, and can't be, independent of the rest of the country. When the President said that the job of planning for the "potential public usefulness of the Tennessee river" was so big that "it touches and gives life to all forms of human concerns," he was right; and the rest of it is that all forms of human concerns touch the job.

You can keep the independence of the Authority in all the obvious ways in which it must deal with outside agencies. The War Department, the Department of Agriculture, the various social agencies of the New Deal, can be dealt with on terms definitely understood; as state agencies—colleges, extension services, experiment stations, departments of health and education—can be, too. Everybody agrees that TVA has done a good, tactful job of co-ordinating all government efforts and creating a new agency with a definite place of its own. The catch comes when you deal with folks living in the Valley, who also live in the world.

In its mere job of planning, the Authority has to think of people every minute. Maybe, in choosing a dam site, you have a choice between scenery and power. Who's going to look at the scenery? They didn't mind when a private power development gave no thought to it at Talullah Falls, down in Alabama. But tourists like scenery— and there you are, out of the Valley.

The questions the planners must decide are often complicated enough in themselves. Will a reservoir be worth more than the bottom land it floods? Will power sale at a low rate make more trouble than it is worth to the consumer? Will farmers learn how to use concentrated fertilizer, and divert their land to better uses? If the farmer decides to grow strawberries, will people up in Chicago buy them? To the question of what is so now, you must add what will be so next year, because a few years ago, as one of the planners remarked, nobody realized that the Smokies would become a national playground, or that tourists would bring in more money than regular industry.

But the real trouble is that the minute your plans involve social and political considerations, and private economic interests, you subject your whole enterprise to a barrage that varies from the expensive propaganda and lawsuits of the corporations to the heckling of resident hill-billies. Southerners say you're ruining the niggers and the National Association for the Advancement of Colored People says you're not fair. Your own zeal makes you seek the right spot for a power pylon—in England the placing of rural lines is a subject for letters to the *Times*—and a countryside happy with billboards laughs at you for a fool. Your job may be, as the President said, "a return to the spirit and vision of the pioneer," or, as Mr. Lilienthal says, the charting of "a new frontier." But you have cause to remember that the pioneers, besides clearing the ground and getting in a crop, had to dodge the arrows and axes of hostile Indians.

Of course the success of the Authority, so far, is evident from the wide variety of commendation as well as of abuse. If every move is criticized, everybody approves some branch of TVA activity. Farm experts praise the fertilizer, women admire the Norris houses, country folks like the lights, and business men hope for a change in the freight rate. These good words add up to approval of the whole program.

Also the success of the project is evident from its own quick coordination of all these varied activities. No doubt the fight for life has helped that. Anyhow, you discover that you can't divide it—cut off a leg and call it farm program, or an arm for navigation, or charge off the other leg to power. People who want to kill TVA all begin that way; in the matter of costs, particularly, they were unable to see the difficulties of charging off so much to your right eye, and so much to your left foot. They want to cut it up and scotch the thing by sections, while the Authority insists that its program is all of a piece.

If you like the idea of order in the world, you come to see this

all-of-a-pieceness as a big advantage. Maybe it is hard to think of
everything at once; maybe men's minds aren't built to do it. One
physical scientist has said that what he calls " 'action-at-a-distance'
. . . as though every bit of the universe knew what other distant
bits were doing, and acted accordingly," [1] is the best indication of
some sort of divine management. But if it could be achieved, it
would also be the best sort of human management, government, or
civil service.

And a curious thing is that so far you can't attribute the development of the Valley to any one person. Edison and Mr. Ford both
saw the significance of the Shoals, but long before that they had been
discovered and boomed. Government enterprise there began under
a Democratic president and was revived by one, but it was the pet
idea of a Republican senator. More, he is a senator from Nebraska;
effective action on the Tennessee has been "action-at-a-distance."

There are people who, besides approving of the Authority as a
living body, would like to see it grow. Alarmists might well have
suggested that the Authority could get to be a dictatorship for the
whole country under one clause of the act, which gives it the duty
of planning for the drainage basin of the Tennessee river and "such
adjacent territory as may be affected by the development," because
it's easy to see that the whole country may be affected before it's
over. But sensible folks down South have confined themselves to
suggesting that TVA is the logical administrator for a larger Southern region, or even for the whole area of "Problem Number One."

But so far TVA has made no bid for the job, and maybe it knows,
better even than its friends and neighbors, how big a job it still has
on its hands. The fact is that it has yet to solve the problem of lasting prosperity for the Valley.

[1] *The Mysterious Universe,* Sir James Jeans.

Hope for the South

And I will make them one nation in the land upon the mountains . . . and
they shall be no more two nations, neither shall they be divided into two king-
doms any more at all.

They have been having hopes of prosperity in the Valley ever
since Daniel Boone told the Indians there was wealth there that they
didn't know about, and since a Chickamauga chief, departing, said
the white men could shoe their horses with silver when they learned
where to find it. But there has always been some slight disagreement
as to what direction prosperity might take. Dr. H. A. Morgan didn't
seem greatly impressed by Dr. Arthur Morgan's plans for dairying,
and on the other hand Dr. Arthur seemed to doubt the value of
Dr. H. A.'s experiments in strawberry culture. Mr. Lilienthal has
said that it is the duty of the Authority to encourage heavy industry,
while the Yankee opponents of the project object so much to that
idea that they speak wistfully, even if humorously, of Dr. Arthur
Morgan's "cottage industries."

No doubt the happy solution all round would be new industries,
new processes, new inventions, to use TVA power and Southern
materials and labor. There is even some hope for such miracles;
air-conditioning and soundproofing require new materials, with in-
sulating qualities, which are available from some of the Valley minerals or as by-products from fertilizer manufacture.

Then the clay-refining experiments made by TVA, now taken
over by the Bureau of Mines, were said to develop a good grade of
hard porcelain not before available in this country. The Valley has
the kaolin—North Carolina clay is similar to the English variety,
having been admired by Josiah Wedgwood himself—and TVA can
supply the furnace heat.

There have always been, in the South, hopes of starch from sweet
potatoes, new uses for peanuts and cotton, and similar ideal disposi-
tions of staple Southern crops. With the University of Tennessee,
TVA has undertaken more experiments in these directions, as well

as research in refrigeration; and if new commercial processes are developed, the Valley will gain while the Authority may get back some tax money through the sale of patents.

Meanwhile there is the unforeseen development of a tourist industry which increased summer visiting at Norris dam from a hundred thousand in 1934 to a million last year, and brings in more every week. Right now they come from curiosity, and because you have to cross the Valley to get to other places. But there is some basis for the hope that, when more people discover the Smokies, there will be regular tourist traffic over the Valley's eastern rim. On a clear day you can see nine folds in the hills above the S-curve in the Hiwassee river where they put the dam. The mists may hide the tops of the mountains, or wrap around their necks so they float like islands in the sky; the picture is never the same but it's always worth seeing, and handier than the Rockies for Easterners to reach. It may prove easier to coax tourists than capital into the Valley, and if the tourists come first, the capital, when it does come, will have to spare some of the scenery as a cash asset.

Most of the planners incline to a picturesque combination of agriculture and industry, anyhow. Dr. Arthur Morgan wanted the Valley to be not the Ruhr, but the Provence of America; he thought of a country of small farmers, cleverly adding to their income by supplemental crafts. Other planners have imagined big industrial plants, "decentralized," with short hours and quick transportation of workers to farm homes. Others still have hoped, as in Mississippi, that the coming of unregulated though subsidized industry would somehow combine with equally unregulated but federally subsidized farming to produce a workable balance.

Before you dismiss the small farm-handicraft idea as impossible, you should take a look at a place on the road between Knoxville and Hiwassee dam, a place that is the prize exhibit of TVA men who hold to this solution. An electrician who lost his business in town, during the slump, has here acquired four acres close to the highway. He has a garden and some fruit trees and a fish pond— "subsistence farming" carried to the elegancies of frogs' legs and trout. He has a small shop where he makes furniture. This shop is a triumph in itself because its tools have been assembled from old Ford parts, sewing and talking machines, a threshing machine, a section of road rail. As TVA current is not available, water power to run the machines and grind meal is supplied by damming a small stream on the place; and the millwheel for this miniature TVA is the paddlewheel from an old river boat. The shop keeps two men and a boy at work, and the busy proprietor has built two tourist cabins on his property in order to cash in on the Valley's newest industry. The tourists no sooner light from their cars than they start bargaining for walnut or cherry chests, and spool beds from the workshop.

However, this individual solution can't be recommended for the Valley. It took unusual skill and a positive genius for adaptation and diversification to make this place work. And suppose a dozen more people along this road tried the same thing—wouldn't there be an oversupply of spool beds?

Here you have to distinguish, as usual, between overproduction in the sense of use, and overproduction in the sense of profit. All the people in the Valley could work from dawn to dark making home-made furniture, and there wouldn't be too much to supply even those people in this country who are capable of appreciating its superiority. But there would mighty quick be too much to supply the people able to pay good prices for it.

So this simple solution of Dr. Arthur Morgan's turns out to be, when you look at it, pretty complicated by implication. When we solve the economic problems of the whole country and of the world —when people in New York and Chicago and Alaska have enough money to buy all the splint-bottomed chairs and handwoven coverlets and carved wooden pigs that they'd really like to have—then the Valley can make a living at these arts. Until then it might be more profitable to stick to moonshining.

This is not to disparage efforts made to sell Southern handicrafts. Shops at Norris, where you can buy the work of some thirty-odd mountain schools and settlements, are co-operatives that actually work. This may be because they co-operate actively in production, not just passively in consumption. And the products sell widely in the Valley, to tourists and to TVA men who are loyal to handwoven ties. But in New York, where a successful branch has been established, the appeal is to the luxury trade of Rockefeller Center.

If you persist in looking for individual effort and self-supporting farms in the Valley, you will note the discovery of some families that buying a washing machine to run on TVA current permits adding to the farm income with returns from a home laundry. But suppose the neighbors in time buy their own washing machines? Even if they don't, what is to become of that Southern institution, the Negro washwoman?

The more you watch these expedients, the more you see that what people need is steady work. But here, if you incline to unfettered private enterprise, you face the likelihood that the Valley will develop more Tupelos, Huntsvilles, and Kingsports, towns where industry and rural life merge only to retain the worst features of each.

There remains the idea of large industry so regulated as to insure a decent rural life for its employees. Here, of course, the objection is to the necessary regulation. Large industry over the country is already sold on decentralization; witness Kingsport, and witness the fact that one large corporation is said to have invested some fifty million dollars, or considerably more than the cost of Norris dam, in a decentralization program. It could be that some sort of truce between big business and government would send factories into the Valley to be surrounded by small farms and homesteads, in the sort of workers' paradise they talked of at Kingsport but failed to achieve. The octopus industry could be trusted, maybe, if it were controlled by the larger power of an active government. Otherwise, whatever its intentions, it is bound to acquire the relationship of a feudal overlord to the surrounding countryside.

A big corporation, public or private, can no more help influencing industry all around it than a big liner can help rocking a rowboat. With the best intentions, TVA has difficulties in keeping to a hands-off policy. Near one of the reservoirs, the Authority had rented a brick building for its own offices. A mill promoter, with machinery to be moved down from Pennsylvania, picked that building as the only one in town suitable for his enterprise, and offered to lease it. Should TVA, or should it not, give up its lease and bring a hosiery mill to a town which needed work? They are welcoming hosiery mills to some of the government homesteads now, but there they can make conditions. The Authority has no power of that sort but, willy-nilly, it was bound to affect the location of the mill.

The TVA men worry over these problems, and where they are capable of solution by goodwill and ingenuity, they solve them, in pleasant contrast to the ways of private industry. Up in the Carolina mountains a power company has deprived the Indians of one source of income; they wove baskets from cane growing wild on the power-company preserves, and the company said, no more cane-cutting. In the same area, TVA men noted holly growing on the reservoir land, and made a note to tell the local people they might as well get it out for the Christmas trade.

This may suggest to you another possibility for the Valley: that the Authority should, in time, extend its objectives to industrial enterprise. You will get no support for this idea from the Authority. The industries division is quite definite in saying that there was never any thought of undertaking the actual manufacture of porcelain. The agriculture division is equally definite in saying there is no idea of government competition in the fertilizer industry.

But the fertilizer business is an interesting example of what happens when you lead industry to water power and invite it to drink of its own accord. Back in 1933, reporting that Nitrate Plant Number Two could supply from ten to fifteen percent of the nation's needs, *Business Week* added that the National Fertilizer Association was opposed, and the probable output would be two percent. That was before the success of the metaphosphate process made it possible for the Authority to change production methods considerably.

The Authority is still co-operating with the fertilizer companies as pretty as you please; it has leased power to the two biggest ones, and one of them is building a new million-dollar plant in Maury county, Tennessee. But the industry, through its official organs, has already shown its opposition to TVA, to the "seven little TVA's" proposal, and to the use of Grand Coulee power for phosphate manufacture by the government.

The fears of the fertilizer industry follow closely the line laid out by power-industry objections. As with power, the government proposal is for a big increase in use; just to keep the soil where it is now, without improving it any, the experts say we should use from three to ten times the amount of phosphate we have been using. The verdict of the industry is that such an increase is "unnecessary, impracticable, and economically impossible," [1] by which it means that it couldn't supply the extra phosphate with its present facilities or hope to sell it at current prices.

So far, while TVA has given away phosphate to the demonstration farms and supplied over half the phosphate distributed by the AAA, the amount has been small in comparison to the commercial sale. But the promise of the TVA experiments is such that it is necessary for the industry to deny that the TVA process is really a new one, really cheaper if you count all costs (capital charges again), and so on. To which the answer is, as before, that by creating a new demand TVA "has done for the fertilizer industry what it was unable or unwilling to do for itself." [2]

In this case the argument over demand and supply has been somewhat complicated by the international implications. Back in 1937 Dr. H. A. Morgan told an Idaho conference that, in his view, "not a spoonful" of phosphates mined in this country should be exported. The next year, a presidential message to Congress suggested that, aside from their importance to national welfare, the disposition of American phosphates should be made a national concern. This naturally alarmed the companies doing an export trade.

They took the attitude that restrictions on export were necessary only if the American supply of phosphate rock was running low;

[1] Editorial in *Fertilizer Review,* June 1938.
[2] Statement of Edward A. O'Neal, president of the American Farm Bureau Federation, to the congressional committee on TVA.

and as the TVA process for using low-grade ore had just increased our resources fifty times over, they were able to arrive at astronomical figures for the reserves. But Dr. H. A. Morgan, in talking against export, had mentioned not only national security but international peace. It is possible that Dr. H. A. Morgan opposes selling American phosphates abroad because he would prefer to swap them for some guarantee against their coming back as poison gas. The next big fertilizer conference, after that one in Idaho at which Dr. H. A. Morgan spoke, was an international one held at Rome in October 1938. Although they were busy with Czecho-Slovakia at the time, delegates from the Fascist and Nazi nations which buy American phosphates outnumbered all others at the meeting.

So the phosphate war, unlike the power war, has both a home and a foreign front. At home there will be no war if Dr. H. A. Morgan's method of getting his way without carrying a gun is given a chance. The Farm Bureau Federation would like to see more action, and has pointed out that TVA has not yet carried out its authorization to arrange for large-scale fertilizer distribution through farm organizations, but TVA and AAA have been going ahead quietly instead of marching into the fertilizer business. There are advantages on the government side which make this possible. The improvements in processing made at Muscle Shoals are, of course, government-owned patents. And the big phosphate deposits up in Idaho are on the public lands. You could let the commercial manufacturers go ahead and wear themselves out. Or you could insist that the international sale of phosphate should be controlled at once, as the government controls the sale of helium. And you could say that the urgent need of the land justifies doing more at home. It's hard for an ordinary citizen to understand why the government can sell power, but can't sell phosphates, or why it shouldn't give them away in larger quantities. Southern farmers, needing the phosphate most, aren't able to buy them; they were also promised part-time work to keep them alive. When they need fertilizer and need employment, and the government has the factories and the phosphate deposits, doesn't it look funny to figure out ways to give farmers cash money enough for them to buy commercial fertilizers?

You can speculate forever about all these things, starting from a gully in the watershed and going on through Dr. H. A. Morgan's remark that "the greatest check to soil erosion would be an increase of industrial opportunity," until you wind up with government manufacture and regulation of export trade. About midway you will part company with official TVA policies, and you can see why that has to be. Whatever the implications may be, it does the present progress of the Authority no good to have Mr. Norman Thomas call it "the only purely socialistic flower in the New Deal garden," or for the *New Republic* to insist that it is "the first large-scale experiment in economic and social planning ever undertaken outside Soviet Russia." With everybody determined to carry the country through its crises without discarding any baggage, it was more likely to help when Mme. Odette Keun called the project "an effort comparable . . . to the admirable performance of the Scandinavian nations . . . an effort to . . . adjust capitalism to the present realities."

You have to plan for what you've got, of course. You can dam a river and use it for practical purposes without deciding the theoretical question: does a river make its own bed, or does the nature of the bed control the river? You simply have to accept the fact that you can't divide the Valley from the rest of the country, or the rest of the country from the Valley; and that government enterprise in the Valley, though a new thing under the sun, is held back by the general assumption over the country that private enterprise must come first.

How the Road Leads

And unto this people thou shalt say, Thus saith the Lord; Behold, I set before you the way of life, and the way of death.

Go thee one way or other, either on the right hand, or on the left, whithersoever thy face is set.

Dr. H. A. Morgan once said he felt that the selection of the Valley area was providential. But the engineers had to draw the lines somewhere, and they were smart in what they left out—West Virginia, and South Carolina, and Harlan county, Kentucky.

The Authority has been equally smart in limiting its own realm of activity. But one thing about a rainbow is that it leads you on, farther than you ever thought it would; and it's hard to see how to escape looking ahead if your job involves that very thing. TVA is there to think and move in what it thinks is the right direction. There are other executive agencies in the country and other planners, just as there are other tree-planters and mosquito-killers, other game-preservers, experimenters in housing, providers of books, other farm-aiders and other good engineers or plumbers; what makes TVA peculiar is its ability at once to plan and to do. That way it does, certainly, violate what some people see as the whole spirit of the constitution—the idea of checks and balances meant to keep a government from doing anything.

It may be that when they tried to give the Authority the powers of a government agency and the flexibility of a private corporation, they upset that idea. The procedure may be justified if TVA can prove that it is not only doing right but headed right.

They had, at the start, what they called a power policy that is interesting as a declaration of where they were headed. It was strictly in accord with the Act, but when the power companies set out to test the law and it developed that the Authority would have to stand or fall not by the Act but by the constitution, or what the judges would say the constitution was, they got more cautious and withdrew the policy. But there is no indication that it does not, right now, represent what TVA is trying to establish. It read: "The interest of the public in the widest possible use of power is superior to any private interest. When the private interest and this public interest conflict, the public interest must be preserved."

What makes this statement important is that you can apply it to other things than power. What about fertilizer, for instance? What about milk and butter? What about strawberries, and shoes? In its simple way, that early power policy of the Authority cut right into the thing that all modern economic arguments are about—whether production should be for use or for profit. Because, of course, the public interest is always in use; it is the private interest that is concerned with dividends.

The private interests set out to test the Act and what they got was a decision that the Authority had a right to sell power, in accordance with the public interest, even if it meant that private interests were destroyed. Now, nobody need be alarmed, because the Authority has given ample proof of intent to be kind to the private interests it is destroying, and it has limited its own field of activity to power. Nevertheless, if you have a simple practical mind, it may occur to you that just as electricity is a by-product of falling water, so a lot of goods could be by-products of electricity. You'd have to manufacture them, but you also had to manufacture the electricity—you don't just plug the percolator into the spillway of the dam.

If you really wanted to stop government progress in the direction of production for use, and keep the government in the role of policeman for private industry, you would have to disagree with the Supreme Court decision and agree with Justice McReynolds, of Tennessee.

The thing to do is keep looking at that phrase "public interest." Isn't that the business of government? If it is, how are you going to avoid that democratic process in business, as in voting, that puts the wants of the many ahead of the wants of the few?

Up to a certain point private business does, of course, consider public interest. Take the coal industry so dear to the heart of Congressman May of Kentucky, and so badly treated by the hydro-electricians in the Valley. Early in the days of the Authority, the president of the

Appalachian Coal Association was reported to say that "the coal industry is determined to destroy the TVA. It will destroy it by political means, by financial means, or by any means in its power." This year, the executive secretary of the National Coal Association complained that TVA had "crucified the coal industry." During the struggle that went between, political speakers told coal-miners that TVA was taking their jobs, and the industry resisted all the efforts to extend power production to other regions. Yet coal was unable to put up anything like the fight made by the power companies, and fought chiefly as their minor ally. The reason was that the coal industry was ailing long before TVA was heard of, and it could do no more than breathe a dying curse. It was not killed by TVA but by improvements in private industry.

You can depend on private industry to make such improvements whenever it can, as it would say, afford them. The reason they didn't build rural power lines, the reason that railroads burn coal, and slums stay with us, and all the other clumsy ways of doing things go on after better ways have been found, is only that doing better doesn't always pay.

That brings up the question they always ask about government enterprise. Admit that the government does a better job, as you have to admit it when you've watched TVA. They do it right, but how can they afford it? Does the far end of the rainbow, the one outside the Valley, reach to a pot of gold? Or is it, as Dayton, Ohio, would say, encumbering the future?

In the first place you have to admit that the money does have to come from outside, because there isn't enough along the Tennessee. Up North they can have associations to improve the scenery of the Hudson, but down South, instead of studying about how to pretty up the rivers, they're fishing for cat to eat. If you say the South is none of your business, that's all right; but then maybe your grandfather should have let the Southern states leave the Union when they tried to.

Once you decide to spend the money, you have a chance to argue that the government can do the job for less than anybody else, and

still do it better. Of course you'll find plenty of people in the Valley
to tell you, as somebody has told them, that the dams would have
cost less under private contract. To balance an opinion like that all
you can do is offer another opinion, such as that of the famous English
engineer who said the Aswan dam could have been built for about
half the price if the British government instead of private enterprise
had built it.

But just by building a series of dams instead of one or two, the
government has made savings that count. They estimate a saving of
a million and a half, so far, by using the same equipment. Then
they've figured savings on quantity buying, and savings on construction of down-river dams because the flow of water can be regulated
from above. All this comes to is that the government, being bigger
than any corporation, is able to cash in on that bigness the way the
big businesses do. As Mr. Lilienthal put it, "What the Authority is
required to do in its power program is to set up an area for power
operation which will be on a comparable basis with typical private
operation."

A utilities man said the one good thing about TVA was that its
size justified the big private companies in their gobbling-up of smaller
companies. It saves a lot of argument to admit that a monopoly is
more economical than a lot of smaller units, and high-school students
who used to debate municipal ownership should have been told by
their teachers that city rates were bound to be high and service inef-
fectual, in many cases, because the unit was too small.

Once you admit the monopoly is cheapest, it comes to a question
of what sort of monopoly you can trust. Most people see, when you
put it to them, that a big private monopoly is dangerous. Some people
object even to government monopoly; a writer in *Public Utilities Fortnightly* suggested that "once the private companies have been elimi-
nated and competition is no longer a factor, the consumer may find
the cost of his electricity increasing per kilowatt-hour, as a result either
of Congressional or local legislation, or both." There were just two
answers to that. One was that, with only one company in an area,
there was no competition in the light business anyhow, and the con-

sumer's only reliance was on legislation. The other answer is that Postmaster Farley and his predecessors have so far overlooked their opportunity as monopolists of the mails.

But even if the government can do a thing economically, it still costs money. If it costs too much, maybe we'd better do without?

Let's go back to that power-policy declaration about the public interests. It's to the interest of the public, isn't it, to have all the things that TVA is doing—the dams, the trees, the park areas, the cheap electricity? And it's to the interest of the public not to have the things that TVA is stopping—the raging floods, the spreading gullies. It's to the interest of the public to have men at work.

But somebody is going to have to pay the bill for materials and wages. Somebody may worry over losing money on utilities stocks. The whole question is whether this somebody is the public under another name, or just part of the public. You know the stockholders are fewer than the consumers; little as the private companies have done for rural electrification, the service has never been that bad. And you know that some stockholders, especially Southern ones, are likely to save instead of lose if Uncle Sam buys the companies out.

But taxpayers will have to put up the money. Again, only part of the consumers are taxpayers; but you've heard that when the government tries to do its taxing in the higher brackets, the loss is always passed right on to the consumer in higher prices. Of course it's an old custom; back in the old days when kings or queens needed money, they used to borrow it from their well-to-do subjects who then got it back by being allowed to "farm," as they said, the taxes. Folks started complaining about it in Queen Elizabeth's time and maybe some of the mountain folks are there because their ancestors couldn't pay. Nowadays they do it a little differently but it comes to the same thing.

The funny thing is that people as a rule don't question what they have to pay for what they buy, while they kick like mules over what they have to pay the government direct. As sensible governments don't impose taxes on people who can't afford to pay them, the taxes that business imposes are worse. They are paid only because people don't realize.

Of course business always says it couldn't possibly afford to pay, and when you work out a tax that can't be passed on, like the one on profits, Senator Pat Harrison of Mississippi isn't happy until he releases business from this burden. But you have only the word of the business men that they can't manage any better, and sometimes you'd think people would worry more over how business spends what it gets. Hard-up folks aren't asked by Uncle Sam to contribute to TVA or WPA or any government expenditure; it's business that asks them. Sometimes business pays one of its executives a hundred or more times what Uncle Sam pays his workers; maybe business could save that and pay its own taxes or lower prices. Nobody knows; usually there is no way of telling how much of what you pay for anything is indirect tax, and how much is actual cost, and how much is fair or unfair profit or loss due to mismanagement.

Here's where a yardstick can really work, by disclosing the make-up of the price tag. How much is government tax, how much is private profit; how much of what was intended for tax on profits is paid by the people who don't get the profits? Maybe it won't be enough to have a yardstick in just one industry, power. But get yourself a few more industries. Let the schools set them up, if the government can't do it officially—only be sure the industry is a social-science project, as in the school at Norris, and not a private project as in the school in Mississippi. Then watch what happens to the transfer of high-bracket taxes to low-bracket customers.

And then what happens if your industry sits down and won't play? If it applies the argument that business depends on the incentive of big profits to people at the top? Well, of course it doesn't really mean that, and when it balks, it is just a temporary measure until it can arrange a change in government. But it can happen partially; it happened, in a way, when the power industry declined to build rural lines. And the remedy happened too: the government built the lines, finding no difficulty at all in hiring people to do the work. Ordinary working people do not ask fancy profits as an incentive; all they ask is a living wage.

But suppose that when you get all your yardsticks working, there are no big profits, and therefore no taxes to pay for new enterprises like TVA? In that case maybe you will have to come clear down to earth. You will have to decide whether you want things—houses with lights in them, dams to stop floods, trees growing on the hills, maybe even strawberries and cows and shoes—or whether you want to keep on playing with what some call the profit system, and some confuse with the American system of government.

Getting the things will be easy—the engineers can tell you how. Paying for them is harder, and the bankers whose job is managing money can't tell you how, at all. They can't tell you why or how it is that in this country, where the pioneers came with their axes, and cut down the trees to build cabins, it should now be government extravagance for a CCC boy to plant a tree, or a TVA man to build a house. They only know it is extravagance, and where will the money come from?

Maybe they do need a separate coinage in the Valley, because a child can see that they could solve their problems all right if they just took what they have in raw materials, and power, and people to work, and put them together—using shells, as the Indians did, for exchange.

It could be, though, that the whole country is in the same fix, and what we need is to look hard enough at the Valley to see the answer. Or just look at the rainbow—one end in middle Tennessee where they dig phosphates, and one end up in Kentucky where they bury gold. Maybe we've been looking at the wrong end.

You could give money to people who think a lot of it, the same way the Indians thought a lot of trade beads and blankets because they didn't understand how they were made. Lots of people don't understand how money is made; they think it is made by business, when as a matter of fact only the government is entitled to make it. The constitution says so. Money can be made by the government the way the corporations issue stock, only no sane government would ever approach the dropsy of the private companies.

But you can pay out money to people who howl and scream for it the way the Cherokees whooped when they went to war, and started the rebel yell. Then you can turn around and get the money back by taxes; and if you pay it to people entitled to it because they are selling stocks or materials or work, and then tax it back out of incomes able to spare it, maybe you've improved things all around. Because some of the people you pay for materials or work, maybe even some of the people from whom you buy stocks, may not have money enough to spend for the things they need. In fact that's pretty certain to be the case if they are people down South. So whatever you pay them they will spend again, and keep in circulation, buying things made by other people who need to sell their work.

The people you tax, on the other hand, will have so much money that they don't need to spend it and may be, as they say, too "frightened" to put it into anything, even anything as safe as building lines to carry current that people want to buy.

If the government has the spunk to do that work and similar work that needs doing, it will naturally stand to profit from the results, the way the people with money might have profited if they hadn't been scared. Not being greedy, the government won't need to profit so much, but it can still make a little even while selling at lower prices. It will, that is, "make" money the way private business does; and it will have increased its real assets, and resources and property of the country, which are its security for actually making money at the mint.

They never mention these things when they talk about spending, but look what the government gets for its money, just in the Valley. To begin with, there's security from flood damage. For the Valley, the army engineers estimated the annual damage at $1,780,000; this estimate took no account of loss of life, or to business, and was an average yearly expectancy with no insurance against peak disasters. The army engineers considered that the losses in Tennessee at the time of the 1926 floods, amounting to $2,650,000, could largely have been prevented. For Chattanooga alone, with an average annual damage of $400,000, it was estimated that the TVA dams saved a loss of $750,000 in the floods of 1937. At Cairo, they figure the money savings went up to a million, based on the damage done at Paducah. And going down into the Mississippi valley, they say potential savings there, when TVA is able to take those two feet off a Mississippi flood, will be around twenty millions a year.

Then there is the economic salvage of bankrupt counties like Grainger, with its bill, you remember, of $206,000 for state and federal aid in one year.

There is the saving of the soil, making more progress in five years of TVA phosphates than in twenty-five years of moral suasion.

There is the potential cash value of trees and uncounted fish.

There is the saving in transportation costs to be made by river traffic, both actual and potential if they change the freight rates.

There is the saving to users of electricity, directly through the low TVA rates, indirectly as other rates go down. Back in 1931 a public-power advocate said that the public was paying a million dollars a day more than it needed to pay for light and power; that bill has been cut.

Understand that the Authority does not count these savings when it says that the dams will pay for themselves, as the Panama Canal did. It is selling electricity to pay back the taxpayers' money. But the other profits are there—profits for what you might, if your mind runs that way, call the holding company behind TVA. That holding company is, like some others, a commonwealth—with "Southern" not an addition to the firm name, but part of the commonwealth of the United States.

They Don't Have to Hurry

For a thousand years in thy sight are but as yesterday when it is past.

He that believeth shall not make haste.

They certainly didn't intend, when they started building dams in the Valley, to affect the American system. Right now they will argue earnestly that they have no such intention.

And certainly the economic determinists, the people who think the world will be all right as soon as we give everybody enough calories and vitamins and gadgets, aren't going to get much support from Valley dwellers. Hill folks may not know much about modern contraptions but they certainly know about right and wrong, and how, rich or poor, high or low, you are bound to get what's coming to you in this world and the next.

As for the planner, he says, sure you're going to get what's coming to you, so why not improve it? And that's where planners and free-will people see eye to eye. You won't find an out-and-out determinist in a carload of TVA men either.

Maybe the most important thing happening in the Valley is the meeting of minds between Valley folks, who know about right and wrong from never having lost their old-time religion, and the new-fangled planners, who hold to a new set of rights and wrongs with an equally firm conviction. These people learn to respect each other, because the word that covers both attitudes is responsibility. Maybe you couldn't have called it the Tennessee Valley Responsibility, but that, more than authority, is what they've got.

There are some good reasons these days for questioning authority, but whenever a lot of people are converted to anything, there must be some reason for it; and maybe the one percent of sense in dictatorship is Herr Hitler's discovery that you shouldn't shrink from responsibility. Of course he carries that too far. But you have to admit that the mess the world has worked itself into is mainly due to the desire of ordinary people to escape thinking about government, their wish to avoid thinking of it or doing anything about it, and the desire of all politicians in democratic governments to pass the buck.

Voters were busy with their own affairs, like people before the flood, and the politicians never took any action, so they said, unless the people demanded it. Nobody suggested that it was the business of government to see that people didn't starve or freeze or die of malaria. We freed the Negroes from slavery, we freed the slave-owners from any obligation to take care of them, and we freed everybody from trouble, we hoped.

Then trouble came, and in time came the TVA to say in the name of the government, all right, I can take it, I'll do what I can. The

Authority is no authority at all as government authority is known elsewhere; the most it can do is to assume part of the freedom, if you please, of a private corporation, and to compete with the corporation, and it gets criticized for that. You hear, from the corporations, that the liberties people came here to find are endangered.

But nowadays people are coming over here again. The other day the Yankee papers published a picture of a group of refugees in Europe, camped out on a road. They had been forced out of a Fascist country and now other countries, it was said, would have to take care of them. They looked a good deal like people down South evicted from mill houses, as people were evicted in Tupelo, Mississippi, and as they have been thrown on public charity in places everywhere when mills and factories closed or machinery replaced cropping. You'll find them camping along Southern roads for other people to take care of—for the government to help.

And which is the dictatorship, the government that helps them, or the industry that uses them and then pushes them out? The industry that, besides using up people, has used up woods and mines and soil just as it pleased, and left only wreckage for the government to reclaim?

You can look at these things and get right mad, and people down South will put up with just so much. They won't complain when they think it's necessary to do without and work hard. They put up with slavery once; they plow with oxen, and oxen are patient. But there are flint rocks in the hills, and flints strike fire. There are rivers that rise fast when they get going.

There is the Tennessee Valley Authority to dam the rivers and harness their power to build, and not destroy. It will save cities, maybe save capitalism, they say. Maybe it's too late for that, but maybe they can slow up the changes so they will make less trouble for everybody. The Yankees went through fast once, said the Southerner at Shiloh.

Now the job is going slow—not a five-year plan, a twenty-five-year one; and with elections coming on how can you be sure? There are people who think it would be nice for Uncle Sam to leave the dams in the Valley, as a little souvenir of the depression, the way he left harbor improvements over in France.

But they tried leaving Wilson dam that way, and it wouldn't work. The Authority has created a precedent, not only for government enterprise, but for the salvage of former enterprise. Should worse come to worst, that precedent might come in handy, but however you look at it, you can be pretty sure the dams are there to stay.

There they sit, and they have an authority of their own. Napoleon said, back in Egypt, that you could have no more absolute authority than control over the waters that cover the earth. So it's an authority that must be exercised carefully, cautiously, by men unlike Napoleon and not admiring him—men willing to walk humbly with the power they are given. The power moves upon the face of the waters to make a land, to create order, and a world fit to live in. And the men, maybe, had to be as they are—careful and cautious Yankees alongside slow-moving Southerners, the Yankees knowing about kilowatts, and the Southerners fearing God.

The Lord sat back and looked at Satan.

Satan had just got back from walking to and fro on the earth, and up and down in it, the way he does, and he was making his regular report.

"And how," the Lord asked him, "did you find things in the Valley?"

"Which valley you mean?" said Satan.

"You know which one I mean," the Lord told him. "The same one where you stirred up that monkey business a while back."

"Oh," says Satan, grinning. "You mean Tennessee. Well, they've been having more lawsuits, and a little trouble down there among themselves, with Congress settin' in on it——"

"I know all about that," said the Lord. "I can read the papers. All I want to know is what the people think. You know more about that than I do."

"Some think one thing and some think another, the way they always do down there," said Satan.

"Yes," said the Lord, patient like, "but do they think the same things they always did?"

"Mostly," said Satan.

The Lord sighed, and looked down into the Valley. He could see some changes in it, even from a long way off. They'd begun the way He always liked to, with moving the waters and making a light. They were still working on the river, and rearranging the

304

mountains, and building some houses and planting out little trees. Here and there, where the sun shone through the mist, He could see a glint like new copper wire. It didn't look quite the same, but it was too far to tell about the people.

"And you don't think they'll change much?" He asked Satan.

"Not in a thousand years," said Satan. "You know what I think about human nature, in the Valley or outside of it."

The Lord sighed again. Then He remembered He could afford to be patient.

"A thousand years," He said, after Satan. "Well, today's only Tuesday. What's one day more?"

FACTS AND FIGURES

The Valley

The Tennessee basin is an area of 40,600 square miles in Tennessee, North Carolina, Virginia, Georgia, Mississippi, Alabama, and Kentucky. Its longest measure, east and west, is over 400 miles. Measured north and south, it varies from nearly 200 to less than 50 miles.

Some 13,500,000 acres of this area are wooded. Of the farm land, 2,000,000 acres are badly gullied, 1,000,000 more going, and 7,000,000 less seriously eroded.

The area has a population estimated to be 2,500,000. The largest cities are Chattanooga, 119,798; Knoxville, 105,802; and Asheville, 50,193.

The River

Numerous tributaries make the Tennessee river system one of the largest in the United States, although the river, measured from its junction with the Ohio at Paducah to its source in the junction of the Holston and the French Broad, is only 648 miles long. Other principal tributaries are the Powell, Clinch, Nolichucky, Pigeon, Little Tennessee, Hiwassee, Sequatchie, Elk, Buffalo, Duck, and Big Sandy rivers.

The profile of the river shows a fall of 800 feet, 200 feet in the Muscle Shoals section between Guntersville and Pickwick Landing.

The Dams

Wilson dam, on the Tennessee near Florence, Alabama, was begun in 1918 and finished in 1924.

Height, 137 feet; length, 4860 feet.
Power, 184,000 k.w.; ultimate installation, 444,000 k.w.
Cost, $46,950,748; present value, $34,989,790.

Norris dam, on the Clinch river 20 miles northwest of Knoxville, Tennessee, was finished in 1936.

Height, 265 feet; length, 1860 feet.
Power, 100,800 k.w.
Cost, $30,749,776.

Wheeler dam, on the Tennessee river 15 miles above Wilson dam, was finished in 1936.

Height, 72 feet; length, 6502 feet.
Power, 64,800 k.w.; ultimate installation, 259,200 k.w.
Cost, $31,586,564.

Pickwick Landing dam, on the Tennessee river near Shiloh, was finished in 1938.

Height, 113 feet; length, 7715 feet.
Power, 72,000 k.w.; ultimate installation, 216,000 k.w.
Cost, $31,837,000.

Guntersville dam, 10 miles downstream from Guntersville, Alabama, is to be finished in 1940.

Height, 94 feet; length, 3985 feet.
Power, 72,900 k.w.; ultimate installation, 97,200 k.w.
Estimated cost, $33,400,000.

Chickamauga dam, on the Tennessee 7 miles above Chattanooga, is to be finished in 1940.

Height, 108 feet; length, 5794 feet.
Power, 81,000 k.w.; ultimate installation, 108,000 k.w.
Estimated cost, $37,000,000.

Hiwassee dam, on the Hiwassee river 20 miles below Murphy, North Carolina, is to be finished in 1940.

Height, 307½ feet; length, 1265 feet.
Power, 57,600 k.w.; ultimate installation, 115,200 k.w.
Estimated cost, $20,000,000.

Gilbertsville dam, on the Tennessee at Paducah, Kentucky, is in an early stage, with construction to be completed in 1945.

Height, 150 feet; length, 8655 feet.
No initial power; ultimate installation, 160,000 k.w.
Estimated cost, $95,000,000.

Other projected construction includes dams at Watts Bar and Coulter Shoals on the Tennessee, and a dam on the Little Tennessee.

The Authority

The Tennessee Valley Authority was created by act of the 73rd Congress, in May 1933, "for the purpose of maintaining and operating the properties now owned by the United States in the vicinity of Muscle Shoals, Alabama, in the interest of the national defense and for agricultural and industrial development, and to improve navigation in the Tennessee River and to control the destructive flood waters in the Tennessee River and Mississippi River Basins."

Described in the Act as a body corporate, the Authority is directed to construct such dams and reservoirs on the Tennessee river and its tributaries as will provide a nine-foot channel from Knoxville to the river mouth; to "advise and co-operate in the readjustment of the population displaced by the construction of dams"; to manufacture and sell fertilizer at Muscle Shoals, and to contract with commercial producers for such fertilizers as may be needed in excess of that produced by government plants; to manufacture explosives for the United States government, upon requisition of the Secretary of War; to produce, distribute, and sell electric power.

Work Accomplished

In the course of building three dams and beginning those under construction, the Authority has acquired for the government 497,610 acres of land at an average cost of $51.82 per acre; and has assisted in the removal of 5002 families from reservoir areas.

Additional activities, summarized for the fiscal year ended June 30, 1938, include:

Reforestation: a total of 61,426,000 seedlings planted.

Navigation: 195.4 miles of 9-foot channel and 349 miles of 6-foot channel opened to shipping. Completion of the total mileage of 9-foot channel requires building all projected dams.

Power sale: Latest available reports show a total of some 150,000 domestic, commercial, and industrial consumers served, through 43 small city plants and 19 rural co-operatives, with Memphis and Chattanooga under contract for but not receiving power. Purchase of Tennessee Electric Power company properties will, it is estimated, more than double this distribution.

Domestic consumers of TVA power used an annual average of 1270
kilowatt-hours, compared with a national average of 802 kilowatt-hours.
They paid an average rate of 1.99 cents per kilowatt-hour, compared to a
national average of 4.40 cents.

Basic residential rates under TVA contracts are:

3¢ per kilowatt-hour for the first   50 k.w. hrs. per mo.
2¢   "   "   "   "   " next 150 "   "   "   "
1¢   "   "   "   "   "   200 "   "   "   "
4   mills   "   "   "   "   " 1000 "   "   "   "

Gross revenue from power sale, for the fiscal year ending June 30, 1938,
was $2,305,877. Present contracts indicate that gross revenue for 1939 will
be $5,000,000, and for 1940, $6,500,000.

Power sale is not restricted to the Tennessee basin, but is governed by
transmission distance from the dams. Arkansas is now buying TVA
power. Cities in the transmission area, not yet served, include Nashville,
Louisville, Birmingham, and Atlanta.

Costs

Total expenditures, to June 30, 1938: $213,458,609.48.
Estimated additional cost of completing present construction program,
$306,000,000.

In a statement allocating costs for Norris, Wheeler, and Wilson dams,
the Authority charged 52 percent to power production, 28 percent to navigation, and 20 percent to flood control. At the same time the Authority
reported that sale of power from these three dams, operated at normal
capacity, should be sufficient to "cover all costs of operation, including depreciation, and 3 percent interest on the investment allocated to power,
and in addition to return in 30 years the entire investment allocated to
navigation and flood control."

Sources of Information

Five annual reports, issued by the Tennessee Valley Authority, are ob-
tainable either from the Authority or from the Government Printing
Office, Washington, D.C. To these should be added, when available, the
report of the congressional committee of investigation, and court decisions
affecting the Authority.

Excellent bibliographies can be obtained from the Information Division
of the Tennessee Valley Authority, Knoxville, Tennessee.

INDEX

AAA, 49, 62, 63, 102, 289, 290

Aberdeen, Miss., 160, 162

Adams, John Quincy, 201

Adventure, 28

Advertising, 193, 195, 225

Alabama, 5, 6, 7, 172, 198, 253, 281; in Civil War, 6, 14, 17, 165; electricity, use of, 202, 203, 207, 218, 234; illiteracy in, 22; Negroes in, 116, 134, 248; pellagra in, 121; politics, 244-246, 250; sharecroppers, 99, 116; taxes, 138, 230, 256, 257, 267; textile industry, 166-176; WPA wages, 124; Yazoo land, 199. *See also* Birmingham, Huntsville, Muscle Shoals

Alabama Power Company, 69, 111, 151, 166, 169, 171, 173, 175, 192, 193, 196, 202, 205, 210, 211, 212, 215, 216, 218, 222, 225, 234, 237, 264

Alcorn county, Miss., 207, 209

Allen, Judge Florence, 222

Allen, Private John, 243

Aluminum Company of America, 244, 270-272

American Cotton Association, 102

American Federation of Labor, 106, 151, 185, 189

American Legion, 156

American Liberty League, 226

American Statisticians' Association, 207

Amoskeag Mills, 195

Anderson county, Tenn., 64

Antioch college, 147, 150

Antioch Notes, 135

Appalachian Coal Association, 294

Appalachian mountains, 7. *See also* Smokies, Blue Ridge, Cumberlands

Appliances, electric, 214-216

Appomattox, 16

Arkansas, 102, 103

Arkansas Power and Light Corporation, 272

Arkwright, Preston, 210

Arnold School for Boys, 29

Asheville, N.C., 5, 91, 195

Ashwander case, 222

Athens, Ala., 206, 207, 235

Atlanta, Ga., 41, 42, 123, 195

Atlanta Constitution, 251

Atlantic Monthly, 236

Avengers of Blood, 28

Aylesworth, Merlin H., 225, 233

Bailey, Senator, 244

Baker, Newton D., 222

Ballads, 11, 82

Bank deposits, 15, 256

Bankhead Act, 62, 138

Banner Elk, N.C., 15

311